The War That Never Was

The War That Never Was

Evolution and Christian Theology

KENNETH W. KEMP

CASCADE *Books* · Eugene, Oregon

THE WAR THAT NEVER WAS
Evolution and Christian Theology

Copyright © 2020 Kenneth W. Kemp. All rights reserved. Except for brief quotations in critical publications or reviews, no part of this book may be reproduced in any manner without prior written permission from the publisher. Write: Permissions, Wipf and Stock Publishers, 199 W. 8th Ave., Suite 3, Eugene, OR 97401.

Cascade Books
An Imprint of Wipf and Stock Publishers
199 W. 8th Ave., Suite 3
Eugene, OR 97401

www.wipfandstock.com

PAPERBACK ISBN: 978-1-5326-9498-1
HARDCOVER ISBN: 978-1-5326-9499-8
EBOOK ISBN: 978-1-5326-9500-1

Cataloguing-in-Publication data:

Names: Kemp, Kenneth W., author.

Title: The war that never was : evolution and Christian theology / Kenneth W. Kemp.

Description: Eugene, OR: Cascade Books, 2020. | Includes bibliographical references and index.

Identifiers: ISBN 978-1-5326-9498-1 (paperback). | ISBN 978-1-5326-9499-8 (hardcover). | ISBN 978-1-5326-9500-1 (ebook).

Subjects: LCSH: Evolution (Biology)—Religious aspects—Christianity. | Evolution (Biology)—Religious aspects—Christianity—History. | Creationism | Creationism—History. | Scopes, John Thomas—Trials, litigation, etc. | Intelligent design (Teleology).

Classification: BT712 K40 2020 (paperback). | BT712 (ebook).

Manufactured in the U.S.A.   05/28/20

Contents

CHAPTER 1
Introduction | 1

CHAPTER 2
The Historical Origins of the Warfare Thesis | 25

CHAPTER 3
Christianity, Geology, & Cosmology before 1859 | 39

CHAPTER 4
Christianity & Evolution in the Nineteenth Century | 68

CHAPTER 5
William Jennings Bryan, John T. Scopes,
& the First Curriculum War | 96

CHAPTER 6
Creation Science, Intelligent-Design Theory,
& the Second Curriculum War | 141

CHAPTER 7
Conclusion | 189

Bibliography | 193

Index | 221

CHAPTER 1

Introduction

THIS BOOK IS A partial account of the history of the relations between theology and science, two of the central projects in the intellectual history of Western civilization, from the seventeenth century until today. Such accounts sometimes meet with the objection that *science*, in particular, has been understood variously over the course of the centuries. The term was understood differently by Aristotelians such as St. Robert Bellarmine (and St. Albert the Great before him) and by the founders of the modern sciences (Galileo Galilei, René Descartes, Isaac Newton, Charles Lyell, and Charles Darwin, who would have differed with one another). Nevertheless, we can characterize science (*natural philosophy* before about 1800) broadly, if somewhat vaguely, as the attempt to offer a descriptive and explanatory account of natural phenomena by reference to natural causes. Scientific inquiry is rational and empirical, or in other words it is based on the human powers of observation and inference. Theology, by contrast, is the attempt to offer an account of the existence and nature of God and of the world (both natural and spiritual) by reference to him.[1] Christian (as well as Jewish and Muslim) theological inquiry, whatever role it gives to reason and observation, gives pride of place to revelation. In this it is distinct from deistic theology, which does not recognize revealed truth as a possible source of knowledge.

---

1. I do not consider the words *theology* and *religion* to be interchangeable. Roughly, I use *theology* to refer to the intellectual component of the larger practice which I call *religion*. Although I try to distinguish the terms in this way, nothing in my thesis turns on exactly where the line of demarcation between the two is drawn; often what I say about one is true also of the other, and I will sometimes use one term and sometimes the other, attempting to respect the distinction just drawn and the focus of those whose work I am discussing.

This book is a partial account in having as its subject only one part of science, the part which (following nineteenth-century philosopher of science William Whewell) I will call the paleoetiological sciences,[2] the science of "ancient causes." It will focus also on only one part of theology, the doctrines at the center of what might broadly be called the theology of nature—creation, providence, and anthropology. The history of these ideas, taken separately, and their eventual logical relations, I am leaving for another book. In this book I will focus on the *historical relations* between the paleoetiological sciences and the theology of nature.

One of the enduring myths of our age is that Western intellectual history includes a long-running war between science and theology (or sometimes religion generally)—a war in which the fight was once over the sphericity of the earth and its place in relation to the sun, planets, and stars; a war in which the fight is at present not over the structure of the universe but over its origin and history. It is, according to that myth, a war that has also included battles on other fronts, ranging from the obstetric use of anesthesia to the destruction of human embryos in medical research.

Its renarration is a standard weapon in the arsenal of militant atheists and is the first resort of any journalist struggling to formulate a lede. But what is it that the purveyors of the idea of a war between science and theology have on offer? Is it a thesis, an interpretive lens, or just a metaphor? Who or what is it that is at war? Are the belligerents groups of people—scientists, on the one hand, and theologians, or religious people generally, on the other? Is the idea only that there has in fact been a war, or that such warfare is inevitable? Is the war perhaps just between actual groups of people, or is it somehow between two disciplines—perhaps between two mutually inconsistent approaches to the study of the same subject matter? Or is the "war" a logical contradiction between the *content* of science and of theology? Is there something in the stories of Galileo and Pope Urban VIII, of John T. Scopes and William Jennings Bryan, that provides some insight into the nature of the relationship between science and theology? Something that will show that that relationship is essentially conflictual? Most generally, is it grounded just in the contingencies of history, or does it show us something about the essential nature of science and theology?

Colin Russell, not himself a defender of what I will call the Warfare Thesis, has suggested that we can distinguish four kinds of putative

---

2. Whewell, *Philosophy of the Inductive Sciences*, 1:xxxv–xxxvi. Whewell used a haplological version, "palætiology," which seems to me to be both less euphonious and less clear.

conflict—moral, institutional, methodological, and substantive.³ Grouping the latter two as variants of epistemic conflict, we can organize these possibilities as in the diagram.

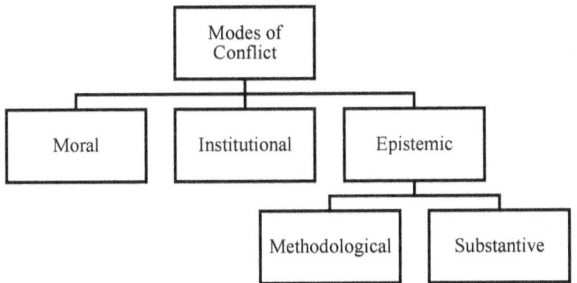

Non-epistemic Conflict

For some people, the idea of a conflict (or war) between science and religion calls *first* to mind questions of ethics, so let us begin there. Andrew Dickson White, in his *History of the Warfare of Science and Theology in Christendom*, about which much more will be said in chapter 2 below, presented alleged religious objections to the obstetric use of anesthesia as evidence for his thesis.⁴ He got his facts wrong—there were no significant religious objections to this practice,⁵ but the fact that he included the matter in his *History* at all does show that what I will call the Warfare Thesis is sometimes extended to what are really moral controversies.

Engineers, physicians, and policymakers must, after all, address moral questions about the development of certain technologies and techniques and about the use of others already available. Questions about research into new biological weapons would be an example of the former type. Eugenics presents an example of the latter. George William Hunter's *Civic Biology*, one of the most popular biology texts in early twentieth-century America and one that will figure prominently in chapter 5 below, only went as far as recommending the prevention of the marriage of the immoral and the feeble-minded, but his contemporaries were already using putatively

---

3. Russell, "Conflict." Russell uses the term *ethical* rather than *moral*.
4. White, *History*, 2:62–63.
5. See Farr, "Early Opposition to Obstetric Anaesthesia"; and Farr, "Religious Opposition to Obstetric Anaesthesia: A Myth?"

scientific insights to justify forced sterilization in the United States, Germany, and elsewhere.[6]

Scientists must also address questions of what might, in a narrower sense, be called research ethics. Although questions might sometimes be raised about whether certain kinds of knowledge should be sought at all, the more common kind of question is about the moral permissibility of certain research methods. A prominent recent example is, of course, the destruction of human embryos in order to obtain stem cells for medical research. Objection to this practice is sometimes cited as an example of intrusion *ab extra* into scientific matters.[7] Scientists, generally responsible though they may be, have no more immunity from moral error than do the rest of us. Prominent among the moral failures of research scientists were the classical conditioning experiments of John D. Watson and Rosalie Rayner on Little Albert (at Johns Hopkins University in 1920),[8] the US Public Health Service's Untreated Syphilis Study (at Tuskegee Institute between 1932 and 1972),[9] and Stanley Milgram's experiments on the willingness to obey authority figures (at Yale in 1963).[10] These sufficiently canvas the range, though they do not exhaust the list, of experiments now universally condemned.

Whether it is permissible to conduct a certain kind of experiment, however, is fundamentally a moral question, not a scientific one. It is surely possible to address these issues in a purely philosophical (i.e., in a nonreligious) way, though of course many people find it more natural to bring theological resources to the resolution of such questions. Seldom, if ever, do theologians doing research ethics argue for conclusions that cannot also be defended philosophically. Nevertheless, when objections to certain lines of research come from moral theologians or bishops, those who chafe at the proposed moral constraints on their research work often complain about *religious* objections against the proposed research. If there is, in those cases,

---

6. Hunter, *Civic Biology*, 261–64. For a more radical policy, see, for example, Laughlin, "Model Eugenical Sterilization Law." Virginia's version of that model law was upheld by the US Supreme Court in *Buck v. Bell* in 1927. The law served as the model for Germany's 1933 (so, Nazi-era) Gesetz zur Verhütung erbkranken Nachwuchses. For a history, see Kevles, *In the Name of Eugenics*.

7. "Religious groups are turning scientific matters like stem cells . . . into political issues"—Gross, "Scientific Illiteracy," 680. Of course the religious groups say nothing about the purely *scientific* side of the matters in question.

8. See Watson and Rayner, "Conditioned Emotional Reactions," and the discussion in Beck et al., "Finding Little Albert."

9. See Jones, *Bad Blood*.

10. Milgram, "Behavioral Study of Obedience"; and Milgram, *Obedience to Authority*. For a critique of the pervasive, if less outrageous, reliance on deception in social science research, see Korn, *Illusions of Reality*.

something to the idea that religion is one of the participants in a conflict with science, it is a conflict with science only contingently, and even then only in the institutional sense. Why a certain segment of the community seems to consider appeal to religious principles to be acceptable in the moral evaluation of immigration policy, capital punishment, and war, but not of scientific research, remains one of the mysteries of contemporary political liberalism.

The question of which is the greater problem—unjustifiable restrictions on scientific research or research outrages like those mentioned above—is an interesting one, but the proponents of the Warfare Thesis seem primarily to have in mind a problem about the relationship between scientific and theological claims about what is true—about what we know rather than about what we should do. In any case, the paleoetiological sciences that are the subject of this book seldom raise questions of research ethics and so I will say no more about these issues here.

Questions about institutional conflict are not really *about* science and religion at all. It may happen that conflict between religious and scientific institutions arise in the same way that they arise between competing religious institutions (between Roman and Greek Catholics in Poland and Ukraine, between Jesuits and Dominicans in the Chinese missions, or between Franciscans and the diocesan clergy over the apparitions at Medugorje), or between competing scientific institutions (as between the Institute of Geography at the Soviet Academy of Sciences and the Department of Geography at Moscow State University in the 1940s[11]), or between institutions that are neither religious nor scientific (between the US Navy and the US Air Force over airpower spending priorities). Interesting questions could be asked about whether, and if so how, conflicts between scientific and religious institutions differ from intrareligious or intrascientific conflicts, but the interest of those who promote the Warfare Thesis does not seem to be in the light it might shed on, say, the Revolt of the Admirals over spending priorities (mentioned above). We will notice it only to the extent that it exacerbates, or is mistaken for, epistemic conflict.

Epistemic Conflict

Questions about the relation between Christianity and the paleoetiological sciences are in the first instance questions about epistemic conflict—questions about methodology and about content.

---

11. See Shaw and Oldfield, "Scientific, Institutional and Personal Rivalries."

Questions of Method: Science, Theology and Naturalism

Some philosophers have argued that there is an inherent conflict in the methodologies of these sciences and of theology. On their view, science, and perhaps in particular the paleoetiological sciences (though critics are often not clear on this point), is inherently naturalistic *in a way that is inconsistent with religion*, or at least with Christianity. In discussions of the connections between science and *naturalism*, however, it is important to distinguish two different theses—ontological naturalism and methodological naturalism.

Ontological naturalism is an account of what exists in the world. Alan Lacey characterized it as the view that "the world of nature . . . form[s] a single sphere without incursion from outside by souls or spirits, divine or human, and without having to accommodate strange entities like nonnatural values or substantive abstract universals."[12] A naturalist might think this on the basis of an even stronger thesis, namely

(O1)   Only natural beings exist.

or, focusing on participation in the causal nexus rather than on existence itself, he might take it just as Lacey gives it, asserting only that

(O2)   Nonnatural beings (if they exist at all) have no causal influence on the natural world.

For the purposes of most of what follows, it does not much matter exactly where one draws the line between natural and nonnatural beings (e.g., whether Aristotelian forms or human souls having free will are natural or not[13]) as long as one puts chemicals, plants, and animals on one side of the line and God on the other.

Methodological naturalism is a precept about the proper way of doing science. In its strongest version, it can be put as follows:

(M1) Scientific explanations of natural events must refer exclusively to natural causes.

M1 would seem to follow from O2, but even someone who accepted the existence and causal efficacy of nonnatural beings might accept M1, thinking that such beings can play no role in *scientific*, as opposed to other, kinds of explanation.

---

12. Lacey, "Naturalism," 604.

13. This can be left to the side because what is at issue in discussing the relation between the paleoetiological sciences and theology is not human action in the world or even divine influence on human actions, but rather divine influence on nonhuman objects and human bodies (at the physiological rather than the mental level).

O1 and O2 can be contrasted with two other ideas, each constituted by a pair of theses. These ideas must be, but often are not, distinguished from one another.

The first of those alternative ideas states that

(O3a) Nonnatural beings exist, but they only occasionally act as direct causes[14] of what happens in the natural world.

(O3b) The effects of nonnatural causes will generally be identifiable as due to such causes.

If O3a is true, then the causal powers of natural objects (the object of scientific research) are sufficient to explain most, but not all, of what happens in the natural world. Appeals to other causes will require special justification, and an elaboration of O3b will tell us what such a justification should look like. There is, in other words, a strong presumption in favor of natural explanation.

Moving yet further from O1 and O2 are another pair of ideas. One might think either or both of the following:

(O4a) Nonnatural beings not only exist, but frequently act as direct causes of what happens in the natural world.

(O4b) Cases of nonnatural causality are not readily and reliably identifiable as such.

In such a world, much of what happens could not be explained as the result of the interaction of natural objects.

What logical or practical connection does science have with any of these theses? What logical or practical connection do they have with theology? Answering these questions, requires us first to address two other questions.

How Much Naturalism Does Science Require?

O1, if it does not exclude everything that could be called religion, is surely inconsistent with Christianity and indeed all forms of theism that postulate a transcendent God. The slightly weaker O2, however, is still strong enough to be inconsistent with Christianity (if not with deism) and has been a particularly popular foundation for attacks on Christianity. The argument (or at least the assertion) underlying these attacks is that the acceptance of O2

---

14. By "direct causes" I mean "causes not mediated by the secondary causality of natural objects."

is required by science. Los Alamos physicist Marvin Mueller wrote that if appeal to supernatural agency can be made "all scientific discussion and all rational discourse must perforce cease."[15] Physiologist Sheldon F. Gottlieb, in a response to a journalistic religious critique of evolution, wrote: "In the world of the supernatural, anything goes, and the only limitation is the extent of one's imagination. No evidence is required to substantiate any claims."[16]

Evolutionary biologist Richard C. Lewontin wrote, with a special focus on science and the religious doctrine of creation:

> Either the world of phenomena is a consequence of the regular operation of repeatable causes and their repeatable effects . . . or else at every instant all physical regularities may be ruptured and a totally unforeseeable set of events may occur. One must take sides on the issue of whether the sun is sure to rise tomorrow. We cannot live simultaneously in a world of natural causation and of miracles, for if one miracle can occur, then there is no limit.[17]

These authors claim that the very existence (*contra* O_1 and O_2) of non-natural beings capable of acting on the natural world would make science impossible and that the practice of science, therefore, presupposes that at least O_2, if not O_1 itself, is true. Are they correct in making that claim?

Science is a method of coming to know about the natural world, i.e., about the natures of material objects. It is a method that begins with the attempt to identify the best explanation for the behavior of some natural object and then goes on to test the explanation by new observations (often under the artificially constructed conditions central to what have come to be called experiments). It cannot tell us whether material objects always act in accordance with their natures. C. S. Lewis once wrote:

> The laws [of Nature] will tell you how a billiard ball will travel on a smooth surface if you hit it in a particular way—but only provided no one interferes. If, after it's already in motion, someone snatches up a cue and gives it a biff on one side—why, then, you won't get what the scientist predicted . . . In the same way, if there was anything outside nature, and if it interfered—then the events which the scientist expected wouldn't follow. That would be what we call a miracle . . . [But] it isn't the physicist who can tell you how likely I am to catch up a cue and spoil his

---

15. Mueller, "Shroud of Turin," 27.
16. Gottlieb, Letter to the Editor.
17. Lewontin, "Introduction," xxvi.

> experiment with the billiard ball; you'd better ask a psychologist. And it isn't the scientist who can tell you how likely Nature is to be interfered with from outside. You must go to the metaphysician.[18]

Science does not presuppose, entail, or have any other logical connection to O2.

O4b would make it difficult to do science. If science investigates the nature of things by studying their behavior as they interact with other natural objects, then behavior too frequently under the influence of nonnatural agents, under conditions difficult to identify, would make the doing of science very difficult, if not impossible. It would be simply too hard to know when the behavior reported as scientific data was the result of natural causes and when it was not.

O4a alone would seem not to have this consequence, though it would make science a less important component of our understanding of the world than we generally take it to be.

O3, by contrast, is entirely compatible with doing science and with the idea that science makes an important contribution to our understanding of the world. Science is possible as long as most of what we observe is caused by natural interactions and the exceptions are generally either unnoticeable or identifiable. Science no more requires that all of what we observe be caused by natural interaction than it requires perfect observation on the part of scientists or the absolute impossibility of scientific fraud. To see that this is so, imagine someone objecting that (replacing Lewontin's words, quoted above, with the underlined modifications):

> Either the world of phenomena is <u>exactly as it is reported in laboratory notebooks</u> . . . or else <u>all the data in all our laboratory notebooks could be completely wrong</u> . . . We cannot simultaneously <u>rely on science and admit that scientists can make mistakes</u>, for if one <u>mistake</u> can occur, then there is no limit.

Phenomena are not exactly as reported in laboratory notebooks; scientists make imperfect measurements. The errors, however, are not common, and often we can identify the causes of those that they do make. The scientific method thus provides us with a reliable account of how the world works despite the fact of measurement error. It can also do so in a world that includes occasional, and generally identifiable, supernatural interventions.

---

18. Lewis, "Religion and Science," 73–74.

How Much Non-Naturalism Does Religion Require?

Theistic religion is inconsistent with O1. The Christian doctrine of miracles is an elaboration (though not a *logical* consequence) of the doctrine of providence—that God, through his providence, protects and guides all that he has created.

The doctrines of the Virgin Birth and the Resurrection are sufficient to establish that orthodox Christianity is incompatible with O2.

Does O3 provide enough space for Christianity, or does Christianity require O4? If doing science is compatible with O3, but not with O4, and religion (or at least Christianity) needed O4, then there would still be a science-religion problem for Christianity. So, the next task is to determine how much nonnaturalism Christianity needs. It is, of course, possible that different versions of Christianity would need different amounts. To keep the discussion focused, I will address the question in terms of what Catholicism needs.

What does Catholicism require? How much causal relation is there between nonnatural agents and the natural world? In one sense, the answer is, a lot. First, there are the doctrine of creation and two central principles of the theology of nature. Sufficient here are the following:

(C1) God created the world out of nothing.

(C2) Every individual soul was immediately (i.e., without the mediation of any secondary causes) created out of nothing by God.

(TN1) God keeps all things in existence.

(TN2) God cooperates immediately in every act of his creatures.

Second, there is the effect of grace on voluntary human actions. Third, and the heart of this matter for those particularly interested in science, is the doctrine of special providence (such as the occurrence of miracles and, more generally, the response to petitionary prayer). I mean, of course, miracles in the etymological sense—events whose occurrence creates amazement or wonder in those who witness them. They are signs (see John 2:11) in a way that creation, conservation, and for that matter Transubstantiation, for example, are not.

Do any of these doctrines require the kind of frequent or unidentifiable supernatural agency that make O4 rather than O3 the correct account of the world?

The doctrine of the creation of the world, insofar as it tells us how the world came into existence in the first place, is not about what happens *in* the world. Although it is not compatible with O1, its silence about how the world works makes it compatible with O3 and O4 (and, for that matter, with O2).

The doctrine of the creation of the human soul is a little different since the creation of human souls occurs as a correlate of (or, is occasioned by) a natural phenomenon—human zygosis. Nevertheless, if this is supernatural agency, it is clearly identifiable as such in virtue of the explicit teaching of the Church.[19] Catholic doctrine does not require O4 to accommodate the direct creation of each individual human soul.

The occurrence of miracles is the doctrine that has the most relevance to this question. Miracles are not everyday occurrences and there are generally ways of recognizing them when they occur. Evidence is required. The signs of a miraculous cure, for example, were given a more or less definitive formulation by Prospero Lambertini (later Benedict XIV) in the eighteenth century:

> In order for the cure of an illness or infirmity to be considered a miracle, a number of features must be present:
>
> (1) that it be grave and difficult or impossible to cure;
>
> (2) that it not be at a stage shortly after which improvement would be expected;
>
> (3) that no medications were used, or, if any were, that it is certain that they did not help;
>
> (4) that the cure be sudden and follow closely [after prayers for the cure];
>
> (5) that the healing be complete, not partial or temporary;
>
> (6) that it not be preceded by any noteworthy weakening of symptoms or turning point [*crisis*];
>
> and finally (7) that the disease not return.[20]

The recognition of miracles is part of the ordinary work of the Congregation for the Causes of Saints.[21] If miracles were not recognizable, they would not be able to fulfill their theological function; they might be providential

---

19. Pope Piux XII, *Humani Generis*, 575 (*Some False Opinions*, para. 36); John Paul II, "Message on Evolution."

20. Pope Benedict XIV, *De Servorum Dei Beatificatione et Beatorum Canonizatione*, 4.1.8.

21. I discussed this in more detail in Kemp, "Scientific Method."

interventions, but they would not be *miracles*. No scientist need worry about the provenance of the wine served at Cana; there is no theological reason for suspecting that such a transformation might occur in the laboratory or winery. It could, but it won't.

Modest Methodological Naturalism

So, O1 and O2 would create problems for Christianity, but science neither requires them nor even suggests that they are true. O4 would create problems for science, but Christianity neither requires it nor even suggests that it is true. That leaves O3 as both sufficient for Christian theology and compatible with scientific research.

The methodological consequence of O3 for science might be called modest methodological naturalism. Such naturalism grants a strong presumption in favor of appeal to natural causes in the attempt to understand something that happens in the world but allows that presumption to be overridden for a sufficiently good (theological) reason. The resultant appeal to supernatural agency would not, because it cannot be confirmed by further scientific research, count as a *scientific* explanation, but it would not be considered any the worse as an explanation for that. This is, for example, the approach used by the Congregation for the Causes of Saints in the investigation of miracle claims.

The mere fact that God *could* have acted directly, by contrast, is not sufficient to make appeal to supernatural agency a good explanation. Christians have a good reason for adhering to modest methodological naturalism rather than making the more frequent appeal to supernatural agency suggested by Philip Johnson (and many other proponents of Intelligent-Design Theory). Johnson once wrote: "Occasionally, a scientist . . . will suggest that perhaps supernatural creation [Johnson probably just means 'immediate divine action'] is a tenable hypothesis in this one instance. Sophisticated naturalists instantly recoil in horror, because they know that there is no way to tell God when he has to stop."[22]

The danger (and potential harm) created by following Johnson here is manifest in the fate of the eighteenth-century English tradition of physicotheology. In 1692-3, Isaac Newton suggested to Richard Bentley that intelligent design was the only possible explanation for the structure of the solar system (and hence was evidence for the existence of God).[23] In 1802, William Paley, whose *Natural Theology* stands as a culmination of the

---

22. Johnson, "Evolution as Dogma," 18.
23. Newton, "Four Letters."

physicotheological tradition so important in eighteenth-century English thought, appealed to direct supernatural agency to explain the adaptedness of plants and animals to their environments. In the first instance, Pierre-Simon Laplace, in book 5 of his *Exposition du système du monde*, was able to offer a plausible natural account for the origin of the solar system or at least of the peculiarities of planetary orbits. In the second, Charles Darwin, in his *Origin of Species*, was able to show that there were other ways of explaining adaptation. The scandal that such appeals caused was well characterized by Stephen Toulmin, who wrote:

> From the year 1700 on, religious-minded men in the Protestant world . . . had always hoped and expected that the new science would eventually confirm and reinforce the fundamental doctrines of Christianity; and they were correspondingly ready to see in their observations of Nature evidences of 'wisdom,' 'foresight,' and 'design.' . . . All the hitherto unsolved problems of geology, astronomy, physiology and natural history were presented as demonstrating that the world of Nature had been created as we now find it 'by the Counsel of an intelligent Agent' . . . The result of this enthusiasm for the teleological argument from design was to give a hundred hostages to fortune; and as the physical and biological sciences succeeded in explaining the supposedly supernatural *inexplicabilia*, all of these hostages in turn had to be ransomed, one after another.[24]

Questions of Substantive Content: Nondescriptivist Irenicism

With respect to the substantive content of science and theology, there are, to be sure, scientists, theologians, and philosophers who have argued that a war (indeed even a contradiction) between science and theology is, if not absolutely impossible, at least impossible as long as both science and religion (including theology) are properly practiced.

One way of defending the thesis that contradiction between scientific and theological claims is impossible would be to claim that only one of them describes the world, the other having some other function. In 1905, the French Catholic physicist and historian of science Pierre Duhem attempted to do just that. In reference to some of the particular problems of his day he wrote:

---

24. Toulmin, *Return to Cosmology*, 123.

> It has been fashionable for some time to oppose the great theories of physics to the fundamental doctrines on which spiritualistic philosophy and the Catholic faith rest; these doctrines are really expected to be seen crumbling under the ramming blows of scientific systems. Of course, these struggles of science against faith impassion those who are very poorly acquainted with the teachings of science and who are not at all acquainted with the dogmas of faith; but at times they preoccupy and disturb men whose intelligence and conscience are far above those of village scholars and café physicists.[25]

He went on to propose a positivist understanding of the nature of scientific theory that would, he thought provide a solution. A metaphysical proposition (he includes here religious dogma) is, he said:

> a judgment bearing on an objective reality, affirming or denying that a certain real being does or does not possess a certain attribute. Judgments like 'Man is free,' 'The soul is immortal,' 'The Pope is infallible in matters of faith' are metaphysical propositions or religious dogmas; they all affirm that certain objective realities possess certain attributes.[26]

A principle of theoretical physics, by contrast, is "a mathematical form suited to summarize and classify laws established by experiment."[27] So, while facts of experience and empirical laws could conflict with religious dogmas, the theories of physics could not. The principle of the conservation of energy, for example, cannot contradict a claim about freedom of the will.[28] In that way, Duhem thought, his system could "eliminate the alleged objections of physical science to spiritualistic metaphysics and the Catholic faith."[29]

More recently, Bas van Fraassen has argued that "a theory is empirically adequate exactly if what it says about the *observable* things and events in the world, is true."[30] Both men are Catholics who take their faith quite seriously, though neither thought that their theological commitments were necessary for their conclusions. It is not clear, however, that their work can reach (or that they intended it to reach) beyond the science of physics. Whatever plausibility antirealism has for theoretical physics vanishes when

---

25. Duhem, "Physics of a Believer," 283.
26. Duhem, "Physics of a Believer," 283.
27. Duhem, "Physics of a Believer," 285.
28. Duhem, "Physics of a Believer," 286–87.
29. Duhem, "Physics of a Believer," 282.
30. Van Fraassen, *Scientific Image*, 12 (italics added). See also Van Fraassen, "Constructive Empiricism Now."

the matter under discussion is not quarks but tyrannosaurs. The two are simply not "unobservable" in quite the same sense.

Perhaps more widespread is the idea that the risk of conflict stems from misunderstanding the true nature of theology and religion. Ian Barbour offered as examples of such views the neo-orthodoxy of Karl Barth, the existentialist theology of Rudolf Bultmann, and the philosophy of religion grounded in the linguistic analysis of Ludwig Wittgenstein.[31] A more recent attempt to draw a principled separation between the two, with explicit reference to the relation between the paleoetiological sciences and theology, one that has had a favorable reception in many quarters, was made by Stephen Jay Gould. Gould was by profession a paleontologist who had made interesting and important contributions both to evolutionary theory and to the history of science. In addition, he wrote, every month for many years, popular science articles for *Natural History*. His family religious background was Jewish, and while he himself was an agnostic, he maintained a certain respect for the place of religion in human life.

In his widely acclaimed essay "Non-overlapping Magisteria," and in more detail in his book *Rocks of Ages: Science & Religion in the Fullness of Life*, Gould explicated and defended what he called the Non-Overlapping Magisteria Principle—namely, that science and religion are independent, each constituting a "domain [. . .] where one form of teaching holds the appropriate tools for discourse and resolution."[32] These two magisteria, he went on to say, have equal status but separate subject matters. Science has as its domain matters of fact; the domain of religion is matters of value. Gould suggested that this solution is not only "a proper and principled solution—based on sound philosophy" but is "humane, sensible, and wonderfully workable."[33] He argued that this view of the relation between science and religion can be found in the writings of the most careful scientists and theologians ranging from Charles Darwin to John Paul II.

I have learned much from Gould's writings and admire his determination to give a careful hearing even to those with whom he is in deep disagreement, but, as the saying goes, *Magis amicus veritas*. As much as I appreciate the irenicist spirit of his work, I cannot agree with his thesis. I also think that the thesis is not found in all of the authors to whom he attributes it.

First, although he claimed that there are two domains and thus implicitly two sets of appropriate tools, it is never clear exactly what the religious

---

31. Barbour *Religion and Science*, 85–89.
32. Gould, *Rocks*, 5; see also Gould, *Rocks*, 52–53.
33. Gould, *Rocks*, 92.

tools are. There is a clear negative heuristic—"Don't look to nature" is said to be his principle's chief piece of advice for theologians.[34] The positive heuristic, by contrast, is very vague—"Look within oneself."[35] Indeed, although Gould in one passage refers to the logic of religious arguments, more often he suggests that this is merely the realm of taste.[36] It is, he says at one point, a realm where resolution relies upon "compromise and consensus."[37] In sum, Gould acknowledges no real teaching authority in religion and has little to say about the tools by which we can arrive at the truth in religious matters. It is unclear how he can acknowledge a religious magisterium at all.

Second, his account of religion is surely too narrow. Sometimes it seems as though Gould should have subtitled his book *Science and Ethics*. Catholicism, to focus on a particular religion, does, of course, make claims about matters of value (about what is good and what bad, about how we should act and what we should avoid doing). But it makes claims about matters of fact as well—about the existence of God and the immortality of the soul, to begin with the salient claims, but also about the creation of the world and of each human soul by God, about the Virgin Birth and the bodily Resurrection of Christ, about the Real Presence of Our Lord in the elements of the Eucharist, and about the resurrection of the bodies of us all on the Last Day. Without the resurrection of Christ, Christianity is not Christianity—"If Christ be not risen again, then is our preaching vain, and your faith is also vain," says St. Paul (1 Cor 15:14). The other doctrines are also, according to most Christians, in various ways constitutive of Christian belief. These are factual claims. Gould's characterization of the proper domain of religion may accommodate deism, but it cannot accommodate Christianity, which (though Gould does not acknowledge this) it will adjudge inherently a trespasser into an alien domain.

Gould did not seem to see this problem. He avoided it by including some of the facts just mentioned within the domain of values. The clear line of demarcation of the opening passages of his book becomes obscure in its application. In certain passages, the domain of religion is extended to values *and meaning*.[38] Elsewhere in the book, he broadened his characterizations yet further. There, the existence of God is also a value claim, not a factual one. At another point he said that claims about "the origin and constitution

---

34. Gould, *Rocks*, 162; see also Gould, *Rocks*, 184.
35. Gould, *Rocks*, 197; and Gould, *Rocks*, 204.
36. Gould, *Rocks*, 210.
37. Gould, *Rocks*, 62.
38. E.g., Gould, *Rocks*, 62.

of the human soul" are not factual matters.[39] Neither, he said yet elsewhere, is discussion of the ultimate beginning of all material things.[40] It is hard to see how these are not matters of fact. One wonders where the claims about free will or the occurrence of miracles lie. Are they factual matters for science to resolve or matters of value which can be left to religion?

Two doctrines in particular are too close to the subject matter of the paleoetiological sciences to allow resort to any variant of Gould's solution—the doctrines of the creation of the world and of the origin of man. Generous in spirit Gould may be, but the misunderstanding of religion that underlies his solution is too deep to permit its acceptance. The reality of such an overlap is inconsistent with Gould's irenicist hope that one can identify complementary subject matters, respect for which will render impossible any conflict between these two important human activities.

The possibility of conflict between science and religion (or theology), even when both are properly practiced, cannot be ruled out in advance. Conflict cannot be dismissed a priori as the result of some kind of epistemic malpractice. Where could it occur?

The Possibility of Substantive Epistemic Conflict between Science and Theology

Claims about substantive conflict between science and theology have been advanced with respect to a variety of theories and doctrines—the doctrines of free will, the efficacy of prayer, and the occurrence of miracles, for example, are sometimes contrasted with allegedly scientific materialism or determinism. The subject of this book, of course, is rather the relationship between the products of the paleoetiological sciences and the doctrine of creation.

We can define an evolutionary theory by generalizing a remark of Msgr. Georges Lemaître, one of the originators of the big bang theory, who wrote: "The purpose of any cosmogonic theory is to seek out ideally simple conditions which could have initiated the world and from which, by the play of recognized physical forces, that world, in all its complexity, may have resulted."[41] University of Notre Dame philosopher of science Fr. Ernan McMullin characterized evolutionary theories as the attempt "to explain

---

39. Gould, *Rocks*, 75.
40. Gould, *Rocks*, 217–18.
41. Lemaître, *Primeval Atom*, 162.

diversity by postulating an earlier, different [and simpler] stage from which the present diversity developed in an intelligible way."[42]

Although the idea of creation is sometimes associated by definition with divine action, it is, I want to say, *essentially* exnihilation—the bringing of something into being out of nothing.[43] Since only God can do that, the association of creation with divine action would be a consequence of the definition, but not part of the definition itself.

There are three ways in which conflict might occur.

The first possible type of conflict is direct logical conflict between the very idea that the world was created by God and the idea that its current state is the result of natural, evolutionary processes. There is, however, no such logical conflict. If there is some internal incoherence in the very idea of an evolving world, or in the idea of exnihilation, then, while the idea would be false, the impossibility would have nothing to do with any relation *between science and theology*. There can, however, in fact be no conflict between the ideas themselves because if an evolving world is possible at all, there is no reason why an omnipotent God could not have created it. If creation is possible, there is no reason why the resulting created world could not be a world that changes (evolves) over time. The ideas of creation and evolution are answers to fundamentally different questions. The doctrine of creation offers an account of the very existence of the world, of its dependence for that existence on God. Theories of evolution, by contrast, explain not the existence of the world, but how it got to be the way it is. They explain the transition from one state to another—from Jurassic fauna, say, to Triassic—not a *transition* (if that word can even be used here) from nonexistence to existence.

The second possible type is conflict between a particular evolutionary theory and a particular doctrine of creation (or an associated theology of nature, theory of divine action, and so forth). The goal of science is not just to show that, for example, species originate by descent with modification from earlier kinds, but to show which are descended from which (for example, that mammals are descended from reptiles). The goal of theology includes a proper understanding and a correct expression of the truths found in the sources of theological knowledge—in Scripture and Tradition. These may (Christians believe they do) go beyond the bare fact of creation to particular details such as the fact that the world is not only dependent on God for its existence, but that it had a beginning in time, i.e., that it is not

---

42. McMullin, "Introduction," 3.
43. See, e.g., Thomas Aquinas, *Summa Theologica*, Ia, Q. 45, a. 1.

eternal.[44] On a Christian view of God and revelation, of course, there will be no contradiction between an accurate account of the evolution of the world and the contents of revelation. Truth cannot contradict truth, as the fathers of the First Vatican Council had put it.[45] Non-Christians, of course, thinking that Scripture and Tradition are at best fallible sources of knowledge, would not rule out the possibility of such a conflict.

There is, however, a third possible kind of conflict—namely, that between the actual (perhaps as yet imperfect) results of scientists and theologians contemporary with one another. If competent scientists trying to work out an account of the origins of various features of the world in fact frequently and significantly (even if contingently) found themselves in conflict with competent theologians trying to understand revelation then one could, I suppose, say in a meaningful sense that there was a conflict between science and religion *simpliciter*.

Here, I am interested in the third possible kind of conflict.[46] The purpose of this book is to argue that the war that did occur, and that continues to be waged, between the practitioners of the paleoetiological sciences (in particular historical geology and evolutionary biology) and their opponents cannot be understood as a war between science and theology or religion.

To challenge ideas to the contrary, I will begin by examining the nineteenth-century origins of the Warfare Thesis, focusing in particular on the two books that nearly everyone sees as the *loci classici* of the theory. Then I will go on to discuss the incidents that proponents of the thesis cite as evidence in its favor—in particular the Huxley-Wilberforce exchange, the Scopes Trial and the larger anti-evolution campaign in which it was embedded, and finally the more recent curriculum wars centered at first on Creation Science and now on Intelligent-Design Theory.

---

44. Lateran Council IV, *Constitutio Dogmatica De Fide Catholica*.

45. Vatican Council I, *Constitutio Dogmatica de Fide Catholica* (First Vatican Council), 4. See also Leo XIII, *Providentissimus Deus*, 291. John Herschel had put the same point in his seminal *Preliminary Discourse*, 9: "truth can never be opposed to truth."

46. In a future book, I intend to address the second possibility and to argue that the theories of evolution that modern scientists have produced are the result of good scientific work done by Christians (both Catholics and Protestants), deists, and atheists. When kept distinct from ideas with which it is sometimes associated by the philosophically less careful of its proponents, it contains nothing incompatible with Christian doctrine. The doctrine of creation, in turn, presents rich and important truths about the material (and spiritual) world, none of which are inconsistent with the results of the paleoetiological sciences. The defense of that thesis, however, requires a book of its own.

What History Will Reveal

What can we learn from reviewing the incidents from the history of the paleoetiological sciences around which the warfare theorists have built their case?

What we learn is that the history of science is *not*, as John W. Draper put it, "a narrative of the conflict of two contending powers."[47] The Warfare Thesis is rather the result of its proponents' conflation of two partially overlapping conflicts.

The first of these is the conflict of new ideas with old ones—a war that was, and continues to be, fought between evolutionists and anti-evolutionists. The attempt to reduce this to a war between science and theology is misleading. It is a war that was fought *within* science (until, if evolution is taken to include natural selection, the 1930s) and *within* various churches. The fact that the theory of evolution (especially the Common Ancestry Thesis) prevailed quickly within the scientific community and won the assent of people whose primary interests were theological only somewhat later (and even then not of all) has sometimes made this war *look* like a war between scientists and Christians. The claim that it was a war between science and theology, however, distorts historical reality. If Christians have been slower to embrace the new idea, it is because they had more work to do in ensuring that the new theory was consistent with the rest of what they know about the world. There have, to be sure, been extremists on both sides of this conflict—Thomas Huxley and William Jennings Bryan, Richard Dawkins and Henry Morris, the author of *Hell and the High School* and the author of *Darwin's Dangerous Idea*[48]—who are partially responsible for this misperception. They cannot, however, fairly be said somehow to represent science and religion. They are in fact belligerents in an entirely different war.

What different war? At least since the first publication of Darwin's *Origin of Species*, there has been a mix of anticlericals, agnostics, and atheists who have been eager to put science in general, and evolutionary biology in particular, to use in a war on religion—not science's war, but their own *philosophical* war. The false identification of anti-evolutionism with religion, saying "religion" when one is only entitled to say "anti-evolutionism" (or at most "religiously inspired anti-evolutionism") is only reinforced by the existence of this different war—the war of those assorted antireligious types against religion and theology. The work of these secularist scientists (or, perhaps better, evolutionist-philosophizers) has been the aggressive promotion

---

47. Draper, *History*, vi.

48. Those authors were T. T. Martin, for the former, and Daniel C. Dennett, for the latter.

of one or the other of two theses about the implications and significance of science, in general, and evolutionary biology, in particular, for matters strictly outside the domain of science. Although the exact theses vary from author to author, the gist is that[49]

(S1) Science presupposes or otherwise shows that Christianity is false.

(S2) Evolution has, by itself, important consequences relevant to our understanding of man's place in nature.

Let us begin with S1. One can find some version of this view in the nineteenth century in the works of Thomas H. Huxley, John Tyndall, Clémence Royer, Carl Vogt, and Ernst Haeckel, among others. Twentieth-century exponents include Richard Dawkins, William Provine, and Daniel Dennett. In 1859, for example, Huxley wrote in a letter to a friend that "both [Theology and Parsondom] are in my mind the natural and irreconcilable enemies of Science. Few see it but I believe we are on the eve of a new Reformation and if I have a wish to live thirty years, it is that I may see the foot of Science on the necks of her enemies."[50] Royer, Darwin's first French translator, began her long preface to *De l'origine des espèces* with the sentence, "Yes, I believe in revelation, but in a permanent revelation of man to himself and by himself."[51] Haeckel, perhaps Germany's leading evolutionary biologist, and evolutionist-philosophizer, wrote that "in our day, Charles Darwin, has destroyed the prevailing false doctrines of the mystical dogmas of creation and, through his reformation of the theory of evolution, directed the feelings, thought, and will of mankind onto higher pathways."[52] William B. Provine, an historian of biology at Cornell University, which Andrew Dickson White cofounded, once wrote:

> [Darwin] understood immediately that if natural selection explained adaptations, and evolution by descent were true, then the argument from design was dead and all that went with it, namely the existence of a personal god, free will, life after death, immutable moral laws, and ultimate meaning in life.[53]

49. These theses are logically distinct. S1's claim about the incompatibility of science and Christianity does not imply that the evolutionary sciences themselves have anything to offer about man's place in nature, so one could assert S1 without going on to endorse S2. Whether one thinks that S1 would follow from S2 would depend on what one thinks are the implications of evolutionary theory and what one thinks that Christianity asserts.

50. Huxley, Letter to Dyster.

51. Royer, "Préface," v.

52. Haeckel, "Über die Naturanschauung," 81.

53. Provine, "Response to Phillip Johnson," 23.

And Harvard geneticist Richard Lewontin asserted that: "Whatever the desire to reconcile science and religion may be, there is no escape from the fundamental contradiction between evolution and creationism. They are irreconcilable world views."[54] Unsurprisingly, remarks like these elicit anti-*evolutionist* reactions in some Christian circles. Some people who care little about where grapevines come from care a lot about where the wine at Cana came from. If some scientific theory implies that there could have been no miracle at that wedding feast, then, in their view (and, for that matter, in mine), so much the worse for the scientific theory. I would be more confident about the theological truths in question than I would be about the truth of *that particular* scientific theory.

S2 does not directly address the truth of Christianity, but nevertheless in its own way calls the religious neutrality of evolutionary biology into question. In his popular (and in other respects generally good) book, *Why Evolution Is True*, University of Chicago biologist Jerry A. Coyne wrote:

> Learning about evolution can transform us in a deep way. It shows us our place in the whole splendid and extraordinary panoply of life. It unites us with every living thing on the earth today and with myriads of creatures long dead. Evolution gives us the true account of our origins, replacing the myths that satisfied us for thousands of years.[55]

This is not quite biology. What is it?

In *Natural Law and Natural Rights*, John Finnis identified religion as one of what he called "seven basic forms of [human] good." He defined religion as reflection on two fundamental questions:

> (1) How are all these orders [means and ends, priorities], which have their immediate origin in human initiative and pass away in death, related to the lasting order of the whole cosmos and to the origin, if any, of that order?
>
> (2) Is . . . human freedom . . . itself somehow subordinate to something that makes that human freedom, human intelligence, and human mastery possible . . . ?[56]

In the passage quoted above, Coyne put evolution to religious use (in Finnis's sense). People who make evolutionary biology into a source of religion should not be surprised when other people, with different religious views,

---

54. Lewontin, "Introduction," xxvi.
55. Coyne, *Why Evolution Is True*, xv.
56. Finnis, *Natural Law*, 89.

reject it outright (and seek to exclude evolutionary biology from the science curriculum of the public (and by law religiously neutral) schools).

The various disagreements that constitute the fight over evolution differ from one another in ways that are so important that the incidents cannot be aggregated with, say, the dispute over heliocentric astronomy into a larger picture of a war between science and religion (or theology). The conflicts cited by proponents of the Warfare Thesis are different from one another, and different in revealing ways. As an interpretive lens, the Warfare Thesis puts the incidents which it is used to view out of focus.

So how shall we think of the relationship between science (on the one hand) and theology or religion (on the other) if not by reference to either Draper and White's Warfare Thesis or to Gould's principle of Non-Overlapping Magisteria? John Hedley Brooke has suggested the term "Complexity Thesis" as a name for the results of the more careful histories of the relation between science and religion that have emerged over the past thirty years.[57] This approach to the study of the relationship emphasizes that it is sometimes a case of conflict, sometimes of mutual irrelevance, sometimes of mutual support. A study of the relationship between evolution and Christianity reinforces the soundness of Brooke's suggestion.

The only way to show that the Warfare Thesis is profoundly mistaken is to review the history of the conflicts that are cited as evidence in its favor. This book will offer an account of the historical relations between theology and the paleoetiological sciences.

Prospective readers might want to know, as they read my account of this history, where I stand on the substantive issues of the evolution and creation. I think no answer to that question is better than that once offered by the great geneticist, one of the founders of the neo-Darwinian synthesis of Darwinism and Mendelism, Theodosius Dobzhansky: "I am a creationist and an evolutionist."[58] Like Dobzhansky, I believe that God created out of nothing a world that slowly changes over the course of time in accordance with the laws of nature which he established. I believe that scientists have given a generally accurate account of the age of the world and of the processes which have effected its change over time.[59]

---

57. Brooke, "Science, Religion, and Historical Complexity." For a sample of the kind of historical writing that this alternative thesis produces, see Brooke, *Science and Religion;* or Lindberg and Numbers, *God and Nature;* as well as Numbers, *Galileo Goes to Jail.*

58. Dobzhansky, "Nothing in Biology Makes Sense," 182.

59. A detailed, substantive account of each idea, and a general defense of their compatibility, I am leaving for another book.

The purpose of this book is to tell the history of the relationship between the paleoetiological sciences and Christian theology in a way the demonstrates the historical claims asserted above.

CHAPTER 2

The Historical Origins of the Warfare Thesis

Draper, White, and the Invention of the Warfare Thesis

THE IDEA THAT THE best way to think of the relation between science and religion is as a kind of warfare is a product of the nineteenth century. That this idea had not only a logical side (contradiction of doctrine), but also an historical side, was expressed already by Thomas H. Huxley, who wrote in a review of Darwin's *Origin of Species* that

> Extinguished theologians lie about the cradle of every science as the strangled snakes beside that of Hercules; and history records that whenever science and orthodoxy have been fairly opposed, the latter has been forced to retire from the lists, bleeding and crushed if not annihilated; scotched, if not slain.[1]

The historical thesis was given a more extended treatment by two nineteenth-century American authors—John William Draper and Andrew Dickson White. No more recent book of a scope comparable to their work has since been written, and White, in particular, continues to have influence. White's *History* was commended as "a very useful book" by that eminent historian of science George Sarton in 1955,[2] and though its flaws are recognized by today's historians of science, it continues to inspire the ardently antireligious (though, unlike today's "new atheists," neither author is antireligious)

---

1. Huxley, Review of *The Origin of Species*, 556. The review, in accordance with the custom of the day, was published anonymously.
2. Sarton, "Introductory Essay," 14.

and to misinform the unwary. It is, therefore, worth beginning with a review of these two books.

John William Draper

Draper was born in England in 1811, the son of a Wesleyan clergyman. He came to America as a young man and there made a name for himself as a chemist, with a particular interest in the chemical effects of light. He was a pioneer in the development of photography and, among other accomplishments, was the first to make a photograph of the moon. In 1841, he helped to found the New York University School of Medicine and in 1876 was elected first president of the American Chemical Society.

In 1850, he published his last piece of scientific research and turned his attention to intellectual history, publishing in 1863 a *History of the Intellectual Development of Europe* and then, in 1874, a *History of the Conflict between Religion and Science*. The thesis of the latter book Draper put in the following terms: "The history of Science is not a mere record of isolated discoveries; it is a narrative of the conflict of two contending powers, the expansive force of the human intellect on one side and the compression arising from traditionary faith and human interests on the other."[3] The second belligerent, "traditionary faith," the reader quickly comes to realize, is not, despite the book's title, religion: "The tranquillity of society depends so much on the stability of its religious convictions, that no one can be justified in wantonly disturbing them."[4] It is rather Catholicism, "partly because its adherents compose the majority of Christendom, partly because its demands are the most pretentious."[5] This was no doubt a reaction partly against Bl. Pius IX's encyclical *Quanta Cura* (1864), with its associated Syllabus of Errors, and partly against the declaration of papal infallibility issued at Vatican I (1870).

Draper's work is characterized by lack of precision in the handling of concepts and arguments. He did not, for example, distinguish infallibility, omniscience, and impeccability:

> Infallibility means omniscience... There is no need to dwell on the unphilosophical nature of this conception [sc. of an infallible pope]; it is destroyed by an examination of the political history of the papacy, and the biography of the popes. The former

---

3. Draper, *History*, vi.
4. Draper, *History*, vii.
5. Draper, *History*, x–xi.

exhibits all the errors and mistakes to which institutions of a confessedly human character have been found liable; the latter is only too frequently a story of sin and shame.[6]

In another passage, he posed this false dichotomy: "Two interpretations may be given of the government of the world. It may be by incessant divine interventions or by the operation of unvarying law."[7] His understanding of intellectual history is tenuous. In his treatment of astronomy he wrote: "When Kepler announced his three laws, they were received with condemnation by the spiritual authorities, . . . partly because it was judged inexpedient to admit the prevalence of law of any kind as opposed to providential intervention."[8] The idea that providential *intervention* is key to the ordinary operations of the natural world is not the idea articulated in, for example, the *Summa Theologica* of St. Thomas Aquinas, where we read that "all that is in things created by God, whether it be contingent or necessary, is subject to the eternal law."[9] If the concern of "spiritual authorities" were laws of nature, they would also have objected to René Descartes's analysis of motion by reference to law,[10] or to Niels Stensen's use of the concept of law in geology,[11] which they did not.[12]

Andrew Dickson White

At about the same time, however, the history of the relations between science and theology caught the interest of another American, this one a professional historian (though also a university president and a diplomat). Andrew Dickson White was born into a Protestant Episcopal family in New York in 1832. The claims of his church (and most of the other churches in his native Syracuse), that the members of all the other churches were on the road to hell, provoked in him a lifelong reaction against (as he later put it) "the absurdity of distinctions between Christians on account of beliefs which individuals or communities have happened to inherit."[13] Later,

---

6. Draper, *History*, 225–26. For more examples, see pages 352 and 361–62.

7. Draper, *History*, 228.

8. Draper, *History*, 237.

9. Thomas Aquinas, *Summa Theologica*, IaIIae, 93. 4.

10. Descartes, *Principia philosophiae*, II.37–52; and Descartes, *Discours de la Méthode*, V.

11. Stensen, *Canis Carchariae Dissectum Caput*.

12. For recent work on the Christian foundations of the scientific conception of laws of nature, see Harrison, "Laws of Nature."

13. White, *Autobiography*, 2:561.

his efforts, with Quaker philanthropist Ezra Cornell, to establish Cornell University as the first private nondenominational university in the United States met with considerable resistance from New York's religious colleges.[14] "Then it was," he later wrote, "that there was borne in upon me a sense of the real difficulty—the antagonism between the theological and scientific view of the universe and of education in relation to it."[15] In 1869, the year after White succeeded in opening his new university, he was invited to give a lecture at the Cooper Union in New York. There he "determined to go on the offensive" against his clerical adversaries in a talk titled "The Battle-fields of Science."[16] He continued work on this subject for nearly three decades until, in 1896, he was finally ready to publish a two-volume *History of the Warfare of Science with Theology in Christendom*, a history of "the conflict between two epochs in the evolution of human thought."[17]

White's thesis, articulated already in 1869, but repeated unchanged in 1896, was that

> In all modern history, interferences with science in the supposed interests of religion, no matter how conscientious such interferences may have been, have resulted in the direst evils both to religion and to science, and invariably.
>
> All untrammelled scientific investigation, no matter how dangerous to religion some of its stages may have seemed for the time to be, has invariably resulted in the highest good both of religion and of science.[18]

That thesis is a strong one, but it is narrow. Its strength he made clear in the original lecture: "I say *invariably*—I mean exactly that. It is a rule to which history shows not one exception."

Its narrowness, however, must also be acknowledged. White did not say that religion has never benefitted science. "The work of Christianity . . . for science . . . has been great. It has fostered science often and developed it. It has given great minds to it." He did not say that it invariably *interferes* with science:

> The search for each of these kinds of truth must be followed out in its own lines by its own methods, without any interference

---

14. White, *Autobiography*, 1:422–26.
15. White, *History*, 1:viii.
16. White, *Autobiography*, 1:425.
17. White, *History*, 1:ix.
18. White, "Battle-fields," the source of the passages quoted in this and the two following paragraphs. The thesis also appears in White, *History*, 1:viii.

from investigators along other lines by other methods. And it would seem logical that we might work on in absolute confidence that . . . they must at last come together.[19]

What he said (in the narrow thesis) is that *when* religion interferes with science, it invariably harms both, and that science untrammeled invariably benefits both.

In the end, however, he said more than this. He said that "history is full of interferences."[20] These interferences, he went on to say, are not isolated instances, but a prominent feature of the intellectual history of mankind. "Religious men started centuries ago with the idea that pure scientific investigation is unsafe—that theology must intervene. So began this great modern war."[21] There is much in the tone of his *History*, and in the consistent direction of the errors which he made, to justify critics' concerns that the work constitutes in fact, if not in intent, an attack of religion—as a matter of history, to pick up on a distinction White himself once deployed, if not as a matter of logic. And it is as just such a critique that the book has always been understood. The breadth of its influence is suggested by the fact that translations (though sometimes only partial) appeared in French, Spanish, Italian, Portuguese, German, Russian, Ukrainian, Arabic, Chinese, and Japanese.

White mentioned Draper as an influence on his thought, and indeed their works are similar in some respects, but the differences are not trivial.

They differ in the respect which they accord to Sacred Scripture. Draper said of the Pentateuch:

> It is to be regretted that the Christian Church has burdened itself with the defense of these books, and voluntarily made itself answerable for their manifest contradictions and errors. Their vindication, if it were possible, should have been resigned to the Jews, among whom they originated, and by whom they have been transmitted to us. Still more, it is to be deeply regretted that the Pentateuch, a production so imperfect as to be unable to stand the touch of modern criticism, should be put forth as the arbiter of science.[22]

White, by contrast, began his final chapter ("From the Divine Oracles to the Higher Criticism") by remarking that "The great sacred books of the world are the most sacred of human possessions . . . These books, no matter

19. White, *Warfare of Science*, 8–9.
20. White, *Warfare of Science*, 9.
21. White, *Warfare of Science*, 9–10.
22. Draper, *History*, 225.

how unhistorical in parts and at times, are profoundly true."[23] He did not, however, hold an orthodox Christian understanding of the nature of Sacred Scripture, which he saw as the product of "laws governing the evolution of sacred literature,"[24] not the product of divine revelation.

White also lacked Draper's strong anti-Catholic sentiments. He was scrupulously careful to balance the examples of what he did not like between Catholics and Protestants.[25] He did, however, sometimes make serious blunders in his presentation of Catholic doctrine. For example, White understood the doctrine of papal infallibility to extend to "everything relating to faith and morals," even to the *Martyrologium Romanum*.[26] One wonders why he was not tipped off on this point by the prefatory material printed in nearly every edition of the *Martyrologium*. Among that material is the Apostolic Letter that Pope Benedict XIV wrote to King John V of Portugal, as an introduction to the new (1748) edition of the martyrology. There, among other things, he explained that the earlier edition erred in saying that St. Sulpicius was a disciple of St. Martin of Tours. The Sulpicius of the *Martyrologium* was the sixth-century bishop of Bourges, not the fourth-century biographer of St. Martin.[27] The pope's approval of the *Martyrologium* authorizes its use in official contexts; it does not certify it as free from error.

White explicitly tried to distinguish his work from Draper's on one particular point. His 1896 title describes the conflict as one between science and "dogmatic theology," rather than with religion generally as Draper had done in his title. White characterized religion as "the bringing of humanity into normal relations with that Power, not ourselves, in the universe, which makes for righteousness" and as "a need absolute, pressing, and increasing."[28]

23. White, *History*, 2:288.

24. White, *History*, 2:288–93.

25. See, for example, his discussion of anti-Copernicanism, where he wrote: "Nothing is more unjust than to cast especial blame for all this resistance to science upon the Roman Church. The Protestant Church, though rarely able to be so severe, has been more blameworthy" (White, *History*, 1:168), or his discussion of geology: "There is much reason to believe that the fetters upon scientific thought were closer under the strict interpretation of Scripture by the early Protestants than they had been under the older Church" (White, *History*, 1:212). Kind remarks about Catholicism are also easy to find in the *Autobiography*. See, for example, 2:540–41, 545, and 549–50.

26. White, *History*, 2:382. White points to the inclusion in the *Martyrologium* of Barlaam and Josaphat (27 November), whose legend, nineteenth-century scholars had come to realize, was a Christianization of a second-century life of the Buddha.

27. Pope Benedict XIV, *De Nova Martyrologii* (*Postquam intelleximus*), xiv. The entry for Saint Sulpicius is for 29 January.

28. White, *Autobiography*, 2:568.

His distinction between religion and theology found its ground in his dislike for creeds, which were, he thought, "made no one knows where or by whom, and of which no human being can adjust the meanings to modern knowledge, or indeed to human comprehension."[29] White blamed the harm done in the name of religion on theology.[30] Nevertheless, when White attempted to make the case against theology in his *History*, what he discussed is not really theology *per se* at all. The problems that his history identifies are rather, properly speaking, tradition-respecting methodologies and (in the parts of most concern to us) a non-evolutionary philosophy of nature.

Let us first take up White's concern for method. What did White have in mind when he contrasted "the naturally opposing tendencies of theology and science"?[31] Early in the book he said that "the theological method as applied to science"—he meant nature—"consists largely in accepting tradition and in spinning arguments to fit it."[32] This is not so very different from Draper's concern about the harm done by "traditionary faith." He quotes several times the fifth-century Vincentian canon—"all possible care must be taken, that we hold that faith which has been believed everywhere, always, by all."[33]

As a "triumph of this theological method" White cites the *De Proprietatibus Rerum* of Bartholomew the Englishman, perhaps the most popular encyclopedia of the thirteenth century (and indeed of several centuries thereafter). White criticized the book for its uncritical acceptance of what Bartholomew found in his sources (works such as St. Isidore's seventh-century *Etymologiae* and Pliny's first-century *Historia Naturalis*): "It was only when the great voyages of discovery substituted ascertained fact for theological reasoning in this province that its authority was broken."[34] As an example of the scientific approach, which he acknowledged to have been anticipated by St. Albert the Great, but saw as coming to flower only in the Renaissance, he cited Edward Wotton's *De Differentiis Animalium Libri Decem* (1552) and Konrad Gesner's *Historiae Animalium* (1551–1558). There is, to be sure, a significant difference between Bartholomew's work[35] and that of Wotton and Gesner, but it is not what White said it is.

29. White, *Autobiography*, 2:532.
30. White, *Autobiography*, 2:533.
31. White, *History*, 2:41.
32. White, *History*, 2:34.
33. Vincent of Lérins, *Commonitoria*, 2. See, for example, White, *History*, 1:13, 104, and 113.
34. White, *History*, 1:35.
35. For an introduction, see Se Boyar, "Bartholomaeus Anglicus and his Encyclopedia"; and Greetham, "Concept of Nature in Bartholomaeus Anglicus."

All three of those authors relied on the work of earlier naturalists. Alwynne Wheeler remarked of the two later authors that "Modern naturalists may view Wotton's book, . . . and much of Gesner's, as overweighted with information from the literature and short on original observation."[36] If Bartholomew repeated Pliny's story of the basilisk that can kill with a glance (which White reports), Gesner reported that elephants worship the stars (which White omits to mention).[37] Bartholomew, biblical commentator and renarrator of classical texts though he was, did sometimes make his own observations. Greetham, while acknowledging his "almost total reliance upon the notoriously credulous Solinus's *De Mirabilibus Mundi* for the description of Ireland," adds that "for other Western European countries [he] often seems to have based his accounts upon direct personal observation or upon other eye-witness reports."[38]

It is fair to emphasize the difference in the extent to which Gesner and Bartholomew relied on observation. Less sound is White's idea that this is because Bartholomew is a theologian and Gesner is not. It is rather because Gesner, however much he feels a responsibility to try to "bring together the literature,"[39] is trying to make a contribution to natural history while Bartholomew, however much his personal curiosity leads him beyond a strict delimitation of his task, is trying to write a commentary on Scripture. It is not the responsibility of the biblical scholar to do original research in natural history in order to write a guide to animals mentioned in the Bible. But it was not the *theological* method he was using when he got to his treatment of chameleons and spiders, it is the method of the encyclopedist.

White's idiosyncratic understanding of the nature of theology is clear from two other comments. First, he said of Cardinal Nicholas of Cusa, who showed in 1464 that a number of the decretals in the collection attributed to Isidore Mercator were in fact forgeries, that he was *not a theologian*, but a "searcher for truth by scientific methods."[40] Second and more tellingly, about Voltaire's refusal to accept the biological origins of the fossil seashells found high in the mountains, White wrote that "he, too, had a theologic system to support."[41]

36. Wheeler, "Wotton," 507.
37. Bartholomew, *De Proprietatibus*, 18.15; Gesner, *Historiae*, 1:553.
38. Greetham, "Concept of Nature," 669n38.
39. Wheeler, "Wotton," 507.

40. White, *History*, 2:314. The defenders of the authenticity of the documents in question can perhaps be faulted for their uncritical acceptance, but their method cannot fairly be called theological.

41. White, *History*, 1:229.

It is true that, theology being unavoidably tradition-bound on some matters (e.g., the Trinity), the use of tradition-respecting methods plays a more important role in that subject than it does in the natural sciences. That does create the risk that someone trained in theology might misuse recourse to authority in natural history or law, or for that matter might overuse it even in theology. But Cusa did not cease to be a theologian when he applied a critical methodology to distinguish the authentic from the forged documents among the Pseudo-Isidorian Decretals. Nor did Cesare Cardinal Barone cease to be a theologian when he used critical methods in his preparation of the *Martyrologium Romanum*. And the same can be said about the Bollandists who have been doing critical hagiography now for four hundred years.

What White saw as a war between science and theology is in fact nothing more than the struggle to determine the proper line between respect for tradition and reliance on the observational methods of the natural sciences (or on more critical methods in historical research).

White's second target, at least in the chapters most relevant to our inquiry, he called creation. White was not, however, really concerned with creation in the theological sense of the term at all. When he talked about creation, he had in mind, not the ontological dependence of the world on God, or even whether it had an origin in time; he used the term merely to name the opposite of evolution—fixity of species and other features of a static world. Whether that static world was created or existed eternally and independently of God seems not to have been of much concern to him. Either of those variants of staticism, in his judgment, would constitute a misconception of a world that manifests "evolution"—of solar systems, of flora and fauna, of languages, and of sacred texts. The reality of that process, he seems to think, would be evident to anyone but a tradition-bound "theologian." That there might ever have been legitimate scientific concerns about the truth of the new evolutionary ideas he never acknowledged.

White's *History* has, as has often been noted, several significant defects. Although he sometimes spoke generously of those who, in his view, were impeding the growth of scientific knowledge, at other times he described them as going into hysterics and shrieking, screaming in rage, and the like.[42] Sometimes he put a matter completely out of focus. Whom did he cite as exemplifying thirteenth-century theology? Not Albert the Great, teacher of the greatest Catholic theologian of the millennium and (now, though not in White's day) officially a Doctor of the Church, but Bartholomew the Englishman.

---

42. See, for example, White, *History*, 1:73 and 1:134.

Sometimes, he simply misstated the facts. One item on his bill of particulars against dogmatic theology is its rejection of the idea (accepted in ancient Greece) of the sphericity of the earth. "The great majority of the early fathers of the Church, and especially Lactantius, had sought to crush it," he said,[43] though he acknowledged that there were dissenters—Origen, SS. Ambrose and Augustine, SS. Isidore of Seville and Bede the Venerable, SS. Albert the Great and Thomas Aquinas. Who joined Lactantius in this majority? Well, there is the monk-geographer Cosmas Indicopleustes in his sixth-century *Christian Topography*. Two men, with or without courage, do not make a majority.

Another particularly significant error was his account of religious opposition to the obstetric use of anesthesia, a procedure first tried by James Young Simpson in 1847. "From pulpit after pulpit Simpson's use of chloroform was denounced as impious and contrary to Holy Writ," White wrote,[44] but he had misread his source. A. D. Farr concluded a careful study of the question with the remark that "despite a spirited battle between the proponents and the opponents of anaesthesia upon medical, physiological, and even moral grounds, the religious issue was never a real factor in this particular medical development."[45]

At other times, White misquoted his sources. He quoted St. Augustine as saying that "Nothing is to be accepted save on the authority of Scripture, since greater is that authority than all the powers of the human mind." While the second half of the sentence can be found in the passage of St. Augustine which White cited,[46] the first part cannot.

White's problem is that he was using a faulty lens. He was, in the end, guided (or rather misguided) by his acceptance of Draper's thesis that "the history of Science is . . . a narrative of the conflict of two contending powers, the expansive force of the human intellect on one side and the compression arising from traditionary faith . . . on the other."[47] White was looking for events that exemplify a conflict between science and theology. What he found was a conflict between traditional and investigational methodologies. Since Christian theology has its foundation in revelation (and therefore has tradition as an ineluctable part of its method), and since science depends ultimately on human reasoning, the identification—or misidentification—is

---

43. White, *History*, 1:97.

44. White, *History*, 2:62–63.

45. Farr, "Early Opposition to Obstetric Anaesthesia"; and Farr, "Religious Opposition to Obstetric Anaesthesia."

46. White, *History*, 1:25, 210, and 325; Augustine, *De Genesi ad Litteram*, 2.5.

47. Draper, *History*, vi.

made: theology has a tradition-respecting methodology, so any disciplinary reliance on tradition is theological. Science is open to new ideas, so reliance on tradition is antiscientific.

Evolution & the Warfare Thesis

Draper and White wrote histories of a war of many campaigns—ranging from cosmology, geography, meteorology, biology, and geology, to medicine, economics, and literary studies. Of all of the areas of conflict which they claimed to have identified, two or perhaps three remain in the popular imagination: the reception of Copernicanism, the reception of Darwinism, and the question of the shape of the earth. The last of these, on which White spends ten pages, can be set aside for the simple reason that no such debate between science and theology (Christian theology, at least) ever occurred.[48] The reception of Copernicanism, though more serious a problem, is too remote from the topic of this book to justify a detour; fortunately, the topic has been well canvassed elsewhere.[49] How does the Draper-White Thesis hold up with respect to the paleoetiological sciences?

White's version of the alleged war against these sciences includes three central phases. The first, "From Genesis to Geology," focuses on the age of the earth and what might be called its formational economy, and so is centered on the Hexaëmeron and on the story of Noah's Flood. The second stage, "From Creation to Evolution," focuses on the origin of biological species. The third stage concerns the antiquity of man and the doctrine of the Fall.[50]

What do the incidents in the history of the relations between Christian theological doctrine and the paleoetiological sciences look like when seen through the lens of the Warfare Thesis? We can get some feel for this by looking at popular accounts of two of the incidents that inevitably feature in the warfare narratives—the Wilberforce-Huxley exchange, which occurred at Oxford in 1860, and the Scopes Trial, held in Dayton, Tennessee, in 1925.

The first of those, of which historian James R. Moore said, "No battle of the nineteenth century, save Waterloo, has been better known,"[51] arose,

48. See Russell, *Inventing the Flat Earth*.

49. See, for an introduction to the issue, Langford, *Galileo*. For more recent scholarship on the question, see McMullin, ed., *Church and Galileo*.

50. These three phases are discussed in White, *History*, chapters 5, 1, and 6–10 (pages 1:209–48, 1–23, and 249–322), respectively. The quoted phrases are from chapter titles. There is also much that is relevant to these topics in White's final chapter, "From the Divine Oracles to the Higher Criticism," 2:288–396.

51. Moore, *Post-Darwinian Controversies*, 60.

curiously enough, in the discussion of a paper given by Draper, though he made no mention of it in his book, which appeared sixteen years after the event. White did mention the incident in 1896, along with several other incidents.[52] The Oxford incident has since attained a kind of paradigmatic status. Here is a typical modern account of the details:

> For half an hour the Bishop spoke, savagely ridiculing Darwin and Huxley, and then he turned to Huxley, who sat next to him on the platform. In tones icy with sarcasm he put his famous question: was it through his grandfather or his grandmother that he claimed descent from an ape? . . . [Huxley] tore into the arguments Wilberforce had used . . . Working himself up to his climax, he shouted that he would feel no shame in having an ape as an ancestor, but that he would be ashamed of a brilliant man who plunged into scientific questions of which he knew nothing.
>
> The room dissolved into an uproar. Men jumped to their feet, shouting at this direct insult to the clergy . . . Admiral Fitzroy, the former Captain of the *Beagle*, waved a Bible aloft, shouting over the tumult that it, rather than that viper that he had harbored in his ship, was the true and unimpeachable authority . . .
>
> The issue had been joined. From that hour on, the quarrel over the elemental issue that the world believed was involved, science versus religion, was to rage unabated.[53]

The second paradigmatic incident in warfare historiography, the Scopes trial, was merely the most famous event in a decade-long campaign against the teaching of the evolution of man in American public schools, a campaign that began about 1920, just two years after White's death. Law professor Samuel Walker has called the trial itself "one of the most famous courtroom battles in American history."[54] Journalistic historian Frederick Lewis Allen, in a book used in American college classrooms for decades, wrote that

> All through the decade the three-sided conflict [between Fundamentalism, Modernism, and skepticism] reverberated. [That conflict] reached its climax in the Scopes case of 1925.

---

52. White, *History*, 1:184. I will discuss these in chapter 3.
53. Moore, *Charles Darwin*, 126.
54. Walker, *In Defense of American Liberties*, 72.

> The Scopes Trial ... dramatized one of the most momentous struggles of the age—the conflict between religion and science ...[55]

It is now known to most Americans chiefly through the dramatic efforts of Jerome Lawrence and Robert E. Lee, whose 1955 play *Inherit the Wind* was later made into a movie, advertised by United Artists as being "all about the fabulous 'Monkey Trial' that rocked America!" The work has since been read, watched, or produced by countless classes of American high-school students, and too often not so much for its literary quality as for the insight it allegedly provides into attitudes towards science and religion in the 1920s (and, by implication, more generally). Lawrence and Lee explicitly deny that their play is a history of the Scopes Trial. Lawrence has even denied that the play is about the relation between science and religion.[56] Nevertheless, the play has etched into the public consciousness the image of Scopes as a courageous schoolteacher persecuted for teaching evolution in his classroom by the religious fanatics who inhabit the Bible Belt. The incident, thus understood, has become, in the words of liberal journalist Joseph Wood Krutch, who covered the trial for *The Nation* in 1925, part of "the folklore of liberalism."[57]

Maynard Shipley, atheist and founder of the Science League of America, wrote a history of the larger anti-evolution campaign as the battle neared its close. He opened the work with this declaration: "The forces of obscurantism in the United States are in open revolt! More than twenty-five millions of men and women ... have declared war on modern science."[58]

Shipley, to his partial credit, kept his focus on fundamentalism rather than on religion itself. It is less clear that the attack on modernism, which he also mentions in his subtitle, is a war on modern science.

Conclusion

How can we test the Warfare Thesis? The first step will be to extract from the work of the Draper-White historians its central ideas. I would suggest that at the heart of this approach to intellectual history lie the following theses:

---

55. Allen, *Only Yesterday*, 201 and 195.
56. Lawrence told a reporter during the play's 1996 Broadway revival, "It's not about science versus religion. It's about the right to think" (Mandell, "Inherit the Controversy," 10).
57. Krutch, "Monkey Trial," 83–84.
58. Shipley, *War on Modern Science*, 3.

W1. There is something important that all of the incidents these historians cite have in common.

W2. The incidents involve two groups of participants—scientists (and their allies) and theologians (and their allies).

W3. The relation between these two groups is best characterized as a war in which

    a. theology (or religion) harms science by resisting the acceptance of scientific conclusions; and

    b. theology (or religion) is culpable and science is not.

Disagreements or conflicts between a scientist and a theologian are presumptively (if not automatically) presented as new instances of the established type (W1), i.e., as episodes in which W2–3 serve as guides in the determination of relevant facts and in their interpretation. We need to investigate the canonical list of cases cited in support of the Warfare Thesis in order to see whether its central ideas are consistent with the historical record.

CHAPTER 3

Christianity, Geology & Cosmology before 1859

It might seem appropriate to begin our history with the story of the confrontation that occurred at Oxford in 1860. It is, after all, with Darwinism that popular histories of the supposed war between Christian theology and the paleoetiological sciences typically begin. For example, in its obituary of Charles Darwin, *The New York Times* wrote:

> from the moment when the Darwinian theory of evolution was publicly stated the modern struggle between science and theological dogma took its rise. There had been skeptics and atheists and deists and what not before, but what grave essayists call scientific unbelief sprang primarily from the works of Charles Darwin.[1]

There are, however, two problems with the popular view.

The first problem is with the identification of Darwinism as the cause of the nineteenth-century change in attitudes towards religion. There was much in the air in the 1860s. The year 1859 had seen not only the publication of Darwin's *Origin of Species*, but also the quite distinct scientific acceptance of the antiquity of man.[2] This was followed shortly by the publication of two major challenges, both from within the Church of England, to a variety of traditional Christian doctrines, though without any special emphasis on scientific ideas. Those books were the *Essays and Reviews* (1860), whose

---

1. *New York Times*, "Death of Charles Darwin."

2. For an early synthesis of the evidence that caused the rapid conversion on this issue, see Lyell, *Geological Evidences*. For a history, see Grayson, *Human Antiquity*.

authors their opponents promptly dubbed the Seven against Christ, and *The Pentateuch and the Book of Joshua Critically Examined* (1862), written by John Colenso, the Anglican bishop of Natal. I suspect that any unbelief (scientific or otherwise) that arose in the 1860s was due at least as much to those two books as to the new ideas in biology. Indeed Darwin himself, for what it is worth, owed his loss of belief to matters unconnected with his scientific work, a point that will be discussed in more detail below.

The second problem is with the date. Historian Owen Chadwick did write in his *Victorian Church* that "From 1864 the controversy between 'science' and 'religion' took fire. The *Times* newspaper first wrote a leading article upon the subject in May 1864."[3] But whatever the correct apportionment of causal responsibility for any newly emergent unbelief, it is clear that the question of the compatibility of the Bible with the paleoetiological sciences in fact arose rather earlier. John Ruskin had written to his friend Henry Acland in 1851:

> [My faith], which was never very strong, is being beaten into mere gold leaf, and flutters in weak rags from the letter of its old forms; . . . If only the Geologists would let me alone, I could do very well, but those dreadful Hammers! I hear the clink of them at the end of every cadence of the Bible verses.[4]

The origins of the paleoetiological sciences, which are alleged to have caused the disharmony between science and religion, lie not in the middle of the nineteenth century, but in the seventeenth.

One can, to be sure, find in two places antecedents to the paleoetiological sciences even in Greco-Roman antiquity. The outlines of a comprehensive cosmogony appeared in Lucretius's *De rerum natura* (c. 55 BC) though this work, when it was known at all (and it appears to have been lost from about the tenth century to 1417), had too strong an element of hedonism and atheism to be of real interest to ancient or medieval Christians.

Aristotle's *Meteorology* (c. 350 BC) contains a more limited antecedent in his assertion of the reality of gradual, but significant, topographical change: "Mainland and sea change places and one area does not remain earth, another sea, for all time, but sea replaces what was once dry land, and where there is now sea there is at another time land. This process must, however, be supposed to take place in an orderly cycle."[5] Aristotle nevertheless blurred any distinction between paleoetiological science and the

---

3. Chadwick, *Victorian Church*, 2:3. The article in question must be that published on 25 May 1864, on pages 8–9.

4. Ruskin, *Works*, 36:114–15.

5. Aristotle, *Meteorologica*, I.14.

more ordinary scientific account of events that take place over shorter time periods:

> Those whose vision is limited think that the cause of these effects is a universal process of change, the whole universe being in process of growth. So they say the sea is becoming less because it is drying up, their reason being that we find more places so affected now than in former times. There is some truth in this, but some falsehood also. For it is true that there is an increase in the number of places that have become dry land and were formerly submerged; but the opposite is also true... It is absurd to argue that the whole is in process of change because of small changes of brief duration like these; for the mass and size of the earth are of course nothing compared to that of the universe. Rather we should suppose that the cause of all these changes is that, just as there is a winter among the yearly seasons, so at fixed intervals in some great period of time there is a great winter and excess of rains.

Medieval scholars who took an interest in these questions (from St. Albert the Great to Albert of Saxony), and their successors, seemed not to find anything in Aristotle's approach theologically problematic and felt free to attribute, for example, the origins of mountains to natural causes.[6]

Whatever modern paleoetiology may owe to Lucretius and to the Aristotelians, I think it is fair to give considerable credit for the birth of the modern idea of a comprehensive scientific history of nature to René Descartes, who, in his *Discourse on the Method of Rightly Conducting the Reason* (1637), had asked:

> What would happen in a world, if God were now to create somewhere in imaginary space enough matter to compose it, and if He agitated the parts of this matter diversely and without order, so that He made of it a chaos as confused as the poets can imagine and if He afterwards did nothing else except lend His ordinary support to nature and leave it to act according to the laws which he established?

He went on to suggest that

> The greatest part of the matter of this chaos must, according to these laws, become disposed and arranged in a certain way which would make it similar to our heavens... Some of its parts

---

6. For one example, see Faventius, *De Montium Origine* (1561). Faventius was a Dominican priest. For a more general history, see Duhem, "Origines de la Géologie" or Adams, *Geological Sciences*, 329–98.

must compose an earth, some compose planets and comets, and some others a sun and fixed stars... There is nothing to be seen in the phenomena of this world which would not, or at least which could not, appear in the same way in the phenomena of the world I was describing.[7]

Descartes himself took some preliminary steps towards implementing this paleoetiological program with respect to both the heavens and the earth in Parts III and IV of his *Principia Philosophiae* (1644). About the relation between these ideas and the text of Genesis Descartes said nothing. Perhaps his presentation of the account hypothetically (exactly the approach that Pope Urban VIII had proposed to Galileo in 1624)—"what would happen in a world, if God were now to create," etc.—made that unnecessary. Censors who reviewed these works for the Holy Office in 1663 raised theological and philosophical concerns about other aspects of the work, but not about this.[8]

Although Descartes's hypothetical approach to the paleoetiological sciences allowed him to avoid the questions of the compatibility of his account with the text of Sacred Scripture, others interested in the question, beginning with Thomas Burnet in his *Sacred Theory of the Earth* (1681–1690), took a realist approach. That gave defenders of the old ideas (both scientific and theological) an occasion to attack the paleoetiological sciences and gave proponents of the new ideas the task of composing a compatibilist synthesis of paleoetiological and theological ideas.

Questions about the relevance of theology for the paleoetiological sciences and *vice versa* were thus not new in 1859. Indeed, some three decades before that date, Fr. Nicholas Wiseman, then rector of his church's English College in Rome, later Cardinal Archbishop of Westminster, opened his *Twelve Lectures on the Connexion between Science and Revealed Religion*, with a characterization of the problem he intended to address in the following terms:

> Some men in their writings, and many in their discourse, go so far as to suppose that they may enjoy a dualism of opinions, holding one set which they believe as Christians, and another whereof they are convinced as philosophers.[9] ... One does not see how it is possible to make accordance between the Mosaic creation and Cuvier's discoveries [e.g., of prehistoric mammals]; another thinks the history of the dispersion incompatible with

7. Descartes, *Discours*, Part V.

8. See Armogathe and Carraud, "La Première Condamnation."

9. [Wiseman meant what we would call scientists, but that term barely existed when he wrote, gaining currency only after about 1865.]

the number of dissimilar languages now existing; a third considers it extremely difficult to explain the origin of all mankind from one common parentage.[10]

Descartes's idea led, over the course of the intervening two centuries, to the rise of three related, but nevertheless distinct, lines of (sometimes rather speculative) scientific inquiry[11] encompassing several related questions. It led, that is to say, to the emergence of three new, paleoetiological, sciences. These scientific ideas were closely examined for their consistency with, or relation to, a variety of theological doctrines and opinions. It is with these controversies that the story of the relation between Christian theology and the paleoetiological sciences must begin.

The first of the three lines of inquiry was the attempt to make sense of the structure of the earth—of its mountains and valleys, and in particular of its strata. This line of research, not entirely absent in earlier centuries, as noted above, took a definite step forward with the publication of Blessed Niels Stensen's *De Solido intra Solidum Naturaliter Contento Dissertationis Prodromus* [*Prodromus of a Dissertation concerning a Solid Body Enclosed by Process of Nature within a Solid*] in 1669[12] and reached its maturity in about 1830 with Léonce Élie de Beaumont's "Researches on some of the Revolutions which have taken place on the Surface of the Globe,"[13] and Charles Lyell's *Principles of Geology*, the subtitle of which describes it as "an attempt to explain the former changes of the earth's surface by reference to causes now in operation." The effort to explain the origin of these features required those early geologists to address a number of related questions, such as whether the natural agent causally responsible for geological formations was water (Neptunism) or fire (Plutonism and Vulcanism), whether the processes involved were rapid (Catastrophism) or gradual (Uniformitarianism), and whether the pattern of earth history was linear or cyclical.

The second line of inquiry was the attempt to offer an account of the origin of the solar system (including, of course, the earth).[14] Georges-Louis Leclerc, Comte de Buffon, had proposed in his *Théorie de la Terre* (1749), the first part of his great *Histoire Naturelle*, that the planets came into existence

10. Wiseman, *Twelve Lectures*, 1:3.

11. I mean by "scientific inquiry" inquiry that is aimed at explaining observational data by appeal to natural processes. Though the term took on that meaning only in the nineteenth century, the practice (so broadly understood) is identifiable before that date.

12. Stensen is also commonly referred to by the Latin version of his name, Nicolaus Steno.

13. Beaumont, "Researches" is a brief version of Beaumont's much longer "Recherches."

14. For an overview, see Numbers, "Cosmogonies from 1700 to 1900."

when a passing comet tore some solar matter off the surface of the sun.[15] Unfortunately for Buffon, within thirty-five years the work of Fr. Alexandre Guy Pingré had established that comets lacked the mass necessary to do the work required of them.[16] The second half of the century, however, saw the appearance of another, and, in the judgment of most scientists of the day, more plausible alternative.[17] Pierre Simon de Laplace, in his *Exposition du Système du Monde* (1796), suggested that the solar system originated with nebulous matter, an idea which seemed to gain support from the telescopic observation of "nebulae" then being made by William Herschel.[18] Despite their differences, the theories of Buffon and Laplace converged at their point of contact with geology. On both accounts, the earth began as a very hot object in whose history cooling had a prominent place.[19]

The third line of inquiry was focused on fossils. Recognition of their organic origins led to two further questions.

The first question was, how did marine organisms end up far from the sea or high in the mountains? This question had been raised already in classical antiquity. We find it in Strabo's *Geography* (c. AD 17–25):

> Eratosthenes says . . . that this question in particular has presented a problem: how does it come about that large quantities of mussel-shells, oyster-shells, scallop-shells and also salt-marshes are found in many places in the interior at a distance of two thousand or three thousand stadia [i.e., 200–300 miles] from the sea—for instance . . . in the neighborhood of the temple of Ammon and along the road, three thousand stadia in length, that leads to it?[20]

This remained an issue for both Renaissance and early modern geologists.

The second question was, what explains their orderly distribution in the geological column? Darwin's account of the origin of species as part of the history of the earth was at least the third in a series of attempts to elaborate upon the idea that species originated by the modification of previously

---

15. Buffon, "Article I: Of the Formation of the Planets" (see Buffon, *Histoire Naturelle*, 1:127–67). The idea appeared again, in a somewhat modified form, in Buffon, *Époques de la Nature* (1778).

16. Pingré, *Cométographie*, 2:115–16.

17. Immanuel Kant's similar cosmogony, published in his *Allgemeine Naturgeschichte und Theorie des Himmels* (1755), went almost unnoticed until the middle of the nineteenth century.

18. The relevant passages of Laplace's *Exposition* are conveniently available in translation in Numbers, *Creation by Natural Law*, 124–32.

19. For a history, see Lawrence, "Heaven and Earth."

20. Strabo, *Geography*, I.3.4.

existing species. The two earlier attempts—Jean-Baptiste de Lamarck's *Philosophie Zoologique* (1809) and Robert Chambers's *Vestiges of the Natural History of Creation* (1844)—had both received wide notice, but neither had won for the idea much acceptance in the scientific community. Indeed, so intensely did Thomas H. Huxley dislike Chambers's *Vestiges* that he began his review of the tenth edition of what he called "a once attractive and still notorious work of fiction" by quoting *Macbeth*:

> In the mind of any one at all practically acquainted with science, the appearance of a new edition of the 'Vestiges' at the present day, has much the effect that the inconvenient pertinacity of *Banquo* had upon *Macbeth*. 'Time was, that when the brains were out, the man would die.'[21]

These three lines of scientific inquiry made contact, in a variety of ways, with a number of distinct theological ideas. Some of those theological ideas, for example the idea that salvation history gives a direction to time itself, were broadly thematic; others were based on particular passages of the Bible, in particular the Hexaëmeron, the genealogies (and other chronological passages),[22] and the account of the Noachian Deluge. Some, for example the idea that the world was created out of nothing, were clearly a matter of doctrine; others, for example the universal extent of the Deluge or the idea that animal death did not antedate the Fall, must, however widely they were accepted, be acknowledged to have had, at best, a weaker note of theological approbation. The connections that could be made between scientific and theological ideas were imprecise—they were often suggestive rather than logical, going beyond what science could demonstrate, even in principle, or beyond what the Bible actually said. Nevertheless, with some extension or extrapolation, whether of biblical text or empirical observation, the connections were sometimes asserted. The true nature of the relations between science and theology becomes clear in a review of the development of thought on several of the topics mentioned above.

The Age of the Earth

Let us begin with chronology. How old is the world? Eusebius of Caesarea, one of the fathers of church history, had warned his readers in the fourth century, in the very first paragraphs of his *Chronicon* against the hope that one can be certain about such matters: "It is not possible—not from the

---

21. Huxley, Review of *Vestiges*, 425.
22. For a review of these texts and problems, see Finegan, *Biblical Chronology*.

Greeks, nor from the barbarians, nor from anyone else, not even from the Jews—to learn with certainty the universal chronology of the world."[23] Nevertheless, Christian chronographers both before and after him attempted to use the Bible to give a date for the life of Adam and, by extension, for the age of the world. Perhaps the first to do so was Theophilus of Antioch, who wrote in his *Apology to Autolycus* (c. 180) that "all the years from the creation of the world amount to a total of 5698 years, and the odd months and days."[24] The first comprehensive Christian chronographer, Sextus Julius Africanus, came to nearly the same conclusion.[25] On this point, the tradition of the Church followed Julius rather than Eusebius. St. Isidore of Seville, for example, made the same assumptions in the seventh century, in his *Chronicon*, as did St. Bede the Venerable in the eighth in his *De Temporibus, sive De Sex Aetatibus Huius Seculi*. So too did the leading Renaissance chronologists, from Joseph Justus Scaliger to James Ussher, whose calculation gained immortality by its inclusion, beginning in 1701, in many editions of the King James Bible.[26] By 1738 there were, by the count of Alphonse des Vignoles, more than two hundred distinct calculations of the date of creation, all putting the age of the earth at something between three and seven thousand years before Christ.[27] Sir Thomas Browne spoke for most of his seventeenth-century contemporaries when he wrote: "Time we may apprehend. It is but five days older than ourselves."[28] New scientific ideas, about the age of the stars and about the age of the earth, posed a challenge to this idea.

The idea that the stars were much older than six thousand years arose as William Herschel combined his estimates of the distance of observable nebulae with the speed of light:

> I shall take notice of an evident consequence attending the result of the computation; . . . when we see an object of the calculated distance at which one of these very remote nebulae may still be perceived, the rays of light which convey its image to the eye, must have been . . . almost two millions of years on their way;

23. Eusebius, *Chronicon*, 2.

24. Theophilus, *Apology to Autolycus*, III.28. The Septuagint, on which Theophilus relied in his calculation, yields a chronology that is about 1500 years longer than that of the Hebrew Bible.

25. Julius Africanus, *Chronographiae*, 130.

26. Scaliger, *Opus de Emendatione Temporum*; Ussher, *Annales Veteris Testamenti*. For more on Ussher and Scaliger, see Gould, "House of Ussher"; or Barr, "Why the World Was Created in 4004."

27. Vignoles, *Chronologie de l'Histoire Sainte*, b4.

28. Browne, *Religio Medici*, i.i.xi.

and that, consequently, so many years ago, this object must already have had an existence in the sidereal heavens, in order to send out those rays by which we now perceive it.[29]

Herschel was silent about the discrepancy between this and the traditional calculations of the age of the world, but other authors did take up the question. John Pye Smith, an influential nineteenth-century Congregationalist theologian and a member of the Geological Society of London, commented: "These views of the antiquity of that vast portion of the Creator's works which Astronomy discloses, may well abate our reluctance to admit the deductions of Geology, concerning the past ages of our planet's existence."[30] Pye Smith, it seems, was an optimist.

As for the age of the earth itself, an earth that owed its origin to the cooling of stellar matter or a protosolar nebula could not have cooled to its present temperature in a mere six thousand years. Buffon, on the basis of experiments with heated spheres, had proposed an age of around seventy-six thousand years.[31] Over the course of the following half-century, a variety of geologists, independent of the idea of internal heat, proposed for mountains and strata formational processes that could not have done their work in a mere six millennia, or even in seventy-five. Abraham Werner proposed an age of a million years.[32] Lyell's world, parsimonious of violence (his gradualist uniformitarianism) and *prodigal of time*,[33] required many millions of years. Just how many Lyell was unwilling to say.

This discrepancy, it was quickly realized, could be resolved by giving up the idea that the human race was nearly as old as the world itself. The biblical chronologies, after all, could do no more than to give an Annus Adam; if the world itself were much older, no biblical text tells us by how much. Empirical evidence began to suggest such a gap. In 1774, Giovanni Arduino published his "Saggio Fisico-Mineralogico di Lythogonia, e Orognosia," in which he distinguished several "orders" of rock formations. The "primary" formations were mountains, which contain metals, but no fossils. "Secondary" mountains, by contrast, contain relatively few metals but are rich in fossilized sea organisms. Neither contained any traces of man. These

29. Herschel, "Catalogue," 498–99.

30. Pye Smith, *Holy Scriptures and Geological Science*, 370.

31. Buffon, "Septième et dernière époque," in *Époques de la Nature*, 241. In private correspondence, he took seriously the possibility that the earth is much older than that.

32. Ospovat, "Werner," 260, on the basis of "Geognosie," an unpublished lecture, the manuscript of which is available in History of Science Collections at the library of the University of Oklahoma.

33. Lyell had objected to his opponents' geology as one presenting a world "parsimonious of time and prodigal of violence" (*Principles,* 1:88).

orders, Arduino said, "are not of the same age, but are successive, produced at various times and caused by various circumstances."³⁴ The earth (and *a fortiori* time), it seemed clear, is, *pace* Browne, more than five days older than ourselves.

Does the text of Genesis 1 not say exactly what Browne said it says about the age of the earth? There are two ways of denying that it does. The first is to posit a long interval between the first verse ("In the beginning God created the heavens and the earth") and the second ("The earth was without form and void, and darkness was upon the face of the deep"). Such a view had already made its appearance before the close of the seventeenth century in Matthew Hale's *The Primitive Origination of Mankind Considered and Examined According to the Light of Nature* (1677). Symon Patrick, then (Anglican) bishop of Ely, advanced the same thesis in his *Commentary on the First Book of Moses, called Genesis* (1695).³⁵ The second way to give natural processes the time they needed was to posit long "days," an alternative to which I will return below.

Before turning to the Hexaëmeron, however, let us pause to note that on another issue Buffon's ideas were more consonant with traditional theological ideas. The idea that God created the world (i.e., the universe) at the beginning of time, combined with the idea of salvation history and the idea that the world would not continue to exist forever, suggested to many Christians that time should be thought of as fundamentally linear—running from Creation to the End of the World—rather than cyclical. The heart of the Christian arrow of time, of course, is found in human history—the creation of man, the Fall, the Incarnation and Redemption, and the Parousia—but it was natural to combine human history and the history of nature and to think that nature itself should not only have a beginning and an end, but should exhibit a similarly linear pattern. The idea of a cooling earth, proposed by Buffon and put to explanatory use by geologists until the end of the nineteenth century, was a congenial natural correlate to, though neither evidence for nor a logical consequence of, the Christian model of time.³⁶ Defenders of cyclical views—for example James Hutton, who had written that "The result . . . of our present enquiry is, that we find no vestige of a beginning,—no prospect of an end"³⁷—could sound like eternalists, even

---

34. Arduino, "Saggio," 229–30.
35. Hale, *Origination*, 295; Patrick, *Commentary*, 11.
36. For more on models of time, see Gould, *Time's Arrow, Time's Cycle*.
37. Hutton, *Theory of the Earth*, 1:200. Emphasis added.

though there is a difference, as Hutton emphasized, between "we find no *vestige* of a beginning" and "we know that there was no beginning at all."[38]

The Six Days of Creation

Let us turn next to the Hexaëmeron.[39] How should one understand the Six Days of Gen 1? Descartes's idea that the solar system, the earth, and its geological features were, or at least could have been, formed by natural processes appealed to many seventeenth- and eighteenth-century scholars interested in the origins of the world, but no such processes could have shaped the world within six days. Could a Christian accept the idea that natural processes actually did this work?

The idea that the six days of the text were not temporal days had been advanced for other reasons as early as the second century, in the Catechetical School of Alexandria, where it was taught together with the doctrine of instantaneous creation.[40] From Alexandria, the idea spread to Hippo, where it was included by St. Augustine in his *Literal Meaning of Genesis* (*De Genesi ad Litteram*), the last of his several attempts to provide a satisfactory interpretation of the early chapters of Genesis.[41] The nontemporality of the six days, though intermittently defended by prominent and orthodox theologians—for example, St. Albert the Great in the thirteenth century and Tommaso de Vio, Cardinal Cajetan, in the sixteenth[42]—was always a minority view. It was subject to severe criticism from all sides in the century

---

38. Ours, he said, "is a world that is not eternal, but which has been the effect of wisdom or design." He went on to write that "in thus tracing back the natural operations which have succeeded each other, and mark to us the course of time past, we come to a period in which we cannot see any farther. This, however, is not the beginning of those operations which proceed in time and according to the wise œconomy of this world; nor is it the establishing of that, which, in the course of time, had no beginning; it is only the limit of our retrospective view of those operations which have come to pass in time, and have been conducted by supreme intelligence." (Hutton, *Theory of the Earth*, 1:223).

39. For more comprehensive treatments, see Robbins, *Hexaemeral Literature*; Mangenot, "Hexaméron"; and Brown, "Days of Creation."

40. See Clement of Alexandria, *Stromata*, VI.16; and Origen, *Contra Celsum*, VI.60.

41. Augustine, *De Genesi ad Litteram*, 4.26.43. It is important to note that for Augustine, the "literal" sense of Scripture covered all that the *words* were intended to mean by their authors (divine and human). Recognizing a passage as containing metaphor or exaggeration was recognizing the *literal* sense of the passage in question. Nonliteral senses were those in which one *thing* (or event) pointed to another, as when the near sacrifice of Isaac on Mount Moriah was seen as a type pointing to the Crucifixion.

42. Albert the Great, *Commentaria*, II.12.1.2; Cajetan, *In Pentateuchum Mosis*, 2v.

immediately preceding the first appearance of paleoetiological sciences—from Martin Luther and John Calvin among the Reformers, and Francisco Suárez and his fellow Jesuits among the Catholics.[43]

Of those authors seeking to flesh out Descartes's idea that natural processes played a prominent role in the formational economy of the world, some passed over the six days in silence. Stensen, for example, in his *Prodromus* said that "with regard to the first configuration [*facies*] of the earth, Scripture and Nature agree that water covered everything,"[44] but makes no further reference to the Hexaëmeron. Others presented the days as temporally real, but as lasting more than twenty-four hours. Isaac Newton suggested this in correspondence with Thomas Burnet as Burnet was writing his *Sacred Theory of the Earth*: "At first wee may suppose þe diurnal rotations of þe earth to have been very slow, soe þt þe first 6 revolutions or nights may containe time enough for þe whole Creation."[45] In 1769, Fr. John Needham, an English Catholic priest and biologist with a strong interest in the relationship between science and theology, wrote in a letter to Buffon that "one must take those six terms of creation as six periods of unknown length."[46] Buffon made no effort to correlate the events that constituted his seven epochs of nature with the events associated with the days of Genesis, a discrepancy for which he was severely criticized by his opponents. Such a correlation is a feature of Jean-André De Luc's *Lettres Physiques et Morales sur l'Histoire de la Terre et de l'Homme* (1779–1780) and after De Luc many Christians who adopted this day-age interpretation of Gen 1 adopted a similar ("concordist") view of the matter.

Pope Pius VII, one might conclude in noting, is reported to have accepted as orthodox an interpretation according to which the days of the Hexaëmeron are epochs of long duration in a conversation with the members of the Institut National des Sciences et Arts (later renamed l'Institut de France), during his visit to Paris in 1804 and 1805.[47]

43. Luther, *Genesisvorlesung*, 1:5; Calvin, *Commentarius*, 3–4; Suárez, *De Opere Sex Dierum* 1.10–12; other Jesuits holding this view included Pereyra, *Commentariorum*; and Lapide, *Commentaria*.

44. Stensen, *Prodromus*, 221.

45. Newton, Letter № 244, 24 December 1680, in *Correspondence*, 2:319.

46. Needham, Letter to Buffon, in Needham, *Nature et la Religion*, 25.

47. The earliest report of this remark that I have been able to find comes from Alexandre-Aimé Giraudet, a graduate of the Institute, in his *Nouveau Traité*, 369, but, having been born only in 1798, Giraudet could not have heard the conversation himself. The pope's remarks did not, however, settle the matter even in Catholic circles. L'abbé Fabre d'Envieu, professor of theology at the University of Paris, acknowledged in his *Origines de la Terre*, 225–26, that the pope had given the idea a certain approval (though only "simply as a theologian"), but did not think that the interpretation was

The Flood of Noah

Finally, the idea of the Deluge, or at least of a deluge, also figured prominently, though variously, in the thought of many early geologists.[48] There is no reason why the developers of the paleoetiological sciences had to address the question of Noah's Flood. Even assuming the historical reality (and universality) of that flood, there is nothing unbiblical about the idea that it was miraculous in its causes and geologically silent in its effects. Nevertheless, the idea that Noah's Flood not only had natural causes but left geological traces (or even played a fundamental role in transforming the surface of the earth into its present state) emerged as one of the central themes in many seventeenth- and eighteenth-century theories of the earth. Such an idea, many thought, had the benefit of drawing from the new sciences new evidence for the reliability of Scripture. There were, however, also two non-biblical reasons for accepting the historical reality of such a flood.

The first is that flood stories are found not only in the Bible but in the traditions of many other cultures as well. The Greek story of the flood of Deucalion was well known, but the age of exploration brought more examples from the ends of the earth. One Jesuit missionary, José de Acosta, reported that the Incas had such stories in his *Historia natural y moral de las Indias* (1590)[49] and another, Martino Martini, reported two such flood stories from China in his *Sinicae Historiae Decas Prima* (1658).[50]

The second reason was that such a flood might resolve one of the paleontological problems mentioned above—the puzzling fact that fossils resembling marine organisms could be found not only far from the sea, but high in the mountains as well. The idea that the fossils only resembled, but had never in fact been, organic beings was one of the targets of Stensen's *Prodromus*, and scientific opinion fell fairly decisively against that possibility as a result of his work (and, of course, that of others, particularly Robert Hooke in his "Discourses of Earthquakes"[51]). That left the question of how the remains of actual marine organisms could have ended up in the mountains. One possibility was that they were left there after a worldwide flood. A second was that the sea floor had been lifted up to mountain heights. Leonardo da Vinci and Girolamo Fracastoro had raised powerful empirical objections to the idea of diluvial deposition already in the sixteenth century.

---

exegetically sound.
48. See Rappaport, "Geology and Orthodoxy."
49. Acosta, *Historia*, VI.19.
50. Martini, *Sinicae Historiae*, 3 and 26.
51. Hooke, "Earthquakes," 280–98.

Although neither seems to have published his ideas, they were not entirely unknown to their contemporaries.[52] Nevertheless, the idea of a world-wide flood seemed to many not only to have the advantage of being a more familiar cause, but that of receiving some confirmation from historical sources.

And so it is not surprising that early theories of the earth included a universal flood. They did so, however, in a variety of ways. One can see the range of approaches by looking at four authors—Stensen and Burnet, from the seventeenth century, whom I have already mentioned, and John Kidd and Georges Cuvier, from the nineteenth.

Kidd spent most of his scientific career studying and teaching anatomy and medicine, but early in his teaching career he was professor of chemistry at Oxford, a responsibility that led him to give some attention also to mineralogy and geology. He was theologically orthodox and indeed was invited to write one of the Bridgewater treatises.[53] The work relevant to our present topic, however, is his *Geological Essay on the Imperfect Evidence in Support of a Theory of the Earth* (1815). Kidd began his *Essay* with a chapter "On the Nature of the Connection between Geological Speculations and the Mosaic History of the Creation and Deluge," in which he argued that

> from such slight materials [as are contained in the book of Genesis] to attempt to explain the detail of Geological phenomena, or to limit the progress of knowledge by the literal interpretation of so brief and mysterious a history, are equally unreasonable.[54]

About the Mosaic history of the Deluge he went on to say that

> the facts, I think, both of the universality of the Deluge and of the destruction of all mankind with the exception of one family, must be admitted by all who admit the general credibility of Scripture: but it evidently was an operation not brought about

---

52. Leonardo left his ideas unpublished, though they are found in his *Nachlaß* in a manuscript now called the *Codex Leicester*. Duhem has suggested that they might have survived in an oral tradition stretching through Girolamo Cardano and Bernard Palissy into the eighteenth century, when they appear in the works of Italian geologists ("Léonard de Vinci, Cardan, et Palissy"). For more on Leonardo, see Duhem's "Léonard et les Origines" or Gould, "Upwardly Mobile Fossils." Fracastoro's views were published by Torello Sarayna in his *De Origine*, 6–7.

53. Inspired by Paley's *Natural Theology*, Francis Henry, Earl of Bridgewater, left, at his death in 1829, some eight thousand pounds, which the president of the Royal Society of London was to use to commission work "On the Power, Wisdom, and Goodness of God, as manifested in the Creation." The president, with the advice of the Archbishop of Canterbury, arranged for the publication of eight works, written by some of the leading British scientists of the day. Kidd's was *On the Adaptation of External Nature to the Physical Condition of Man*. See Robson, "The Fiat and Finger of God."

54. Kidd, *Geological Essay*, 13–14.

by the ordinary course of nature; or, in other words, a miracle; and probably therefore forever inexplicable in its detail by unassisted reason.

There is, of course, as I mentioned above, nothing unbiblical about the idea that the Flood was miraculous or that it left no geological traces. The French Benedictine Augustin Calmet, perhaps the best Catholic exegete of the eighteenth century, had defended the same view in his twenty-three-volume *Commentaire Littéral sur tous les Livres de l'Ancien et du Nouveau Testament* (1707–1716).[55] Nevertheless, partly for the reasons mentioned above, many geologists believed that the Deluge not only had natural causes, but had left its traces in the geological record, a view that has come to be called diluvialism.

One finds a modest version of diluvialism in Stensen's *Prodromus*. That work, as the very title makes clear, is centered on a question about nature—how can nature produce a solid within a solid? How do fossils and crystals, for example, end up inside solid rocks? Stensen's imaginative brilliance allowed him to see the strata that make up the crust of the earth as themselves being another case of this phenomenon.[56] His solution, that "if a solid body has been produced according to the laws of nature, it has been produced from a fluid,"[57] implied the fluid origin of geological strata, and he went on to offer a geological history of Tuscany (and then, by extension, of the whole world):

> Therefore, we recognize six distinct configurations [*facies*] of Etruria: two fluid, two level and dry, and two uneven. I prove this for Etruria by induction from many places which I have inspected myself and confirm it for the rest of the world from the descriptions of various places made by other authors.[58]

Only then did he write: "But lest anyone fear the danger of innovation here, I will provide a brief exposition of the agreement of Nature and Scripture." Some of those six *facies* are revealed in Scripture (and of these, one he associates with the Noachian Deluge); some, by contrast, are knowable only by scientific inference.

The last decades of the seventeenth century saw the emergence of a more radical version of diluvialism in England with a triad of very influential

55. Calmet, *Commentaire*, comment on Gen 7:11.
56. For more on Stensen, see Gould, "Titular Bishop of Titiopolis," or various articles in Rosenberg, *Revolution in Geology*.
57. Stensen, *Prodromus*, 192.
58. Stensen, *Prodromus*, 220.

books—Thomas Burnet's *Sacred Theory of the Earth* (1681–1691), John Woodward's *Essay Toward a Natural History of the Earth* (1695), and William Whiston's *A New Theory of the Earth* (1696). While these books differ in detail, they have in common the idea that Noah's Flood played a major role in the formation of the strata and surface features of the earth. Burnet and Whiston, in particular, embedded their geological ideas into a larger theological project. While Stensen's work has sections on strata, on mountains, on diamonds, and on mollusk shells, Burnet's book is divided into sections on Noah's Flood, Paradise, the burning of the world, and a new heaven and a new earth. Whiston's subtitle offers a theory of the earth "from its Original to the Consummation of all Things[:] the Creation of The World in Six Days, The Universal Deluge, and the General Conflagration as laid down in the Holy Scriptures." Burnet's "sacred theory," no less than Woodward's "natural history," was nevertheless an attempt to identifying natural causes for the Flood: "This Theory being chiefly Philosophical, Reason is to be our first Guide, and where that falls short, or any other just occasion offers itself, we may receive further light and confirmation from the Sacred Writings."[59]

He argued that "there was no new Creation of waters at the Deluge"[60] and discussed "how far the Deluge may be lookt upon as the effect of an ordinary Providence, and how far of an extraordinary."[61] All three were committed to arguing for the reality and universality of that flood by identifying its effects. Woodward, for example, cited in evidence the fact that "Marine Bodies are now found lodged in those Strata according to the Order of their Gravity, those which are heavyest lying deepest in the Earth, and the lighter Sorts . . . shallower or nearer to the Surface."[62] Burnet, it should be noted, was not entirely orthodox in his theology. Absent from his account, critics hastened to point out, were important theological themes (such as the sinfulness of the human race) that, one would think, constitute the main reason for the story's inclusion in the book of Genesis in the first place.[63]

The beginning of the nineteenth century saw the return of more modest versions of diluvialism, perhaps distinguishable from Stensen's in the idea that the history of the earth was characterized by *a series* of catastrophic

---

59. Burnet, *Sacred Theory*, 4.
60. Burnet, *Sacred Theory*, 12.
61. Burnet, *Sacred Theory*, 65.
62. Woodward, *Essay*, A3.

63. Burnet strayed yet further from orthodoxy in his *Archeologia Philosophica*, where, for example, he questioned the historical reality of the Fall. This book delighted deists and freethinkers (who published a translation of the least orthodox passages (in Blount's *Oracles of Reason*), but evoked a critical reaction from Anglicans and may have led to Burnet's loss of his position as chaplain to King William.

floods, the last of which might be associated with the Flood of Noah. One example of this is Georges Cuvier, who, in his *Discours sur les révolutions du globe* (1812),[64] argued that the succession of fauna in the fossil record showed that the history of the earth was a sequence of catastrophes that had wiped out one set of animals after another. The last of these catastrophes, he suggested, could be identified with the Flood of Noah. The approach was particularly popular in England, where it can be found in the work of William Buckland, Kidd's successor as reader of mineralogy at Oxford. Buckland's approach can be appreciated by attention to the titles of two of his works. His inaugural lecture as reader of geology bore the title *Vindiciae geologicae, or the Connexion of Geology with Religion Explained* (1820), the vindication being that "Geology contributes proofs to Natural Theology strictly in harmony with those derived from other branches of natural history."[65] At about the same time he also published his "Description of the Quartz Rock of the Lickey Hill in Worcestershire . . . : With Considerations on the Evidences of a Recent Deluge Afforded by the Gravel Beds of Warwickshire and Oxfordshire . . ."[66] The two titles show the delicate balance between geological interests and theological ones. In the *Vindiciae* he wrote:

> The grand fact of an universal deluge at no very remote period is proved on grounds so decisive and incontrovertible, that, had we never heard of such an event from Scripture, or any other authority, Geology of itself must have called in the assistance of some such catastrophe, to explain the phenomena of diluvian action which are universally presented to us, and which are unintelligible without recourse to a deluge exerting its ravages at a period not more ancient than that announced in the Book of Genesis.[67]

Around 1840, Buckland came to recognize that the "diluvium," the "extensive and general deposits of superficial loam and gravel, which appear to have been produced by the last great convulsion that has affected our planet," and which had formed much of his evidence for the historical reality of the Deluge, had in fact been formed (as Swiss geologist Louis Agassiz was arguing) by glaciation. His willingness to abandon his earlier ideas is, of course, proof that he took science, and not just theology, very seriously.

---

64. Diderot's *Encyclopédie* defined the word *révolution* in this context as meaning merely "the natural events by which the surface of our globe have been and are still continually altered by fire, air, and water" ("Révolutions de la Terre," 14:237–38).

65. Buckland, *Vindiciae*, 17.

66. Buckland, "Description of the Quartz Rock," 506–44.

67. Buckland, *Vindiciae*, 23–24.

Conclusion

What does the history of the relation between the paleoetiological sciences and Christian theology from 1644 to 1859 show us? Do these controversies show us a campaign in a war of theology against science? There was no single incident that has come to have the prominence of the Huxley-Wilberforce exchange or of the Scopes Trial, but of course such *causes célèbres* are not strictly necessary to the Warfare Thesis, and White did claim to see in all this evidence for the alleged warfare of obscurantist and obstructionist theologians against enlightening science.[68] Indeed one *can* find some individuals and institutions that do just what White's thesis says they typically do.

The theologians at the Sorbonne, who had partial responsibility for the censorship of books in eighteenth-century France, had grave concerns about the orthodoxy of Buffon's *Histoire Naturelle* when the first volume appeared in 1749. They composed a list of fourteen passages that in their judgment "seemed contrary to the belief of the Church," including four relevant to our subject. In the first of these four, Buffon had said that the movement of the sea had produced the mountains and valleys of the earth; in the other three, he had said that the earth was formed out of the sun. Buffon and his theologian-critics worked out an agreement whereby he would publish in the next volume of the *Histoire* a declaration that he believed all that was contained in Scripture and renounced anything in his book that was inconsistent with it.[69] He did publish the promised statements in the next volume of the *Histoire*, but new editions of the first volumes left the passages to which objections had been made unchanged. Buffon returned to these questions in his *Époques de la nature* in 1778. His theological opponents at the Sorbonne initiated once again an inquiry into whether Buffon's ideas were compatible with Catholic doctrine, but in the end (for reasons that remain unclear) let the matter drop.[70]

What to make of Buffon's declaration of 1751 has been a matter of scholarly controversy.[71] Buffon was clearly a practicing Catholic, though one who generally stayed away from theology.[72] With respect to the main

---

68. White, *History*, 1:209–48.

69. The declaration appeared in volume 4, published in 1753. A translation is conveniently available in Lyon and Sloan, *From Natural History*, 283–93.

70. See Stengers, "Buffon et la Sorbonne."

71. The case for Buffon's sincerity is presented in Piveteau "La Pensée Religieuse de Buffon." The case against it is made, for example, in Fellows and Milliken, *Buffon*, 81–85.

72. See his letter to Abbé Jean-Baptiste Corgne de Launay, 4 June 1773, in which he wrote, "I don't understand theology and I always refrain from writing about it."

Christianity, Geology & Cosmology before 1859

point at issue in this book, however, the sincerity of his religious beliefs does not matter. Whatever his views, the fact is that the theologians at the Sorbonne, with the approbation of theology departments in other French universities, condemned Buffon's attempt to attribute the formation of the planet and its topography to natural causes.

In addition, the 1820s saw the emergence in England of a group of "Scriptural Geologists" determined to defend a six-day creation six thousand years ago against the newly emerging science of geology.[73] It was of these that White could write:

> The favourite weapon of the orthodox party was the charge that the geologists were "attacking the truth of God." They declared geology "not a subject of lawful inquiry," denouncing it as "a dark art," as "dangerous and disreputable," as "a forbidden province," as "infernal artillery," and as "an awful evasion of the testimony of revelation." This attempt to scare men from the science having failed, various other means were taken.[74]

The question is whether proponents of the Warfare Thesis are entitled to ascribe the actions of the Sorbonne theologians and the writings of the English Scriptural Geologists to "theology." There is reason to object to that ascription.

Why do the Scriptural Geologists have any more claim to be the spokesmen of theology than do others, such as Buckland, selected with the approval of the Archbishop of Canterbury as a Bridgewater author and later dean of Westminster, who was much more open to the paleoetiological sciences?

The condemnation of 1751 was not typical of Catholic reaction to the paleoetiological sciences. Though the Sorbonne may have objected to these new sciences in 1751,[75] other French theologians did not. The Jesuits' *Journal de Trévoux* (formally, *Mémoires pour l'Histoire des Sciences et des Beaux-Arts*), for example, printed favorable reviews of the *Histoire* when the first volumes appeared.[76] Although many of the theologians at the Sorbonne wanted to issue a second condemnation of Buffon's ideas on publication of his *Époques de la nature* in 1778, in the end they did not do so.

What had been the Catholic reaction to Stensen's book in 1669? When Stensen's *Prodromus* was ready for the press, the Vicar General of Florence had it sent to Vincenzo Viviani, who had been a pupil of Galileo late in the Galileo's life, asking Viviani whether there was anything in the work that

---

73. For an introduction, see Millhauser, "Scriptural Geologists."
74. White, *History*, 1:223.
75. As, for that matter, did the Jansenists in their clandestine *Nouvelles Ecclésiastiques*.
76. *Mémoires*, Reviews of Buffon.

was contrary to the Catholic faith. Viviani having reported that there was not, and a similar report having been received from Francesco Redi, biologist and consultor of the Holy Office at Florence, permission was granted for publication of the work. Censorship was not, perhaps, overly strict in Florence. A half century before, Galileo's *Dialogues on the Two Chief World-Systems* (1632) had been approved by the same office. In Stensen's case, however, the matter ended there. There is no evidence that another consultor would have given the book an evaluation any different from those given by Viviani and Redi. Stensen himself was not only ordained (subsequent to publication of the *Prodromus*) but made a bishop.

Eighteenth-century Italy seems generally to have continued that broadly irenicist and compatibilist approach to the relation between theology and the paleoetiological sciences, an approach that Gian Battisa Vai has called "Galilean Catholicism."[77] Although planet-formation, the subject of three of Buffon's four condemned scientific theses, does not seem to have caught the interest of Italian scientists, the formation of mountains and the origin of fossils did. Those scientists appealed to secondary causes in the same way that Buffon had done in the work to which the Sorbonne theologians had taken exception. All of this work passed Italian ecclesiastical censorship. Works singled out for praise by Charles Lyell in the historical chapters with which he introduced his *Principles of Geology*[78] were cleared for publication by theological censors. Antonio Vallisneri's *De' Corpi Marini, che su' Monti si Trovano* and Anton-Lazzaro Moro's *De' Crostacei e degli altri Marini Corpi che si Truovano su' Monti* appeared in Venice; Giuseppe Cirillo Generelli's summary of Moro, "De' Crostacei e dell'Altre Produzioni Marine, che sono ne' Monti" appeared in Milan. Moro was a diocesan priest; Generelli was a Carmelite.

There is also a larger issue to be considered. What of W2, identified in the previous chapter: the idea that the history of science includes a struggle between two groups of participants—scientists (and their allies) and theologians (and theirs)? A superficial and selective reading of history might illustrate this idea by contrasting the supposedly scientific Niels Stenssen and the supposedly theological Thomas Burnet, pointing not only to the titles of their works—*Prodromus of a Dissertation concerning a Solid Body Enclosed by Process of Nature within a Solid* and *Sacred Theory of the Earth*—but also to a key diagram from each book.

---

77. Vai, "Steno's Twofold Conversion"; and Vai, "Liberal Diluvianism," in Vai and Cavazza, eds., *Four Centuries of the Word Geology*, 220-49.

78. Lyell, *Principles*, 1:41-48.

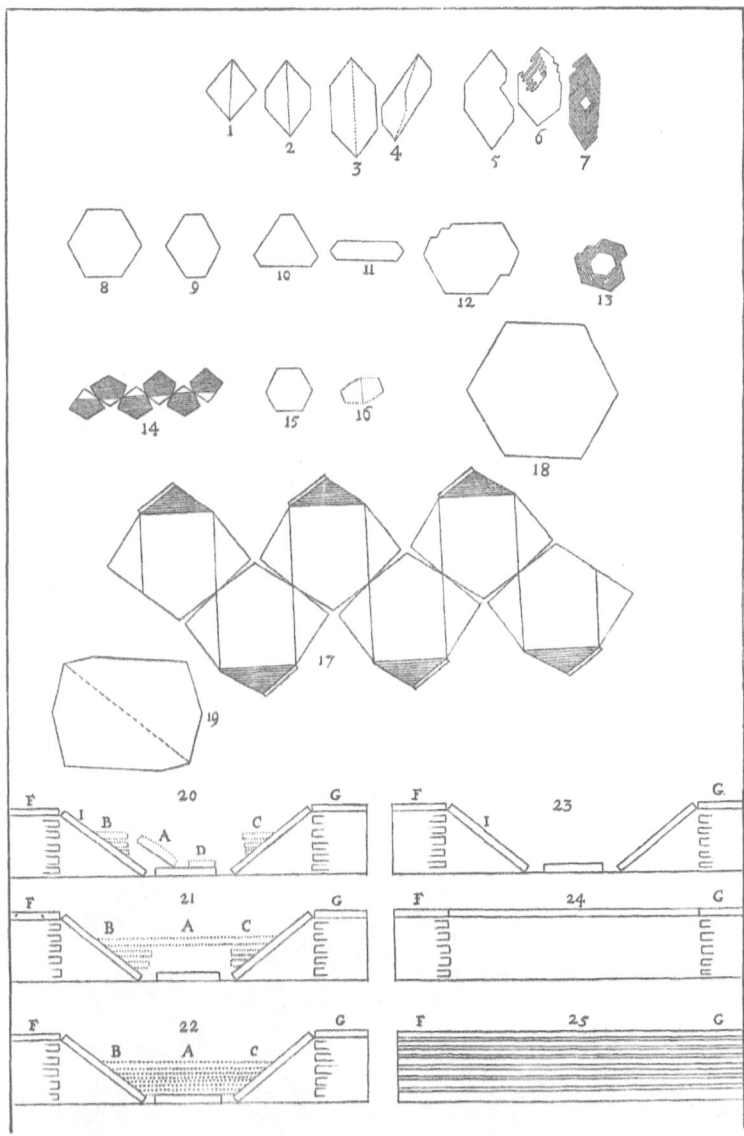

Figures from Stensen's *Prodromus*, depicting (at 25 to 20) successive stages in the geological history of Tuscany—deposition, collapse, redeposition, and recollapse of strata.

The *frontispiece* from Burnet's *Sacred Theory of the Earth*, depicting the successive stages in the history of the earth, from its foundation to its perfection.

On closer inspection, however, the identifications break down. Stensen and Burnet do not fit as easily into the pigeonholes assigned to them as one might at first think. They, and their critics and admirers, show us, not scientists and theologians at war, but savants deeply interested in both God and nature, despite differences in their approaches to the integration of scientific and theological ideas into a larger, comprehensive world picture.

Burnet, whose title, frontispiece, and table of contents look so theological, and who is presented by the warfare theorists as a "champion of orthodoxy,"[79] in fact had, as one of his major goals, to show that Noah's Flood was the result of the operation of natural causes. To achieve this end, however, he was rather less attentive to the text of Gen 1 than his critics (who ranged on this point from Sir Isaac Newton to the bishop of Hereford) thought he should be. He remained obscure on the question of how the Flood could be both the effect of natural causes and the consequence of sin. He was an Anglican clergyman and chaplain to King William, to be sure, but also the independent and imaginative author of an early theory of the earth; not an obscurantist reactionary, but a thinker who was trying to combine Cartesian physics, geological observations, and Holy Scripture into a comprehensive account of (among other things) the origin of the geological features of the earth.

Stensen makes, though he does not emphasize, a connection with Gen 1. He was, shortly before he wrote the *Prodromus*, received into the Catholic Church. His conversion must be seen as a result of theological inquiry and reflection.[80] He took his new religion so seriously that, shortly after finishing the *Prodromus*, he sought ordination to the priesthood, was consecrated as a bishop, and was sent back to northern Europe to minister to the spiritual needs of those Catholics who found themselves living *in partibus infidelium*. There is no sign that he felt any tension between the conclusions he had reached as a result of his scientific research and the doctrines of the Catholic Church into which he was being received. Gian Battista Vai has even argued that his shift of scientific interests (from anatomy to geology) and his religious conversion "cross-fertilized" one another.[81]

The incidents, authors, and movements that provide the Warfare Theorists their best examples must be seen, not as showing us something about the nature of science and theology, but as nothing more than another instance of the generic resistance to new ideas that occurs in the sciences no less than anywhere else. Here, the subjects of the old and the new ideas are several.

Princeton University historian R. R. Palmer characterized one in the following terms:

79. White, *History*, 1:218.

80. For his own account of his conversion, see his letters to Johannes Sylvius, 12 January 1672, and to G. W. Leibniz, November 1677, in Stensen, *Epistolae*, 1:257–60 and 366–69. See also Stensen, *De Propria Conversione*.

81. Vai, "Steno's Twofold Conversion."

> A matter was thought to be more fully understood when, instead of being referred directly to God, it was referred back to a series of other observed events that had preceded it. From this new habit of mind, which the civilization and daily life of Europe had somehow made very general, science and history as we know them both arose. Attention shifted from final to efficient causes, from general reasons for existence to the particulars of what actually happened. The new thinkers conceived of nature more easily than of God, of time more easily than of eternity, of chains of cause and effect more easily than of a single act of universal creation.[82]

As a result, he concluded, "natural knowledge contended with revealed." We can bring that cluster of ideas into focus by concentrating on the task of locating the exact line between the operation of natural processes and the operation of supernatural agency in the formation of the surface of the earth and of the planet itself. Completion of that task requires also answers (possibly new) to questions about the principles of scriptural interpretation.

Second, as Nicolaas A. Rupke has pointed out, many of those interested in the origins of things were not prepared to set aside historical (here, textual) evidence in favor of inference from observation alone.[83] Opponents of the new paleoetiological sciences accused the practitioners of doing just that. The eighteenth-century Irish geologist Richard Kirwan argued that

> past geological facts being of an historical nature, all attempts to deduce a complete knowledge of them merely from their still subsisting consequences, to the exclusion of unexceptionable testimony, must be deemed as absurd as that of deducing the history of ancient Rome solely from the medals or other monuments of antiquity it still exhibits or the scattered ruins of its empire, to the exclusion of a Livy, a Sallust, or a Tacitus.[84]

Granville Penn, one of the Scriptural Geologists, complained that Buckland "concedes *too much* to the authority of the *phenomena*, and *too little* to the authority of *the history*."[85] Proponents of these sciences did not uniformly abandon the textual evidence. Sandra Herbert has suggested, for the approach of Cuvier and Buckland, the term "Cuvierian synthesis."[86] For Hutton, by contrast, (as Dennis R. Dean put it), "the earth's age ... was so much

---

82. Palmer, *Catholics and Unbelievers*, 155–156.
83. See Rupke, *Great Chain of History*, 42–50.
84. Kirwan, *Geological Essays*, 5.
85. Penn, *Comparative Estimate*, 2:356. The italics are Penn's.
86. Herbert, "Between Genesis and Geology," 68–84.

older [than what the Bible had admitted], that not only the Bible but all other historical records were irrelevant."[87]

Finally, the old line of demarcation between supernatural and natural agency, the old principles of scriptural interpretation and the old understandings of the relevant passages of Scripture, seemed familiar and theologically safe. If they do not provide much insight into orogenesis, at least they provide scriptural underpinnings sufficient to protect adventurous Christians from eternalism and other theological errors. Even among scientists, there is always controversy between those eager to embrace new ideas and those appreciative of the power of the old ideas and doubtful of the value of the new. This is all the more so when the controversy requires attention to both theological and scientific concerns. If the rhetoric was more fierce than is found in other controversies, it is in part because the defenders of the old ideas thought that more was at stake. One error of the Warfare Theorists is to have focused on the intransigents as though they, more than their more irenicist and compatibilist contemporaries, spoke for religion.

There was general agreement among Christians and deists (against the eternalists) that the creation (i.e., exnihilation) of the world required supernatural agency. Until the seventeenth century, no Christian had given serious consideration to the idea (found only in the atheist and materialist Lucretius) that the natural powers of material creation (or the natural laws that govern the world) might be sufficient to organize matter into planetary systems. The idea that they might be able to raise up mountains did have its supporters, but that was not a matter of major interest for most Christians. The natural alternative assumption was that supernatural agency played a direct and prominent role not only in the creation of the world but in the topographical details of its present state, and that this formation was accomplished in a short period of time not long ago.

Descartes's idea that the laws of nature were sufficient to organize the world—that the present structure of the world was the result of natural causes and that the world had a reconstructible history, knowledge of which might be had by scientific inquiry—brought the idea, for the first time, into genuine contact with Christian theology even though Descartes himself presented the idea without reference to the Hexaëmeron or to Noah's Flood. The methodology of the project (for most of its practitioners) was well characterized by Burnet, villain in the warfare historiographies though he may be:

> You will say, maybe, that all this is but an *Hypothesis*; that is, a kind of fiction or supposition that things were so and so at first,

---

87. Dean, "Age of the Earth Controversy," 455.

> and by the coherence and agreement of the Effects with such a supposition, you would argue and prove that they were really so. This I confess is true, this is the method, and if we would know any thing in Nature further than our senses go, we can know it no otherwise than by an *Hypothesis*.[88]

He gave as examples the knowledge of the parts of water ("too little to be discerned by the eye") and the nature of a comet (one of the "things inaccessible to us") and went on to say that "this is what we have attempted concerning the Earth and concerning the Deluge." The use of hypotheses in science was, at the time, controversial. Newton, for example, had written in the General Scholium appended to the second edition of his *Principia Mathematica Philosophiae Naturalis*, that "hypotheses, whether metaphysical or physical, whether of occult qualities or of mechanical, have no place in experimental philosophy."[89]

Descartes's idea raised for the first time the possibility that accommodationist interpretive strategies (long accepted in principle, though sometimes controversial in their application) might legitimately be applied to Gen 1 and in a new way.[90] It raised again the issue of the relative place of faith and reason in resolving questions to which both might be relevant. We can see the alternative views on *that* question already well-articulated by St. Bonaventure and St. Albert the Great in the course of the medieval installment of the long-running controversy over instantaneous creation. St. Bonaventure characterized his approach as "the theological way, subordinating reason to faith":

> This view [sc., that all corporeal beings were created over the course of six days], even if it seems less reasonable than the other one, yet is not irrational to maintain. For even though reason does not see the congruity of this position insofar as it relies on its own judgment, reason does see it when it is placed [*captivatur*] under the light of faith.[91]

---

88. Burnet, *Sacred Theory*, 1:100–101.

89. Newton, *Principia Mathematica*, 2:404; Motte and Cajori, trans., *Mathematical Principles*, 2:547.

90. The idea that the authors of sacred Scripture spoke in a way that would be clear to their audience, even at the expense of literal accuracy, can be found at least as early as St. Augustine (*Literal Meaning*, 5.6). Calmet used it in the "Dissertation sur le Système du Monde des Anciens Hébreux" that he put at the front of his Commentary on the Book of Sirach (*Commentaire*, 5:262–71), as did Burnet in his "Review of the Theory of the Earth," 407, and Buffon in his *Époques*, 38.

91. Bonaventure, *Commentaria in Quattuor Libros Sententiarum*, II.12.1.2 *conclusio*.

St. Albert, by contrast, said that

> in matters of faith and morals, Augustine is more to be believed than are the philosophers, if they disagree. But if it is medicine that is under discussion, I would put more trust in Galen or Hippocrates and if it is the natures of things, in Aristotle or in some other expert in the natures of things.[92]

As the issue of the relation between natural and revealed knowledge arose again in the wake of Descartes's new idea, four distinguishable approaches emerged to the relationship between theology and the paleoetiological sciences, with Christians, deists, and anti-religious thinkers scattered among the four.

First, there were incompatibilists, who saw contradictions between theology and science. These included some conservative (but by no means all orthodox) Christians, who used the alleged contradictions to cast doubt on the new scientific ideas, providing the warfare theorists with their whole stock of examples. One might also expect to find here at least those deists who saw it as part of their project to attack Scripture, but one searches in vain for arguments based on the emerging paleoetiological sciences in, for example, Voltaire's *La Bible enfin expliquée* (1776) or in Matthew Tindal's *Christianity as Old as the Creation* (1732), where such arguments should be found if they were being made.[93] For whatever reason (perhaps because of the speculative and controversial character of even the better-developed of the new ideas), antibiblical deists concentrated rather on general arguments and on attacking miracles. Tindal said that "the Scriptural and Philosophical Account of natural things seldom agree" but cites as his examples the immobility of the sun and St. Paul's comment that "that which thou sowest is not quickned, except it die."[94] Thomas Paine called Genesis, "an anonymous book of stories, fables, and traditionary or invented absurdities, or of downright lies" and said that "the Bible-makers have undertaken to give us, in the first chapter of Genesis, an account of the creation; and in doing this they have demonstrated nothing but their ignorance."[95] He cited no particulars.

Second, many of those who addressed these questions not only saw no contradiction, but attempted to construct integrated accounts of the history of the natural world, drawing now on the Bible, now on observations, as

---

92. Albert the Great, *Commentarii in Secundum Sententiarum*, dist. 13, art. 2.

93. For a review of what deists *were* saying against the Bible (without any significant mention of scientific ideas) see Reventlow, "English Rationalism," and Bultmann, "Early Rationalism."

94. Tindal, *Christianity*, 185–86. The biblical passage is 1 Cor 15:36.

95. Paine, *Age of Reason*, Part 2, 431 and 560.

necessary to the completion of their task. Most of those interested in these questions, from Stensen through Buckland, though with varying combinations of emphasis, took this approach.

Third, there were some who made a determined effort to dissociate geology from cosmogony, and especially from theology, altogether.[96] This was implicit in the practice of the Royal Society of London from its foundation in 1660.[97] Sir Charles Lyell, a Unitarian, was loud in his objection to the intrusion of theological considerations into geology; Abraham Werner, apparently a deist, working in the different cultural context of late eighteenth-century Saxony, seems to have ignored the problem altogether.

Finally, there were those who were content simply to await future resolution of the controversy. Robert Chambers, also a deist, included in the "Note Conclusory" to his *Vestiges of the Natural History of Creation* (1844) the following passage:

> My sincere desire in the composition of the book was to give the true view of the history of nature, with as little disturbance as possible to existing beliefs, whether philosophical or religious. I have made little reference to any doctrines of the latter kind which may be thought inconsistent with mine, because to do so would have been to enter upon questions for the settlement of which our knowledge is not yet ripe. Let the reconciliation of whatever is true in my views with whatever is true in other systems come about in the fulness of calm and careful inquiry. I cannot but here remind the reader of what Dr. Wiseman has shewn so strikingly in his lectures, how different new philosophic doctrines are apt to appear after we have become somewhat familiar with them.[98]

A similar note was sounded by the Protestant biologist Albrecht von Haller in some comments on Buffon in the middle of the eighteenth century and by the Catholic Nicholas Wiseman early in the nineteenth.[99]

The two centuries that preceded the publication of the *Origin* show us individual scientists and theologians with widely varying approaches to the question of the relation between the new paleoetiological sciences and theology. They show us a conflict between old ideas and new ideas, and indeed between new ideas and other new ideas. What they do not show us

---

96. For more on this, see Rudwick, "Shape and Meaning."
97. Sprat, *History*, 25–26.
98. Chambers, *Vestiges*, 388–89.
99. Von Haller, *Vorrede*, 122–31; Wiseman, *Twelve Lectures*, 1:7.

is anything that can be characterized, without vitiating qualifications, as a war between science and theology in Christendom.

CHAPTER 4

Christianity & Evolution in the Nineteenth Century

BEFORE UNDERTAKING AN HISTORICAL review of theological and religious reactions to Darwin's evolutionary biology, it will perhaps be helpful to make briefly some conceptual points and to outline the broader history of the reception of Darwinism. Darwin's work presented theologians with several new ideas that were loosely, but not logically, connected with one another. Terms like *Darwinism* and, when it was applied to his ideas, *evolution* were used variously, sometimes with careful distinctions among the related concepts and sometimes not.[1] For the purposes of our story, it will be sufficient to distinguish four central ideas.

The first, the general idea that the origin of particular biological species can be found in the transformation of other, earlier species, had already been advanced in the eighteenth century and had at least two important proponents in the decades before the publication of Darwin's *Origin*. Although transformism was thus not itself new in 1859, and although it had not, even then, won general acceptance, what was relatively new to the idea of evolution was Darwin's second new idea—the Common Ancestry Thesis:

> all living species have been connected with the parent-species of each genus . . . and these parent-species, now generally extinct, have in their turn been similarly connected with more ancient

---

1. Contrast, for example, Erich Wasmann's careful distinctions in his *Berlin Discussion*, 37–41, with Gaetano Moroni's usage in the last of the great Catholic single-author encyclopedias, *Indice generale alfabetico*, II, 437.

species; and so on backwards, always converging to the common ancestor of each great class.[2]

This second central idea, then, goes beyond the evolutionary transformation of species to a particular pattern in the history of life—descent with differential modification resulting in several distinct species sharing a common ancestor.

The third of the four Darwinian ideas relevant to our story is that the cause of the differential modification that turned one or a few first kinds into the millions of species that inhabit the modern world is natural selection:

> As many more individuals of each species are born than can possibly survive; and as, consequently, there is a frequently recurring struggle for existence, it follows that any being, if it vary however slightly in any manner profitable to itself, under the complex and sometimes varying conditions of life, will have a better chance of surviving, and thus be naturally selected. From the strong principle of inheritance, any selected variety will tend to propagate its new and modified form.[3]

The fourth of Darwin's central ideas is that the first three ideas explain the origins of man no less than of other living things. This extension of Darwin's ideas, only hinted at in *The Origin of Species* and presented directly (by Darwin) first in *The Descent of Man*, depended on the thesis that man does not differ in kind from other living things, a thesis for which Darwin gave arguments in the latter book.

We can leave to the side the question of whether natural processes were sufficient to account for the origins of the first living things in a world until then free of life. Although the idea was being advanced by naturalists at that time and, in France at least, rather outdid in prominence the question of the origin of species, it was a thesis that (in the form of whether spontaneous generation was a currently occurring process) was doing rather badly at the hands of Louis Pasteur. The idea that abiogenesis played a role in the origin of life was therefore not a thesis for which any *scientific* argument could then be made. In any case, Darwin was emphatic that that idea was beyond the reach of *his* theory.[4]

Three of Darwin's ideas came in stronger and weaker versions.

How far did the common ancestry thesis reach? Darwin had written:

2. Darwin, *Origin*, 281–82.
3. Darwin, *Origin*, 5.
4. "It is no valid objection that science as yet throws no light on the far higher problem of the essence or origin of life" (Darwin, *Origin*, 3rd ed., 514). For more on this, see Peretó, Bada, and Lazcano, "Darwin and the Origin of Life."

> I cannot doubt that the theory of descent with modification embraces all the members of the same class. I believe that animals have descended from at most only four or five progenitors, and plants from an equal or lesser number. I should infer from analogy that probably all the organic beings which have ever lived on this earth have descended from some one primordial form, into which life was first breathed.[5]

And so there were monophyletic, oligophyletic, and polyphyletic versions of the thesis. Descent with modification was much more plausible when it was limited to the differentiation of closely related species (say, the larks of the Sahara Desert) than it was when extended to the breaking of some proto-avian species into larks, eagles, and penguins, or, more boldly, of a protovertebrate into reptiles, mammals, and birds.

Similarly, natural selection could be conceded a more modest role than Darwin had given it when he called it "the main but not exclusive means of modification."[6] Or it could be given a more comprehensive place, as it was by A. R. Wallace or August Weismann.

Finally, although Darwin thought that evolutionary processes were sufficient to explain the origin of human beings, others thought that they were sufficient only to account for the emergence of the human body and still others that they were at most capable of making a contribution to the origin of the body without being able fully to account even for that.

Darwin's ideas met with varying degrees of acceptance in the scientific community. Some form of common ancestry received general acceptance among scientists fairly quickly. Although the transformation of one species into another that was at the heart of his thesis required some *cause* of the transformations, it did not require *natural selection* as its cause. It was logically possible to accept the evolutionary origin of species, and even common ancestry, without accepting natural selection. Despite the defense Darwin's mechanism got from Wallace and Weismann, many biologists assigned it only a role much more modest than Darwin had suggested. Peter Charles Mitchell, then secretary to the Zoological Society of London, wrote, in his 1910 *Encyclopaedia Britannica* article on "Evolution," that "how far 'natural selection' suffices for the production of species remains to be seen."[7]

---

5. Darwin, *Origin*, 483. By classes, Darwin meant, for example, mammals, birds, and insects.

6. Darwin, *Origin*, 6.

7. Mitchell, "Evolution," 34. For a fuller early twentieth-century account, see Stanford biologist Vernon L. Kellogg, *Darwinism To-day*. For an historical survey, see

Only with the synthesis of Darwinism and Mendelian genetics in the 1930s did natural selection gain acceptance as the primary cause of evolutionary change. In the interim, a variety of non-Darwinian mechanisms were proposed—macromutations, the inheritance of acquired characteristics, and orthogenesis (i.e., an innate tendency to evolve in a preestablished direction) among others.[8]

Evolutionary anthropogenesis, as one might imagine, remained particularly controversial. Thomas H. Huxley endorsed the idea explicitly as early as 1863 in his *Evidence as to Man's Place in Nature*; Wallace, cofounder of the theory of evolution as applied to plants and animals, did not.[9] Fossil evidence (beyond a few Neanderthal skeletons and some fragments of one or two Java Man skeletons) only began to appear in the 1920s.[10]

Each of these four ideas might be juxtaposed with apparently contrary theological doctrines with which it would have to be reconciled, or on the basis of which it would have to be opposed.

The very idea of an evolutionary origin of species might be contrasted with the theological idea that God created each species directly and separately. The attribution of the origin of species to natural processes sounded to some critics, however unreasonably, like some new version of deism. As one anonymous critic put it:

> The obvious tendency of his [sc. Darwin's] doctrines is—if not to eliminate creative action altogether out of the universe of mind and matter, and to reduce the order of harmony of Nature to the results of blind fortuitous forces, which would be to obliterate God altogether—at least to place the Creator at such a distance from His works that His supervision, providence, and justice may be safely ignored.[11]

While an evolutionary explanation might not have provoked any objections had the matter to be explained been only, say, the origin of the various species of beetles or squirrels, nevertheless some Christians thought it did raise questions when applied more comprehensively (in proposing a common ancestry for, say, elephants, sharks, and eagles).

Bowler, *Non-Darwinian Revolution*.

8. For more on this, see Bowler, *Non-Darwinian Revolution*.

9. See Wallace, *Contributions to the Theory*. See also Smith, "Alfred Russel Wallace"; or Kottler, "Wallace."

10. For a history, see Reader, *Missing Links*.

11. J. G. C., "Darwinism," 361.

The role of natural selection in the origin of species was seen by some Christians as a process that included an element of randomness inconsistent with the doctrine of providence. Seton Hall University professor Fr. George Barry O'Toole, for example, wrote that "Natural selection, in making the organism a product of the concurrence of blind forces unguided by Divine intelligence... has furnished the agnostic with a miserable pretext for omitting God from his attempted explanation of the universe."[12]

Finally, and most importantly, Darwin's account of evolutionary anthropogenesis seemed to many to be inconsistent with the distinctive attention that Genesis gives to the origin of the human race and seemed to neglect the place of the human soul in the constitution of the human person.

Wilberforce and Huxley at Oxford, 1860

The first of the famous battles in the alleged war between Darwinism and Christianity, one that, in retrospect at least, came to be seen as (in Owen Chadwick's words) "the symbol of the entire Victorian conflict,"[13] occurred at the 1860 meeting of the British Association for the Advancement of Science. The association, formed in 1831, hosted annual meetings which served both as a forum for the announcement of scientific advances and as one in which scientific ideas could be introduced to a non-professional audience. Some of the papers read at such meetings were fairly technical, or at least specialized. Huxley's 1860 paper, for example, was on the development of Pyrosoma, a genus of marine invertebrate. Others were of more general interest, such as Captain Parker Snow's paper that same year on Franklin's lost polar expedition, which had disappeared in search of the Northwest Passage some fifteen years before. The 1860 meeting was held a mere seven months after the publication of Darwin's *Origin of Species*—though the book was by then already in its second edition—and, in the words of a contemporary journalist, "the chief cause of contention [at the meeting] has been the new theory of the Development of Species by Natural Selection—a theory open ... to a good deal of personal quizzing, without, however, seriously crippling the usefulness of the physiological investigations on which it rests."[14] Darwin, being ill, was not himself in attendance, but most of England's leading scientists—Lyell, Huxley, and Richard Owen, among others—were. To bring the discussion of Darwin's ideas into focus, we can concentrate on two

---

12. O'Toole, *Case against Evolution*, 11.
13. Chadwick, *Victorian Church*, 2:10.
14. *Athenaeum*, № 1706, "Science," 19.

papers that seem most clearly related to Darwin's ideas and on the discussion which followed them.

The first of these papers, Charles Daubeny's "On the Final Causes of the Sexuality of Plants, with particular Reference to Mr. Darwin's Work 'On the Origin of Species by Natural Selection,'" was delivered on Thursday, 28 June. Daubeny recognized the value of Darwin's theory to the problem of distinguishing species from varieties, but he expressed reservations about how far the theory could be extended. The discussion after Daubeny's presentation quickly turned to a general evaluation of Darwin's theory.

Owen, the superintendent of the natural history collections at the British Museum, was asked to speak and focused on the implications of Darwin's work for the origin of the human race, a question that Darwin had tried to skirt. In explicit reference to man, Darwin had gone only so far as to say:

> In the distant future I see open fields for far more important researches. Psychology will be based on a new foundation, that of the necessary acquirement of each mental power and capacity by gradation. Light will be thrown on the origin of man and his history.[15]

Even that was found only on the last pages of the book. But just a few pages earlier he had written: "I should infer from analogy that probably all the organic beings which have ever lived on this earth have descended from some one primordial form into which life was first breathed."[16] The direction of thought, if not the logical implications of the theory itself, was clear, although Darwin addressed the inclusion of man within the theory of evolution explicitly only a decade later. Owen emphasized the importance of testing Darwin's ideas against the facts and returned to the Great Hippocampus Question on which he and Huxley had been sparring since 1857.[17] Owen claimed that the brain of the gorilla showed striking differ-

---

15. Darwin, *Origin*, 488–89.

16. Darwin, *Origin*, 484.

17. The Great Hippocampus Question was a controversy, with Owen and Huxley as principals, over the anatomical difference between man and ape. Begun in 1857, with Owen's claim that the *hippocampus minor* (now called the *calcar avis*) could be found only in human brains, the debate achieved much popular notice before being resolved in favor of Huxley. Illustrative of the public interest in the controversy, "Gorilla" (paleontologist Sir Phillip de Malpas Grey-Egerton, according to Joseph Dalton Hooker—see Darwin's letter to Huxley) wrote in *Punch*:

> Then Huxley and Owen,
> With rivalry glowing,
> With pen and ink rush to the scratch;

ences from the human brain, but was not so different from the brains of the lowest monkeys. This Huxley denied and he immediately took the occasion to object to Owen's conclusions, arguing that the differences among the nonhuman primates were greater than the difference between the highest nonhuman primate and man,[18] and adding that it did not matter to him whether he was descended from a gorilla or not.[19]

The second of the papers touching on Darwin's ideas was William Draper's paper "On the Intellectual Development of Europe, considered with Reference to the Views of Mr. Darwin and others, that the Progression of Organisms is determined by Law." Unlike Daubeny's, this paper was not closely connected to Darwin's own interests and work. It was, as Darwin's friend Joseph Hooker put it, "all a pie of Herbert Spencer & [Henry Thomas] Buckle without the seasoning of either"[20] and seems not to have been well-received. After an initial objection to the very idea that a comparison could be made between the biological evolution of lower animals and the intellectual development of man, discussion turned to the ideas actually found in Darwin's controversial new book.

First to express his views was the prominent physiologist Benjamin Brodie, who offered two reasons why he could not accept Darwin's views. The first was an objection to a strong version of common ancestry, namely, that the existence of the primordial germ that it presupposed had not been demonstrated. The second was a particular objection to the descent of man—Brodie could not see how man's power of self-consciousness, which he identified with the Divine Intelligence, could originate with matter. This was, properly speaking, a philosophical objection and not, despite the reference to Divine Intelligence, a religious one.

    'Tis Brain versus Brain,
    Till one of them's slain,
    By Jove! it will be a good match!
    Says Owen, you can see
        The brain of Chimpanzee
    Is always exceedingly small,
        With the hindermost "horn"
        Of extremity shorn,
    And no "Hippocampus" at all.

For a brief review of the controversy, see C. M. Owen, "*Hippocampus Minor*"; or Gross, "Huxley versus Owen."

18. *Athenaeum*, № 1706, "Science," 25–26.

19. Alfred Newton, Letter to Edward Newton, 25 July 1860, in Wollaston, *Life of Newton*, 119.

20. Hooker, Letter to Darwin, 2 July 1860, in Huxley, *Life and Letters of Hooker*, 526.

Next came Bishop Samuel Wilberforce. Wilberforce, had been appointed Anglican bishop of Oxford in 1845. He was an energetic pastor, a skilled orator both in the pulpit and on the platform, and an author (of a biography of his father—William Wilberforce, the great antislavery campaigner—among other works both literary and historical). He was deeply involved in the theological and ecclesiological disputes of his day, trying to hold the High-Church line against both its Broad-Church critics and the tendency of so many Anglo-Catholics to cross the Tiber (including not only priests of his own diocese—participants in the Oxford movement such as John Henry Newman—but many of his own relatives—all three of his brothers and his two brothers-in-law, one of whom was Henry Edward, later Cardinal, Manning). One of his first biographers emphasized Wilberforce's interest in natural history, particularly ornithology, adding that "it may not always be remembered that his first and his last contributions to the 'Quarterly Review,' were reviews of his friend Mr. Knox's 'Ornithological Rambles in Sussex,' and of his 'Autumns on the Spey.'"[21] These items aside, almost all of his intellectual work was devoted to non-scientific matters. Nevertheless, the editors of the *Quarterly* turned to him for a review of Darwin's *Origin* in 1860. That review, which appeared immediately after the Oxford meeting, must have been written shortly before the meeting was held.

Wilberforce, invited by the chair of the section in which Draper's paper was read to comment on Darwin's ideas, spoke for half an hour. We have no transcript, but can deduce the content of his remarks from the summary published in the *Athenaeum* the next week[22] as well as from the review he published in the *Quarterly*.[23] The bishop's main points were the fixity of species, the unphilosophical (i.e., methodologically unacceptable) character of the *Origin*, and the distinctness of the line between animals and man.

Replies in defense of Darwin came from several of Darwin's friends—first from Huxley and then from Hooker. Huxley had not intended to attend the session at all but had been persuaded to come at the last minute by Robert Chambers, who had entreated him not to desert the cause;[24] his reply was relatively brief. Hooker followed up with a more substantial and more effective, if in the end less memorable, reply.

It was in that context that there occurred the exchange for which the meeting is usually remembered. Adapting a line that he had prepared for his

21. Ashwell, *Life of Wilberforce*, xxi.
22. *Athenaeum*, № 1707, "Science," 64–65.
23. We have it on the authority of Alfred Newton, a scientist who was present at the exchange and who read the review when it appeared, that they were substantially the same. See Newton, "Early Days," 248.
24. Huxley, Letter to Francis Darwin.

review (that "if Mr. Darwin can . . . demonstrate to us our fungular descent, we shall dismiss our pride, and avow, with the characteristic humility of philosophy, our unsuspected cousinship with the mushrooms"[25]) in light of Huxley's remark in his exchange with Owen two days before, Wilberforce put his famous question about simian ancestry. Physicist Balfour Stewart, who was in attendance, provided what must be the most reliable account of the incident in a letter he wrote to a friend a few days later:

> The Bishop said he had been informed that Prof. Huxley had said he didn't care whether his grandfather was an ape. Now he (the Bishop) would not like to go to the Zoological Gardens and find his father's father or his mother's mother in some antiquated ape. To which Prof. Huxley replied that he would rather have for his grandfather an honest ape low in the scale of being than a man of exalted intellect & high attainments who used his power to prevent the truth (which was very imprudent).[26]

Or, as the more delicate account provided by the inimitable *Athenaeum* put it:

> [Some]—conspicuous among these, Prof. Huxley—have expressed their willingness to accept, for themselves, as well as for their friends and enemies, all actual truths, even the last humiliating truth of a pedigree not registered in the Herald's College.[27]

It was, without a doubt, Wilberforce's quip, and Huxley's reply, that elevated this incident to the prominence it has had as an incident in the alleged war between science and religion. It is a great story, but can the Warfare Theorists fairly claim it as evidence for their Thesis? It is undeniable that there was an exchange of views between a bishop critical of Darwin's views and three scientists who supported those views.[28] What is wrong with calling *that* a battle between science and religion? Several things.

---

25. Wilberforce, "Review of *On the Origin of Species*," 121.

26. Stewart, Letter to Forbes, 5 July 1860, MSDEP7, Incoming Letters 1860, Forbes Collection.
The details of the incident vary from one eyewitness account to another and much ink has been spilled over the years in an attempt to determine exactly what form the question, and the reply, took. See, for example, Lucas, "Wilberforce and Huxley"; and James, "'Open Clash'?" The matter of whether either, or both, speakers overstepped the bounds of Victorian propriety, also much discussed, can be left for resolution elsewhere.

27. *Athenaeum*, № 1706, "Science," 19.

28. The third was John Lubbock, much junior to Hooker and Huxley, but about to do important work in evolutionary anthropology.

First, though Wilberforce may well have had theological commitments as well as scientific ones, Huxley surely had antireligious commitments as well as scientific ones. William Flower, a scientific ally of Huxley on the Great Hippocampus Question and later director of the natural history departments of the British Museum, said to Randall Davidson, then dean of Windsor, later archbishop of Canterbury, that

> Both Huxley and [John] Tyndall were anti-religious in a dogmatic sense very long before they had made any mark in science, and . . . their views on these subjects cannot therefore be regarded as the legitimate outcome of scientific thought and scientific knowledge.[29]

Of the two, despite the suggestions of White, Wilberforce seems to have been the more accommodationist.

More generally, in the midst of an 1864 controversy over a proposed "Declaration of Students of the Natural and Physical Sciences" then being circulated for signatures by some earnest young Christians, Augustus De Morgan, after two columns of harsh words about the declaration and its sponsors for what seemed to him (and others) to amount to a kind of religious test, added:

> The men of science are not quite blameless in the matter. Some of them seem to value their studies, as an Orangeman values his religion, chiefly for the opportunity it gives them of making their natural enemies uncomfortable. It is impossible to read some recent speculations upon delicate scientific questions without seeing that the author has his old antagonists, the parsons, in his mind's eye all the time, and is experiencing the same kind of glee as a small boy feels when he is tying a tin-kettle to a dog's tail . . . But science is hardly advanced by this exciting sport. Scientific theories and discoveries do not fulfil their highest function when they are used as long poles to poke up parsons with. If scientific men were more careful of needlessly irritating the prejudices which they find in existence, and if they would abstain from creating fresh prejudice by the announcement of questionable discoveries in a dogmatic tone . . ., the war between science and religion would not have raged so fiercely.[30]

---

29. The conversation, reported in an intermittent journal Davidson was keeping, was dated 18 May 1889. See Bell, *Randall Davidson*, 1:154.

30. De Morgan, "New Test," 386–87.

Even George Sarton, a Warfare Theorist himself, concedes that "Science was, at a time, especially in the eighteenth and nineteenth centuries, excessively arrogant and aggressive . . . At the end of the last [i.e., the nineteenth] century, there were some people who insisted that religion had outlived its usefulness, that intelligent men had no need of such crutches any more."[31]

Second, Wilberforce acknowledged the importance of treating the matter scientifically, not merely theologically. In his review for the *Quarterly*, he said:

> Our readers will not have failed to notice that we have objected to the views with which we have been dealing solely on scientific grounds. We have done so from our fixed conviction that it is thus that the truth or falsehood of such arguments should be tried. We have no sympathy with those who object to any facts or alleged facts in nature, or to any inference logically deduced from them, because they believe them to contradict what it appears to them is taught by Revelation. We think that all such objections savour of a timidity which is really inconsistent with a firm and well-instructed faith—
>
> "Let us for a moment," profoundly remarks Professor Sedgwick, "suppose that there are some religious difficulties in the conclusions of geology. How, then, are we to solve them? Not by making a world after a pattern of our own . . . but by patient investigation, carried on in the sincere love of truth, and by learning to reject every consequence not warranted by physical evidence."[32]

And in fact Wilberforce focused, for the most part, on scientific matters.[33] Darwin acknowledged the appropriateness of the bishop's concerns in a

---

31. Sarton, "Introductory Essay," 7–8.

32. Wilberforce, "Review," 256. The quoted passage is from Sedgwick's *Discourse*, 149.

33. To be sure, Wilberforce also raised theological objections:

> Man's derived supremacy over the earth; man's power of articulate speech; man's gift of reason; man's free-will and responsibility; man's fall and man's redemption; the incarnation of the Eternal Son; the indwelling of the Eternal Spirit,—all are equally and utterly irreconcilable with the degrading notion of the brute origin of him who was created in the image of God, and redeemed by the Eternal Son. (Review, 258)

Oxford philosopher J. R. Lucas has put the justifiability of raising such objections nicely:

> either Darwin's theory was a simple hypothesis, in which case difficulties about hybrids and reversion to type were fair and at the time well-nigh

letter to Hooker: "I have just read the 'Quarterly R[eview].' It is uncommonly clever; it picks out with skill all the most conjectural parts, and brings forward well all difficulties."[34] Biology in the nineteenth century was not such a specialized field that outsiders could not make a contribution. Indeed Darwin himself acknowledged that one of the keenest critiques of his ideas came from Scottish engineer Fleeming Jenkin.[35] The general consensus is that Wilberforce was presenting the views of Owen. The exchange between Huxley and Wilberforce seems not to have been all that different from the exchange between Huxley and Owen two days before.

Third, Huxley cannot be said to represent science and Wilberforce cannot be said to represent religion. Henry Fawcett wrote at the time that "the treatise of Mr. Darwin . . . has for a time divided the scientific world into two great contending sections. A Darwinite and an anti-Darwinite are now the badges of opposing scientific parties. Each side is ably represented."[36] And Huxley himself later wrote about the meeting that

> On the whole . . . the supporters of Mr. Darwin's views in 1860 were numerically extremely insignificant. There is not the slightest doubt that, if a general council of the Church scientific had been held at that time, we should have been condemned by an overwhelming majority.[37]

The session itself saw scientists speak on both sides of the question. Huxley and Hooker defended Darwin's work; Brodie, also a scientist, though not one whose own research had been closely connected with subjects relevant to evolution, raised objections. Wilberforce had spoken against Darwin at the session meeting; Frederick Temple, then Master of Rugby, later archbishop of Canterbury, preached a compatibilist sermon at the University Church on the following Sunday.[38]

---

conclusive arguments against it: or it was a grand interpretative schema, in which case counterintuitive consequences about the nature and dignity of man were relevant and cogent. ("Wilberforce and Huxley," 322)

34. Darwin Letter to Hooker, July 1860, in Francis Darwin, *Life and Letters*, 2:324-25.

35. Darwin's son Francis later wrote, "It is not a little remarkable that the criticisms, which my father, as I believe, felt to be the most valuable ever made on his views should have come, not from a professed naturalist but from a Professor of Engineering" (*Life and Letters of Darwin*, 3:107). For a history, see Bulmer, "Jenkin's Swamping Argument."

36. Fawcett, "Popular Exposition," 81.

37. Francis Darwin, *Life and Letters*, 2:186.

38. Temple, *Present Relations*. For more of Temple's views on the topic, see his later *Eight Lectures*. Temple was, one must acknowledge, one of the contributors to the *Essays and Reviews*.

Fourth, the judgments, even among scientists, about who "won" the exchange are mixed. Each of the principals—Wilberforce, Huxley, and Hooker—thought afterwards that he had acquitted himself well. The Darwinians came away from the meeting unhappy with what they thought was an unscientific approach to the question, but they are not unbiased witnesses. What did others think? We do have eyewitness reports from two scientists not of Darwin's party.

The first is from the letter from Stewart, mentioned above. He wrote that he "thought the Bishop had the best of it."[39] Stewart was a major figure in the science of his day (director, for example, of the Kew Observatory), but it is also important to note that Stewart took religion very seriously.

The second comes from the ornithologist Alfred Newton, shortly thereafter appointed professor of comparative anatomy at Cambridge University.[40] Newton was not a member of Darwin's inner circle (as Huxley and Hooker were) but had been enthusiastic about Darwin's ideas from the moment they first appeared in print in 1858.[41] Shortly after attending the Oxford meeting he wrote in a letter:

> I am quite converted. I was . . . in a 'state of transition,' but Darwin*oid* I might have remained for a whole geological aeon. The Bishop's speech and article have caused me . . . to become something better. I am developed into pure and unmitigated Darwinism.[42]

Newton was there with two other ornithologists, Wilfred Huddleston Simpson and Rev. Henry Baker Tristram, and reports their reactions in addition to reporting his own. One reaction was favorable: "Simpson, who had been very anti-Darwin, declared that if that was all that could be said in favor of the old idea, then he was a convert."[43] The other's reaction was decidedly different. Tristram was perhaps the first scientist to have put the idea of natural selection to use in solving a research problem of his own. Already in 1859, before the publication of *The Origin*, he had written:

> Writing with a series of about 100 Larks of various species from the Sahara before me, I cannot help feeling convinced of the truth of the views set forth by Messrs Darwin and Wallace in their communications to the Linnean Society, to which my

---

39. Letter to David Forbes, 5 July 1860.
40. Wollaston, *Life of Newton*, 118–22.
41. Darwin and Wallace, "Three Papers."
42. Wollaston, *Life of Newton*, 121.
43. Wollaston, *Life of Newton*, 119.

friend Mr A. Newton last year directed my attention, "On the Tendency of Species to form Varieties and on the Perpetuation of Varieties and Species by natural means of selection." It is hardly possible, I should think, to illustrate this theory better than by the Larks and Chats of North Africa.[44]

Natural selection might well create new species, he wrote, though probably not all new desert species originated in this way. He summarized his views by adding,

> Whilst it is contrary alike to sound philosophy and to Christian faith to doubt the creation of many species by the simple exercise of Almighty volition, still, knowing that God ordinarily works by natural means, it might be the presumption of an unnecessary miracle to assume a distinct and separate origin for many of those which we term species.[45]

After listening to Wilberforce, Huxley, and Hooker, however, he came down decidedly on the side of Wilberforce. Newton wrote: "Tristram . . . waxed exceedingly wroth as the discussion went on, and declared himself more and more anti-Darwinian."[46] At the end of the month Tristram wrote to Newton:

> Hanwell [Lunatic Asylum] is the only fit place for a Darwinian. How they can answer the *Quarterly* I cannot tell . . . The more I look into this renovation of Lamarck, the more I see it is one blind plunge into the gulph of atheism and the coarsest materialism.[47]

This is not quite the "re-conversion . . . to the old faith" suggested by Newton's biographer in his account of the incident. It was one thing to use natural selection to explain the origin of the Abyssinian crested lark as the result of the transformation of the crested lark in the desert through application of the ideas suggested in Darwin's paper of 1858. It was quite another thing to argue that natural selection transformed some primordial form into a man in one environment and into a lemur or a mushroom in another, the ideas under discussion at Oxford. It was not illogical to admit that natural selection could change the color of a lark and to deny that it could give language to "primordial forms" or even to protoprimates.

---

44. Tristram, "Ornithology of North Africa," 429.
45. Tristram, "Ornithology of North Africa," 433.
46. Wollaston, *Life of Newton*, 119 (putting "wroth" where the book put "wrath").
47. Wollaston, *Life of Newton*, 121–22.

The entire incident seems to have faded rapidly from memory. Curiously, Draper, whose paper was the occasion for the exchange, makes no mention of it in his *History of the Conflict between Religion and Science* published just thirteen years later. It seems to have come to life again only late in the century, as Francis Darwin and Leonard Huxley prepared the *Life and Letters* of their famous fathers.

Four Other Incidents

It is the Huxley-Wilberforce exchange that has captured the imagination of retailers of the Warfare Thesis, but it was not the only incident mentioned by White in his account of Darwinism. He cites in addition four other incidents—three in the context of American Protestantism and one in the context of Spanish Catholicism.[48] The first two—the firing of American geologist Alexander Winchell at Vanderbilt University and the excommunication of Spanish naturalist Gregorio Chil y Naranjo[49] in the Canary Islands—both occurred in 1878. The third—the forced resignation of Edwin Lewis at the Syrian Protestant College (later the American University of Beirut)—occurred in 1882 and the fourth—the firing of James Woodrow at Columbia (South Carolina) Theological Seminary—happened in 1886. A brief review of these incidents will add to our understanding of the real relations between theology and science.

Confusing Antinaturalism and Anti-evolutionism: The Excommunication of Chil y Naranjo

Let us begin with José María Urquinaona y Bidot, bishop of the Canary Islands (and later of Barcelona), whose condemnation of the first volume of Gregorio Chil y Naranjo's *Estudios históricos, climatológicos y patológicos de las Islas Canarias* (1876), and whose excommunication of its author, White told as follows:

> In the year 1878 a Spanish colonial man of science... published a work on the Canary Islands. But Dr. Chil had the imprudence to sketch, in his introduction, the modern hypothesis of evolution, and to exhibit some proofs, found in the Canary Islands, of the barbarism of primitive man. The ecclesiastical authorities, under the lead of Bishop Urquinaona y Bidot, at once grappled

---

48. White, *History*, 1:184.
49. White, incorrectly, put "Chil y Marango."

with this new idea. By a solemn act they declared it *"falsa, impia, scandalosa"*; all persons possessing copies of the work were ordered to surrender them at once to the proper ecclesiastics, and the author was placed under the major excommunication.[50]

At first glance, of course, this looks like a clear case of conflict between the Church (and of theology) and science. Put in its larger cultural context, however, it is not so clear that it supports the Warfare Thesis. Nineteenth-century Spain was the site of a great intellectual battle (as it was the site of great political battles between liberals and conservatives, republicans and monarchists), but the battle lines are not brought into focus by contrasting theologians and scientists.

Spanish evolutionism[51] was not so much the biological and paleoetiological science of Darwin as it was the monistic philosophy of Ernst Haeckel. This includes Chil's *Estudios*. The introduction to the book presented a materialist account of the origin of the world (along the lines of Darwin and Haeckel, Chil said[52]) in which the word *creation* had been used to mean merely "appearance in the world," and in which man was a modified ape [*simio*], though one differing from other apes insofar as it had the power of abstraction.[53]

It is true that Bishop Urquinaona, in the *Carta Pastoral* in which he condemned Chil's book in 1876, rejected more than just Chil's materialism. Whether Urquinaona's insistence on the account of creation offered by Moses was limited to an exnihilationistic understanding of creation and the immediate divine action in the creation of man, or whether it included also such other aspects of the Hexaëmeron as direct creation of animals Urquinaona does not make clear, but it did also explicitly reject Chil's account of primitive man as a caveman lacking, for example, the use of fire.

Neither Chil nor Urquinaona nor Andrew Dickson White seem to have carefully distinguished the philosophical question of naturalism from the scientific question of evolution. Chil used scientific arguments in support of a philosophical thesis with theological implications; Urquinaona allowed his critique of Chil's excesses to spill over into an attack even on Chil's scientific claims. In that, the bishop went too far, but he is not representative of Catholic attitudes towards evolutionary biology. Only a few years before, English biologist (and Catholic) St. George Mivart had written a relatively

---

50. White, *History*, 1:85.

51. For summaries of the history of the reception of Darwinism in Spain, see Glick, "Spain"; or Núñez, *Darwinismo en España*.

52. Chil y Naranjo, *Estudios*, 14–15.

53. Chil y Naranjo, *Estudios*, 14.

compatibilist account of the interface between theology and evolutionary biology; the year that saw the publication of the *Carta Pastoral* also saw Mivart receive an honorary doctorate from Pope Pius IX.[54]

Intradenominational Conflict over Natural-Scientific Claims: The Lewis Affair at the Syrian Protestant College, 1882

The second of White's examples was an incident that occurred at the Syrian Protestant College, an American missionary institution opened in Beirut in 1866.[55] Edwin Lewis, an ordained Presbyterian minister and professor of chemistry and geology, had been invited to give the commencement address to the graduates of the college and on 19 July 1882 spoke on "Knowledge, Science, and Wisdom."[56] The address is, through and through, an impressive example of its genre. It turned into an incident in our history as a result of two paragraphs found halfway through the address, where, among his examples of scientists, he included Charles Darwin. Without committing himself to the truth of Darwin's ideas, he emphasized their scientific basis and the theological acceptability of what is generally called theistic evolution. To this Daniel Bliss, then president of the college, and some (but not all) of the other members of the faculty took exception. Correspondence between Bliss and David Stuart Dodge, secretary of the Board of Trustees, led to Lewis's resignation.

What can we learn from this incident about the relations between science and religion? Does it provide evidence for the truth of some version of the Warfare Thesis? Does the Warfare Thesis help us understand what happened to Edwin Lewis? Two facts about the affair make it clear that the answer to these questions is no.

First, the small faculty of the college was already factionalized, along lines having nothing to do with evolution, before the address was given. The president of the college had already been attempting for some months to secure Lewis's dismissal on the basis of differences about appropriate personal conduct (for example, Lewis had served wine with dinner at his home) and about institutional policy (Lewis had supported the promotion of Syrian teachers at the college).

Second, the views Lewis expressed about Darwin were shared by other faculty and friends of the college. Fellow professor William van Dyck was

54. *Tablet*, Memorandum.

55. For the full history of the incident, see Jeha, *Crisis*; Farag, "Lewis Affair"; and Leavitt, "Darwinism in the Arab World."

56. The address is available in English translation in Jeha, *Crisis*, 160–70.

in correspondence with Darwin about the publication of some work that he had undertaken in Beirut. Protestant theologian Ibrahim Hurani, who attended Lewis's commencement address, wrote in *al-Nashra al-usbuʻiyya*, the journal of the American Protestant Mission in Beirut, that "Dr. Lewis made a wonderful speech [that] sought to reconcile modern scientific discoveries with religious principles . . . We should indeed thank Dr. Lewis."[57] William Booth, president of the Board of Trustees, also reacted favorably to the translation of the address, which Lewis sent him at his request (though he was later convinced by Lewis's opponents that the translation was unfaithful to the original text).[58]

So, the president of the Syrian Protestant College used Lewis's remarks about Darwin to engineer Lewis's resignation, a result that he wanted anyway and for other reasons. Van Dyck, who was no less sympathetic to Darwin, stayed on, though he resigned a few years later for reasons connected with the general factionalization mentioned above. But, with Christians divided over Darwinism and with so many other issues equally prominent in the events in question, the incident provides little support for, and is little illumined by, the Warfare Thesis.

Theological Rejection of Reconciliatory Syntheses: The Firing of Alexander Winchell at Vanderbilt, 1878

Alexander Winchell, prominent geologist and active member of the Methodist Episcopal Church, had a strong interest in the relations between science and religion, a topic he addressed in a number of his writings over the course of many years.[59] He taught for nearly twenty years at the University of Michigan before accepting (in 1872) a position as chancellor at Syracuse University. When, in 1875, Methodist Bishop Holland N. McTyeire offered him a position teaching historical geology and zoology for half of each academic year at the bishop's new Vanderbilt University, Winchell accepted the offer.

While at Vanderbilt, Winchell published a booklet of about fifty pages titled *Adamites and Preadamites: A Popular Discourse concerning the Remote Representatives of the Human Species and their Relation to the Biblical Adam*.[60] His purpose in writing was "to bring forward certain scientific facts" inconsistent with the idea that "Adam was 'absolutely the first being

---

57. Quoted by Jeha in *Crisis*, 42.
58. Jeha, *Crisis*, 46–47.
59. See for example, Winchell, *Reconciliation*.
60. He later presented his ideas at much greater length in Winchell, *Preadamites*

that could be called a man.'"[61] Shortly after Winchell published *Adamites and Preadamites* he came under attack in the Methodist press,[62] and Bishop McTyeire suggested to Winchell that it would be in the best interests of the university for Winchell to resign his lectureship. When Winchell refused, his part-time lectureship was combined with another part-time scientific lectureship and the resultant chair was given to the occupant of the other part-time position. While there may have been sound administrative reasons for the reorganization,[63] the real problem was surely Winchell's views on Adam. Winchell himself, in an open letter to the *Nashville Daily American*, put it very bluntly: "This action . . . is a *dismissal from office on account of heresy*."[64] That was also how the action was understood both by the Tennessee Methodist Conference, who supported the dismissal, and by the editor of *The Popular Science Monthly*, who opposed it.[65] Andrew Dickson White, who had known Winchell at Michigan, saw the incident as evidence for his Warfare Thesis.[66]

Evaluation of White's claim depends on the answers to two questions: First, what exactly was the controversy over Winchell's views? Second, is the conflict fairly characterized as one between science and theology?

The point in dispute was not, as White has it, evolution. Although T. O. Summers, dean and professor of systematic theology at Vanderbilt, was critical of Winchell's views about evolution,[67] and Bishop McTyeire mentioned the topic in a critical conversation with Winchell, close attention to

61. Winchell, *Adamites*, 4–5. Winchell thought that there were also scriptural arguments for his view.

62. For example, in the *St. Louis Christian Advocate*.

63. On this, see Mims, *History of Vanderbilt*, 101.

64. Winchell, "Science Gagged." The italics are Winchell's; the title is presumably the editor's, but captures the spirit of Winchell's letter.

65. *Popular Science Monthly*, "Religion and Science" and "Vanderbilt Again."

66. White, *History*, 1:84, as well as pages 129, 168, and 313–15.

67. Summers's (Nashville) *Christian Advocate*, "Vanderbilt Commencement." Winchell had addressed the topic of evolution before coming to Vanderbilt in Winchell, *Doctrine of Evolution*, 8; and (for the characterization of evolution, drawn from Herbert Spencer) 15, where he had written that "the doctrine of evolution [the transformation of the homogeneous, through successive differentiation, into the heterogeneous] seems clearly the law of universal intelligence under which complex results are brought into existence." He said that "we are bound to admit the existence of a method of evolution in the physical world" (p. 27) and even that "the succession of forms is, in the main, such as constitutes a method of evolution" (p. 36). Nevertheless, about what he called "the genetic evolution of organic types" (p. 36) he made two points. First, he denied that the "derivative origin of species has been established as a fact." Second, he was insistent such an origin would raise no problems for belief in "the being and providence of a personal God" (both, p. 105)

the controversy reveals that the main problem lay elsewhere.[68] Neither was the problem, as the editors of *The Popular Science Monthly* had it, the *antiquity* of man.[69] The heart of his critics' objections was rather on a strictly theological question—the place of "Adam" in human history.

Winchell's fundamental thesis was that "men must have lived on earth before Adam."[70] This thesis, he pointed out, had been defended by Isaac La Peyrère in the seventeenth century.[71] Winchell emphasized that "[the Bible] was ordained to be interpreted under the concentrated light of all the learning which has been created by a God-given intelligence in man" and proposed to investigate his question "on true anthropological principles." Who, on Winchell's view, was Adam? According to Winchell, the name *properly* refers not to the first man but to the individual ancestor of Moses, Abraham, and Noah specified in the genealogies of Genesis. Whether this ancestor was *also* the first man is precisely what Winchell put into question. Adam was, Winchell thought, a member of the white race who lived between six and fourteen thousand years ago.[72] Winchell's argument for the existence of pre-Adamites began with two key premises. The first was his rejection of the conventional idea that the black races were descendants of Ham, son of Noah. That, and even descent from Adam himself, he thought, was anthropologically impossible: "The time from Adam ... to the date at which we know the Negro type had been fully established is vastly too brief for so great a divergence, in view of the imperceptible amount of divergence since such date."[73] So Winchell's first premise was this:

(W1) Adam was not the ancestor of the black races.

from which, of course, it follows that:

(W2) Adam was not the common ancestor of all men.

---

68. McTyeire, it should be noted, had a few years previously asked Alabama geologist Eugene A. Smith about his views on evolution when McTyeire was considering him as a professor of chemistry. Smith wrote back that he did think that the theory of evolution was true and did not think that it conflicted with any Christian doctrine. This must have satisfied McTyeire, for the bishop nominated Smith for a position on the Vanderbilt faculty, though the Board of Trustees offered the position to a more senior candidate. (Tigert, *McTyeire*, 215–217). Winchell, as mentioned above, had addressed the topic of evolution before his appointment to the Vanderbilt lectureship.

69. White, *History*, 1:84; *Popular Science Monthly*, "Religion and Science," 493.

70. Winchell, *Adamites*, 1–2, for this and the following quotations.

71. La Peyrère, *Pre-Adamitae*.

72. The latter date he defends in the final chapter of Winchell, *Adamites*, 454–74.

73. Winchell, *Adamites*, 47.

Monogenesis was not universally accepted in Winchell's day, but it was then, as now, the orthodox view on the question and Winchell accepted it. That would add to Winchell's premises

(W3) All men have a common ancestor.

That, together with W2, yields

(W4) Adam was not the first human being.

This, the editors of the *St. Louis Christian Advocate* pointed out, raised theological problems. Quite reasonably, the editors wanted to know

> whether these pre-Adamite races are sinners in the sense in which divinity students are usually taught to use the word, and if so, have they any Savior? are they included in the redemptory scheme, did Christ die for them, and should the Gospel be preached to them or, being outside the limits of the Adamic races, have they any part in any of these matters?[74]

These questions Winchell had not addressed, and these are the objections that McTyeire mentioned in his conversation with Winchell prior to Winchell's dismissal. Winchell did attempt to address this question in *Preadamites*[75] a few years after he left Vanderbilt. There he asserted that Christ's redemptive sacrifice could have operated retroactively, but the critics' concern was not about how redemption could be retroactive (i.e., how it could be applied to sinners who had died before the act of redemption itself), but whether the guilt for the original sin could be imputed retroactively. The details of the theological dispute between Winchell and his critics need not detain us.

Important to my thesis are rather several other points.

First, Winchell's work was not a piece of purely scientific work. For all that Winchell's expanded *Preadamites* had to say about the differences between Hottentots and Papuans, Dravidians and Samoyeds, both works were quite explicitly attempts at a synthesis of theology and natural science. This is suggested by the fact that *Adamites* made its first appearance in the pages of the *North Christian Advocate*. It is also clear from the very chapter titles. The booklet opens with a chapter on "A Sagacious Dutchman," the theologian La Peyrère, and closes with a chapter on "Patriarchal Chronology."

Second, the dispute between Winchell and his critics was a *theological* dispute, one about the transmission of original sin and the consequent

---

74. *Christian Advocate*, "Literary."
75. Winchell, *Preadamites*, 283-96.

need for redemption. Any attempt to reconcile salvation history with ordinary secular paleoanthropology had to be faithful to the deposit of faith no less than to the insights of natural scientists. The question was whether Winchell's proposed reconciliation—making the Adam of Genesis merely the ancestor of the patriarchs, but not of all human beings—was theologically sound and that, *pace* Winchell, was not a matter "which *must be settled by scientific evidence*."[76] Indeed it was not a matter that *could* be so settled.

Winchell's dismissal, justified or unjustified, is not, therefore, an incident in a religious war on science. Winchell wrote in *Adamites and Pre-Adamites* that "Religious faith is more enduring than granite. Scientific opinion is uncertain; it may endure like granite, or vanish like a summer cloud ... Let us not adulterate pure faith with corruptible science."[77]

There is not, however, general agreement about exactly where to draw the line between the two. That point could be extracted from a study of Winchell and his critics, but it can be illustrated better by the case of James Woodrow.

Border Adjudication: James Woodrow, Columbia Seminary, and the Southern Presbyterians

This fourth episode, too prolonged to be called just an incident, began at the Columbia Theological Seminary, an institution of the Presbyterian Church in the United States, in 1884-1889.[78] The foundations of this episode had been laid in 1857, when Presbyterian pastor James A. Lyon persuaded Judge John Perkins, a member of his congregation, to endow at the seminary a "Professorship of Natural Science in Connection with Revelation." In 1861, James Woodrow, once a student of America's last great anti-evolutionist scientist, Louis Agassiz of Harvard, became the first holder of the chair. That chair, the first of its kind in the United States, was established, among other reasons, "to furnish ... young theologians with such enlarged views of science, and its relationship to revealed religion, as will prevent them from acting with indiscreet zeal in defending the Bible against the supposed assaults of true science."[79] Woodrow made clear at the time of his appointment his acceptance of the new scientific ideas about the antiquity of the earth[80] and

76. Winchell, "Science Gagged" (italics original).
77. Winchell, *Adamites*, 29-30.
78. The best brief account is Street, "Evolution Controversy." For more detail, see Gustafson, *James Woodrow*; or Thompson, *Presbyterians*, vol. 2.
79. Lyon, "New Theological Professorship," 185.
80. See Adger, "Calm and Candid Review," 390. Woodrow's general views about his

twice engaged in public exchanges of views with fellow Presbyterian Roger L. Dabney over the very possibility of a paleoetiological science,[81] but the events that White had in mind began only in 1882. What are the facts about what White called "the persecution"[82] of James Woodrow?

In 1882, as the seminary was trying to reopen after a two-year closure due to financial difficulties, its Board of Directors included in a report to its controlling synods the remark that theirs was not an institution in which evolution was being taught. Woodrow, ever scrupulous about these matters, remarked in his report to the board in May 1883 that "it is not teaching anything contradicting God's word to say that He may have formed the highest beings from the lower by successive differentiations." This (and assorted rumors) worried the board's secretary, Joseph Bingham Mack,[83] who persuaded it to ask Woodrow "to give fully his views as taught in this institution upon Evolution, as it regards the World, the lower Animals and Man."[84] This Woodrow did in a lecture delivered to the Alumni Association on 7 May 1884 and subsequently published in his *Southern Presbyterian Review*.[85]

Woodrow said that he had sometimes explained, but had never defended, the theory of evolution in his seminary classroom.[86] Indeed, he had long not thought it to be true. But as he prepared his lecture, he came to see the force of the arguments in its favor, at least with respect to the origins of plants and animals. With respect to man, he wrote:

> [T]here would seem to be no ground for attributing a different origin to man's body from that which should be attributed to animals . . . [I]f they were derived from ancestors unlike

---

subject are articulated in his Inaugural Address.

81. The exchanges occurred (mostly) in the pages of Woodrow's *Southern Presbyterian Review*. The first exchange, in which both articles were published anonymously, came shortly after Woodrow's appointment: Dabney, "Geology and the Bible"; and Woodrow, "Geology and its Assailants." The second came a decade later: Dabney, *Caution*; Woodrow, "Examination"; Dabney, "*Caution* Criticised by Dr. Woodrow"; and Woodrow, "Further Examination." Dabney's works have been reprinted in *Discussions*, vol. 3, which contains all the items mentioned above. Woodrow's are reprinted in Marion Woodrow, *Woodrow as Seen by His Friends*.

82. White, *History*, 1:86.

83. For Mack's summary, see Mack, "Other Side," 1. For a negative assessment of Mack's motives, see a personal letter from Woodrow's nephew, Woodrow Wilson, to Ellen Louise Axson.

84. Presbyterian Church, Synod of South Carolina, *Minutes for 1884*, 28.

85. Woodrow, *Evolution*.

86. See Woodrow, Letter to Adger, in Adger, *My Life and Times*, 664; and Fraser, "Evolution," in Woodrow, *Woodrow as Seen by His Friends*, 42.

themselves, so may man have been ... As regards the soul of man, which bears God's image, and which differs so entirely not merely in degree but in kind from anything in the animals, I believe it was immediately created.[87]

The body of Eve, he believed, was produced by God from Adam's rib, just as related in Genesis.[88]

Woodrow's views gave rise to a controversy, first in the Presbyterian press[89] and then in official contexts, that lasted until the end of the decade. The first battle was fought at the September 1884 meeting of the seminary's Board of Trustees and continued at the Annual Sessions of the Synod of South Carolina, held in Greenville the next month.[90] The contrasting positions were well summarized in those initial skirmishes. The Board of Directors, without concurring in Woodrow's views about the origins of Adam's body, expressed its judgment that "'the relations subsisting between the teachings of Scriptures and the teachings of natural science' are plainly, correctly and satisfactorily set forth" in Woodrow's lecture on evolution, and it denied that his view was in any way "inconsistent with perfect soundness in faith."[91] A majority of the session's standing committee on the theological seminary defended Woodrow in its report to the synod, maintaining that "inasmuch as the hypothesis of Evolution concerning the earth, the lower animals, and the body of man ... is a purely scientific and extra-Scriptural hypothesis, the Church ... is not called upon to make any deliverance concerning its truth or falsity."[92] A minority, while explicitly denying that Woodrow's views were heretical, would have prohibited

> the inculcation and defense of the said hypothesis as even a probable one, in the Theological Seminary, as being contrary to the interpretation of the Scriptures by our Church and to her prevailing and recognized views.[93]

The minority report was careful to distinguish between the content of the Bible "in the highest and absolute sense" and "the interpretations of the Bible by the Presbyterian Church in the United States." The synod rejected

---

87. Woodrow, *Evolution*, 17.
88. Woodrow, "Speech before the Synod," 46–47.
89. Thompson, *Presbyterians*, 2:465–69.
90. Presbyterian Church, Synod of South Carolina, *Minutes for 1884*, 11–13, 20–22, and 27–28.
91. Presbyterian Church, Synod of South Carolina, *Minutes for 1884*, 28.
92. Presbyterian Church, Synod of South Carolina, *Minutes for 1884*, 11.
93. Presbyterian Church, Synod of South Carolina, *Minutes for 1884*, 12.

both the majority and minority reports (by a vote of 44–52 in each case) and voted instead (50–45) to disapprove "the teaching of Evolution in the Theological Seminary . . . , except in a purely expository manner, without intention of inculcating its truth."[94]

The controversy thus quickly ramified, adding questions of institutional policy and procedure to the theological and scientific questions with which it began.[95] These questions were addressed at presbyterial and synodal meetings as well as at general assemblies of the entire church. The anti-evolutionists generally, but not always, prevailed. Woodrow was in the end removed from the Perkins Chair but acquitted of heresy at the trial that he had demanded in order to clear his name.[96] The General Assembly held in Augusta in 1886 affirmed that "Adam's body was directly fashioned by Almighty God, of the dust of the ground, without any animal parentage of any kind."[97] Nevertheless, Woodrow not only remained a member of the church in good standing, but continued to be elected to various positions of responsibility within the church (e.g., as Augusta's commissioner to the general assembly in 1889 and moderator of the synod of South Carolina in 1901) up until the end of his life.

Is this, as White has it, a case of persecution and, more generally, of warfare between science and theology? There is undeniably a conflict between anti-evolutionists and their opponents, but that conflict was, even within the Southern Presbyterian Church, a conflict *among theologians*. Some of the anti–anti-evolutionist opposition were evolutionists; others (for example, the majority of the trustees at the 1884 meeting) were not, but did think that the matter was a purely scientific question. It was a fight in which the anti-evolutionists did not always prevail. In 1911, Thornton Whaling, who had authored a minority report defending Woodrow at the general assembly, was appointed to the very Perkins Chair from which Woodrow had been removed.[98] It makes no sense to see a conflict in which there were theologians on both sides as a war between science and *theology*.

---

94. Presbyterian Church, Synod of South Carolina, *Minutes for 1884*, 20–21.

95. There is also reason to believe that the personal unpopularity of Woodrow in some quarters added heat to the controversy. See Street, "Evolution Controversy," 236–38.

96. The whole story of Woodrow's acquittal, like every other aspect of this affair, is in fact more complicated; the acquittal was annulled on appeal by the Georgia Synod in 1886, following which Woodrow filed a complaint against the Synod at the General Assembly in 1888. The complaint was not sustained, but the terms of that decision were not entirely unsatisfactory to Woodrow and his allies. See T.C.W. (presumably, Thornton C. Whaling), "Dr. Woodrow and the General Assembly."

97. Presbyterian Church, General Assembly, *Minutes for 1886*, 7:408 and 18.

98. Whaling later published a book, *Science and Religion Today*, dedicated to

How should we then understand the Woodrow affair? The grand phrases that John William Draper and Andrew Dickson White used to state their thesis—"the conflict of two contending powers, the expansive force of the human intellect on one side and the compression arising from traditionary faith and human interests on the other,"[99] "interference with science in the supposed interests of religion,"[100] a "conflict between two epochs in the evolution of human thought"[101]—do little to help us understand the affair.

It was rather, first, an attempt to determine what should be taught to future Presbyterian ministers at their church's own seminary. The antievolutionist Presbyterians involved in the Woodrow affair drew a careful distinction between "the Bible in its highest and most absolute sense" and "the interpretations of the Bible by the Presbyterian Church in the United States" (i.e., as mediated by the Westminster Confession), and chose to govern their seminary on the basis of their church's traditional interpretation of the latter.

It was, second, an attempt to delimit the frontier between two epistemological methods, faith and scientific inquiry. With how much certainty should Presbyterians accept the traditional understanding of the Westminster Confession's interpretation of the Bible? With how much certainty could the scientist assert that the body of the first human being was actually produced by evolutionary processes? What should the seminary teach in the face of probable arguments that yield opposite conclusions? Is there a way to compare such disparate probabilities? To what extent are those probabilities affected by the tendency to unsettle other well-established ideas? The answer to these questions requires attention to both hermeneutics and the philosophy of science. Disagreement will arise, not only as a result of differences on those two matters, but as a result of varying assessments of the relative danger of theological and of scientific error, not just in general, but about the particular point in dispute.

Conclusion

What, then, should be the verdict on the cases discussed in this chapter? The nineteenth century showed some spirited fights between evolutionists and anti-evolutionists and some no less spirited fights between philosophical naturalists and philosophical antinaturalists. The latter fights may have

Woodrow, "a masterly expounder of the right relations between science and religion."
    99. Draper, *History*, vi.
    100. White, *History*, 1:viii.
    101. White, *History*, 1:ix.

found all Christians on the same side of the barricades, while finding scientists divided. That controversy was over a philosophical issues on which science, as such, is neutral. The former fight was over a scientific issue, but one on which Christians were divided both on its scientific merits and on its logical connection (if any) with Christian doctrine.

As for Oxford, the whole affair was nothing more than a lively exchange between supporters and opponents of a theory that had first seen the light of day less than two years before. Our reporter for the *Athenaeum* summed the meeting up well in saying,

> The flash, and play, and collisions in these Sections have been as interesting and amusing to the audiences as the Battle at Farnborough[102] . . . The Bishop of Oxford, . . . Prof. Huxley [and others] have each found foemen worthy of their steel, and made their charges and countercharges very much to their own satisfaction and the delight of their respective friends.[103]

There is no doubt that many people shared Wilberforce's opposition to Darwin's views for theological reasons, but there were others who did so for scientific reasons. There were also, both then and subsequently, others as serious about theology and religion as was Wilberforce, who did not share this opposition. Darwin had said, "It seems to me absurd to doubt that a man may be an ardent Theist and an evolutionist,"[104] and while this may be attributed to hopefulness on his part, given his wife's piety and his own lack of enthusiasm for public battle, some with more interest in theological matters than he seem to have thought the same.[105]

The two Presbyterian cases show only theological differences within a college or synod, nothing more than a dispute *among Christians* about what to make of Darwin's new scientific ideas. They do not show an opposition between religion or theology and science. Although the Canary Islands case shows what one Catholic bishop thought about evolution, his actions cannot be generalized to his Church as a whole.[106]

---

102. [The reference is to the bare-knuckle boxing match ("world championship") between the English and American champions (Tom Sayers and John Heenan) that had drawn sixty-four train coaches of spectators to the Hampshire village just a few months before.]

103. *Athenaeum*, № 1706, "Science," 19.

104. Darwin, Letter to Fordyce.

105. See, for example, Moore, *Post-Darwinian Controversies*; and Livingstone, *Darwin's Forgotten Defenders*.

106. I will discuss this in detail in a history of Catholic evolutionism now in progress.

In the case of Winchell, the controversy was over the *theological* soundness of a proposed integrated account of the early history (and prehistory) of the human race. In the Woodrow affair, the controversy was over where exactly the line between the theological and the scientific lay.

CHAPTER 5

William Jennings Bryan, John T. Scopes, & the First Curriculum War

THE YEAR 1920 SAW the outbreak of the first of two great wars over the place of evolution in the curriculum of American public schools. Neither popular nor polemical historians make much of a distinction between the two wars, and indeed the two do reveal certain similarities. Nevertheless, they show important differences as well and will have to be treated separately. In this chapter, I will address the question of whether the Scopes Trial and the larger 1920s campaign against evolution in which it was embedded, constitute a battle in a war *between science and theology or religion.*

The Scopes Trial, 1925[1]

The Scopes Trial itself stands, in many respects, in fairly sharp contrast to the image that it has acquired in popular culture. In that popular account, it is the prosecution, if not the persecution, of a schoolteacher for the crime of teaching evolution. Although in a technical legal sense it was a *prosecution,* it was not a *persecution* at all and not even so much a prosecution as a test case. Joseph Wood Krutch, who reported the trial for *The Nation* and was sharply critical of the anti-evolution law, put it nicely: "It was a strange sort

---

1. The best history of the case is Larson's *Summer for the Gods,* which won a Pulitzer Prize in 1998. Also quite readable, and perhaps sufficient for those willing to forego Larson's excellent account of background and context, is Scopes's memoir, *Center of the Storm.* See also, Numbers, *Darwinism Comes to America,* 76–91. For a particularly fair-minded account of the anti-evolutionists, written by an opponent, see Beale's *Are American Teachers Free?,* 249–59.

of witch trial, one in which the accused won a scholarship enabling him to attend graduate school and the only victim was . . . [assistant prosecuting attorney William Jennings] Bryan."[2]

The scientists who went to Dayton in order to testify on behalf of Scopes raised a scholarship fund to enable him to pursue graduate study in the field and at the institution of his choice. Scopes thought seriously of law, but in the end decided on geology, which he studied at the University of Chicago. Bryan, who was eloquent as an orator, suffered, in the eyes of most, humiliation at the hands of defense attorney Clarence Darrow when Bryan agreed to testify about the teachings of the Bible on the witness stand. Neither Darrow nor Bryan were particularly nuanced thinkers, but Darrow was quicker on his feet, and had the advantage of getting to ask questions rather than having to answer them. In addition, the heat of Dayton's midsummer days, and the strain of the trial, may well have been the immediate cause of Bryan's death just five days after the end of the trial.

Krutch might have added that it was a strange sort of witch trial in which the defendant has to persuade the prosecution's witnesses to testify, in which the prosecutor offers to pay the defendant's fine, and after which the defendant was offered a renewal of his teaching contract. But that is exactly what happened at Dayton.[3]

In the men responsible for setting the Scopes case up, one can distinguish two very different (though not incompatible) motives. Some were opponents of Tennessee's new anti-evolution law who wanted to challenge the act's constitutionality; others were civic boosters who hoped that hosting a test case would bring some notice (and some business) to a city facing hard economic times. The background of the story lies in three events.

The first was Tennessee's passage of the Butler Act. Early in 1925, farmer and part-time legislator John Washington Butler, motivated by concern that teaching students the theory of evolution caused them to lose their faith in God, drafted a bill that would make it

---

2. Krutch, "Monkey Trial," 83.

3. "Three of my students . . . were scheduled to testify against me . . . [O]ne of [them] did not want to go on the stand. To prevent his loyalty from delaying the trial I went to see the youngster and told him to go ahead and testify . . . because he would be doing me a favor" (Scopes, *Center of the Storm*, 105).

"I will let the defendant have the money to pay if he needs it" (Bryan, Letter to Sue Hicks, 28 May 1925, Bryan Papers, Box 57).

Scopes mentionsed the school board's offer of another year's work in Scopes, *Center of the Storm*, 206–7. He chose to accept the scholarship instead and went to the University of Chicago to study geology.

unlawful for any teacher in any of the Universities, Normals and all other public schools of the State which are supported in whole or in part by the public school funds of the State, to teach any theory that denies the Story of the Divine Creation of man as taught in the Bible, and to teach instead that man has descended from a lower order of animals.[4]

The House passed the bill (71–5) without debate and the Senate, after a delay of some six weeks but with only brief debate, followed suit (21–6). Governor Austin Peay was clearly in sympathy with the spirit of the law, but seemed to have mixed feelings about it as a piece of legislation. Nevertheless, after some deliberation, he signed into law the first full-fledged instance of what we might call, after their most prominent promoter, the "Bryan laws."

The second event was a decision by the American Civil Liberties Union (ACLU) to challenge the constitutionality of the law. To do this, it needed to find someone with standing to bring the matter into the courts. A schoolteacher would be best situated for that role, and to find one the ACLU distributed to the newspapers of Tennessee an article announcing,

We are looking for a Tennessee teacher who is willing to accept our services in testing this law in the courts. Our lawyers think a friendly test case can be arranged without costing a teacher his or her job. Distinguished counsel have volunteered their services. All we need now is a willing client.[5]

The third event was the response to that announcement by George Rappleyea,[6] a young New Yorker with a doctorate in chemical engineering then working in Dayton as manager of the mines of the Cumberland Coal and Iron Company. Rappleyea saw the announcement in the *Chattanooga Daily Times* just a few days after Dayton's school year had ended and decided that it would be good for Dayton to host such a test case.[7] The next

---

4. Tennessee, Chapter № 27 (Butler Act).

5. *Chattanooga Daily Times*, "Plan Assault."

6. This name is widely misspelled in the secondary literature. The spelling used here is correct.

7. Scopes later wrote, "I don't know what Rappleyea's personal motives were. But I am convinced that he must have had a special reason . . . I knew him well enough to realize he wouldn't have done the things he did if he hadn't had an angle" (Scopes, *Center of the Storm*, 61). Scopes guessed that they might be business or civic reasons. Reporters' interviews suggest that friction between Rappleyea and local fundamentalists may also have played a role. Rappleyea told Charles McD. Puckette of the *New York Times*, "My interest in the law was hereditary. My people were driven from France by religious persecution. I was against the law when it was first mentioned," and added, "Several of my friends and I were on boat trip on the Tennessee River. My host was

day, he went to work on securing the trial for Dayton. He first succeeded in persuading some of his fellow citizens (including F. E. Robinson, the chairman of the school board, and Walter White, the superintendent of schools) that hosting a trial would be good for the town. Some of those citizens favored the law; Rappleyea did not.[8] Both sides, however, agreed that hosting the trial would be good for Dayton, so Rappleyea went in search of a teacher willing to stand as defendant.

The logical choice, of course, would have been the biology teacher, W. F. Ferguson, but Ferguson, who was also principal of the school, had a family to support and decided not to get involved. The second choice was John T. Scopes, who had just finished his first year teaching physics and mathematics at the high school, but who had substituted in Ferguson's biology class during that teacher's illness. Scopes was invited to meet with Rappleyea and the others at Robinson's Drug Store, which served as a kind of social center for the town. Rappleyea began by asking Scopes whether it was possible to teach biology without teaching evolution. Scopes said it was not and, to make his point, pulled a copy of George William Hunter's *Civic Biology*, the state-mandated textbook, off the shelf. (Robinson's Drug Store sold textbooks on the side.) The book said:

> [G]roups [of organisms in the evolutionary series—protozoa, mollusks, insects, mammals, etc.] are believed by scientists to represent stages in complexity of development of life on earth. The theory of evolution . . . is the belief that simple forms of life on the earth slowly and gradually gave rise to those more complex . . .[9]

Man was placed in the evolutionary series along with all other organisms, although Hunter emphasized that "man is separated mentally by a wide gap from all other animals."

Would Scopes be willing to challenge the law? Scopes was not certain that he had actually taught the passages that discussed evolution during

---

a strict Fundamentalist. All of them kidded me. I couldn't argue with my host, but I told the others I would get even." (*New York Times*, "Evolution Arena at Dayton," 10.) He made a point of telling independent reporter Marcet Haldeman-Julius a story about a fundamentalist preacher who, a few months before the trial, was arranging a funeral service for the six-year-old son of one of Rappleyea's employees. The preacher had told the boy's grieving mother that her son, not having been baptized, was burning in the fires of hell. This was to give the reporter some idea of the kind of religion that, in Rappleyea's view, characterized the town (Haldeman-Julius, *Clarence Darrow's Two Great Trials*, 6–7; see also *New York Times*, "Lays Scopes Trial to Publicity Thirst," 10).

8. Rappleyea, Letter to the editor. See also Scopes, *Center of the Storm*, 60.

9. Hunter, *Civic Biology*, 193–96

Ferguson's illness at all,[10] but since he had used the book to help the students review for their final examinations, all present thought that a case against him could be made. Scopes, who had been a student at the University of Kentucky just three years before, when university president Frank McVey had led the successful fight against a Bryan law in that state, consented ("if you can prove that I've taught evolution, and that I qualify as a defendant"). Robinson then called the city desk of the *Chattanooga Daily Times*: "This is F. E. Robinson in Dayton. I'm chairman of the school board here. We've just arrested a man for teaching evolution."[11] Then Scopes went back to the high school to finish the tennis game that had been interrupted by the invitation to come down to the drugstore. Rappleyea notified the ACLU.

Although local lawyers could have handled the prosecution of the case, and the ACLU had already offered to provide lawyers for the defense (i.e., for the challenge to the law), several other lawyers quickly became involved in the case. Their identities, their concerns, and their motives reveal much about the nature of what happened at Dayton on those hot summer days of 1925.

The first non-Dayton lawyer to enter the case was John Randolph Neal. Born not far from Dayton, he had represented Rhea County for two terms in the state legislature and had taught law at the University of Tennessee until 1923 when, having lost his position during the "slaughter of the Ph.D.'s," he opened his own law school in Knoxville.[12] When Neal heard about the Scopes case, he (as Scopes later put it) "appeared in Dayton and more or less appointed himself my counsel." He introduced himself by saying, "Boy, I'm interested in your case and whether you want me or not, I'm going to be here. I'll be available twenty-four hours a day."[13]

A goal of the city being to host an event that would attract some notice, it was perhaps only natural that the prosecution would invite William

---

10. Scopes, *Center of the Storm*, 60. See also De Camp, *Great Monkey Trial*, 432–33.

11. As Edward J. Larson has pointed out (in *Trial and Error*, 60), the charge against Scopes was not legally necessary. Tennessee had passed its Declaratory Judgment Act just two years before, making possible a test of the law's constitutionality without the challenger having to face a criminal trial. Perhaps ignorant of the new law, Dayton's drugstore conspirators brought the matter into the courts the old-fashioned way.

12. Although some people have seen Tennessee's firing of seven professors that year as a free speech or academic freedom case (allegedly originating with university president Harcourt Morgan's attempt to keep professor Jesse Sprowls from using James Herman Randall's *Mind in the Making* and thereby from presenting the topic of evolution in the classroom), this seems not to have been the reason why either Sprowls or Neal was fired. For details, see Montgomery, "Neal and the University of Tennessee"; or Garner et al., "Report."

13. Scopes, *Center of the Storm*, 63.

Jennings Bryan to come to its assistance, which he promptly agreed to do.[14] Bryan, now "The Great Commoner" rather than "The Boy Orator of the Platte," had been active in Democratic Party politics since his election to Congress in 1890. Three times nominated by his party for the presidency, and secretary of state in the Wilson administration (until Wilson's bellicose response to the sinking of the *Lusitania* precipitated his resignation), Bryan had been a tireless advocate for many of the progressive causes of his day—Philippine independence, the direct election of senators, women's suffrage, the income tax, and legislation by initiative and referendum. He had also been a regular and popular speaker on the Chautauqua circuit. The antievolution crusade of the 1920s, which he was largely, though not exclusively, responsible for launching,[15] was to be his last campaign.

Bryan's announcement that he would participate in the prosecution of Scopes prompted Clarence Darrow and Dudley Field Malone to volunteer for Scopes's defense. Darrow had gained national fame (or perhaps notoriety) representing defendants in at least two "crimes of the century" already in a century not yet three decades old. The first of these was the trial of labor leader Big Bill Haywood, charged with complicity in the assassination of Idaho governor Frank Steunenberg in 1905. In the years between his acquittal in the Steunenberg case and the Scopes Trial, Haywood had been convicted of violating the Espionage Act of 1917 (for calling a strike during wartime) and had fled to Soviet Russia. Darrow's second "trial of the century" was the case of Nathan Leopold and Richard Loeb, two brilliant, and rich, Chicago college students who had killed a young neighbor in an unsuccessful attempt to prove that they could commit a perfect crime. Darrow came to Dayton within a year of arguing before a Chicago judge in mitigation of the latter offense (the defendants having pled guilty) that the killers could not be held responsible for their actions. His efforts saved them both from execution, but Darrow's denial of the doctrine of free will and his public defense of agnosticism in other contexts had gained him as much notoriety in some circles as he had gained renown in others. Scopes's was the only case in which Darrow ever volunteered his services.[16] Malone, a

14. The invitation (or perhaps better, suggestion) that he participate seems first to have come from L. M. Aldridge, who invited Bryan to serve as the World Christian Fundamentals Association (WCFA) lawyer in the case (letter of 12 May 1925, Bryan Papers, Box 47), but this was quickly followed up by an invitation from Mr. Sue Hicks, the Dayton city attorney, who took initial responsibility for prosecuting the case (letter of 14 May 1925, Bryan Papers, Box 47).

15. If credit (or blame) is to be shared, Bryan must share it with William Bell Riley, pastor of Minneapolis's First Baptist Church and founder of the WCFA, as well as with less prominent figures in various conservative Protestant churches.

16. Darrow, *Story of My Life*, 244.

friend of Darrow, was a prominent New York divorce lawyer, and a divorced Catholic, who continued to hold broadly Christian theological views.

The ACLU would never have chosen Darrow, whose iconoclastic views on religion and human psychology would have distracted from the narrow constitutional focus that the Union preferred.[17] But Scopes was the defendant, so the choice was his. Representing the ACLU, then, was Arthur Garfield Hays, one of its founders. Hays's later career provides his character note: he defended the right of workers to organize unions and the right of Henry Ford to distribute anti-union literature to his workers; he traveled to Berlin on behalf of the defendants at the Reichstag Fire Trial (though Hays was himself Jewish) and defended the right of the pro-Nazi German American Bund to possess anti-Semitic literature.[18] Hays's view of the Scopes case (expressed later) was that "it was a battle between two definite types of mind—the rigid, orthodox, unyielding, narrow, conventional mind and the broad, liberal, critical, cynical, and tolerant mind."[19]

The city welcomed all of these men. The impression sometimes created by the *Baltimore Sun*'s H. L. Mencken (and indirectly by Lawrence and Lee's play) notwithstanding, Dayton was a good host; hospitality was extended to all sides.[20] Bryan was fêted with a dinner at the Progressive Dayton Club when he arrived to help the prosecution; so was Darrow when *he* arrived in town a few days later to conduct the defense. Bryan was cheered when he spoke at the trial, but defense lawyers—Darrow, but especially the lesser-known Malone—were given even more spirited applause when *they* spoke. When objection was made that the prayers with which the court was opened each day had a uniformly fundamentalist (and "argumentative," one defense lawyer complained[21]) tone, the judge, John T. Raulston, turned the matter over to the Dayton pastors' association, which arranged an alternation between fundamentalist and modernist ministers for the remaining days of the trial. Krutch wrote in a retrospective article forty years later:

> The little town of Dayton behaved on the whole very well. Though ostensibly at least all on the side of the prosecution, many of the businessmen were finally delighted that their town was going to be put on the map as the place where one of the

17. Scopes, "Reflections," 20–21. See also Larson, *Summer for the Gods*, 101–3 and 206–10.

18. See Hays, *City Lawyer*.

19. Hays, *City Lawyer*, 213.

20. Mencken's dispatches from Dayton (thirteen articles published between 29 June and 14 September in the *Baltimore Sun*) show his usual mean-spiritedness, but even he sometimes acknowledges the town's fairness and hospitality.

21. Hays, *Let Freedom Ring*, 34.

greatest questions of the day would be debated by world-famous visitors.[22]

The trial itself began on 10 July 1925 in the courtroom of the Rhea County courthouse, which, despite Dayton's small size, had one of the largest courtrooms in the state. The defense strategy, according to Hays, was based upon three propositions:

> First, that the law was unconstitutional because it attempted to make the Bible the test of truth;
>
> second, that the law was unconstitutional because in the light of present-day knowledge of evolution, to be adduced from scientists, it was unreasonable;
>
> and third, that the evidence of . . . students of the Bible would show not only that there was no inconsistency between an acceptance of the evolution of man and of the Bible, but would also show that the law was indefinite as well as unreasonable, because no two persons understand the Bible alike.[23]

The state's view of the case was put by prosecution attorney Ben McKenzie: "there is but one issue before this court and jury, and that is, did the defendant violate the statute. That statute interprets itself."[24]

The trial opened with the defense's attempt to quash the indictment on the basis of the Butler Act's alleged unconstitutionality under both state and federal constitutions. Prominent among the objections were, of course, infringement on the freedom of speech and of religion. That motion being rejected, the prosecution called as witnesses Superintendent White, two of Scopes's students, and Robinson (as chairman of the school board) to testify to the book Scopes had used and to what he had said in the classroom, testimony that took all of about fifteen minutes.

The defense admitted that everything the prosecution witnesses had said was true. It had planned to build its case on expert testimony in support of the second and third points mentioned above. It had invited to Dayton, for that purpose, eleven scientists and biblical scholars on whom it intended to base its claim that the Butler Act constituted an unreasonable use of the police power.[25] To the use of expert testimony for this purpose the prosecution objected and was sustained,[26] though the judge did allow the defense at-

---

22. Krutch, "Monkey Trial," 83.
23. Hays, "Strategy."
24. Rhea County Court, *World's Most Famous Court Trial*, 119.
25. Rhea County Court, *World's Most Famous Court Trial*, 57.
26. The law on the admissibility of expert testimony was much more restrictive than

torneys to read into the trial record (as an offer of proof for consideration by the appellate court) statements from those scientists and theologians about the testimony they would have given.[27] The only expert witness allowed to testify was Bryan, whom the defense called as an expert on the Bible.[28] This is what led to Darrow's famous examination of Bryan, an examination so mean-spirited that it evoked sharp protests even from the law's opponents.[29] The testimony of the scientists being excluded, the defense had little left to do. Judge Raulston having refused to accept the defense's complaint that the Butler Act was unconstitutional, a conviction was necessary to the attainment of the larger goals of Scopes and his attorneys. If Scopes were to be acquitted, their day in court would come to an end with the law still on the books. Indeed, the *New York World* had been exaggerating only slightly when, before the trial began, it had written:

> Upon [Mr. Darrow] is placed the responsibility of losing the case. Should Mr. Scopes be acquitted, all the plans for testing the law of Tennessee in the State and United States Supreme Courts would have been for nothing. It would be necessary then to obtain a new defendant and lose his case.[30]

Darrow told the jury that on the evidence provided, they had no choice but to find the defendant guilty.[31] After nine minutes of deliberation the jury returned that verdict, as the evidence in fact required that they do.

The judge had told the jury that he would impose the minimum penalty authorized by the Butler Act (a fine of one hundred dollars) unless the

---

it is today, and most commentators agree that Raulston's ruling was a reasonable application of the law. The editors of the *New York World* had argued that "an attempt to prove the validity of the doctrine of evolution [or, it added "to reconcile religion and science"] would be beside the point" ("Strength of Mr. Bryan's Case"). Walter Lippmann was writing editorials for the *World* at the time, but the editorial itself is unsigned.

27. These statements are available in Rhea County Court, *World's Most Famous Court Trial*, 231–80.

28. To this the lead attorney for the state, District Attorney General Tom Stewart also objected, but Bryan's eagerness to testify to the content of (or perhaps rather to bear witness to the truth of) the book of Genesis, combined perhaps with Judge Raulston's eagerness to see the exchange, overcame the judge's better judgment, and Darrow's examination of Bryan was allowed to proceed, though it was, next day, stricken from the record. A transcript of the exchange is available in Rhea County Court, *World's Most Famous Court Trial*, 284–304.

29. George Fort Milton, editor of the *Chattanooga News* and opponent of the law, though a friend of Bryan, called the questioning of Bryan "a thing of immense cruelty" and "a travesty on the processes of justice" ("A Dayton Postscript," 551).

30. *New York World*, "Darrow and Colby."

31. Rhea County Court, *World's Most Famous Court Trial*, 311. See also 306.

jury indicated that a larger amount should be assessed. This, he said, was his usual practice.[32] The jury said nothing about the amount of the fine, so one hundred dollars it remained. It was paid by the *Baltimore Sun*.

An appeal to the state's Supreme Court was heard during its December 1926 term, and a decision was handed down in 1927.[33] Three of the four judges participating in the case upheld the statute. It was, they said "a declaration of a master as to the character of work the master's servant shall, or rather shall not, perform." They applied a rule handed down in an earlier case in which they had upheld the right of the state to "select a uniform series of textbooks for the public schools," despite constitutional provisions against establishing a monopoly, on the principle that:

> If the authority to regulate and control schools is legislative, then it must have an unrestricted right to prescribe methods, and the courts cannot interfere with it unless some scheme is devised which is contrary to other provisions of the Constitution.[34]

No such exception, they thought, applied here. The act did not violate the Religious Preferences Clause of the state constitution[35] since: "Protestants, Catholics, and Jews are divided among themselves in their beliefs, . . . there is no unanimity among the members of any religious establishment as to this subject." The act only forbade the teaching of some things; it did not require the teaching of anything. Justice Colin P. McKinney, in the lone dissent, would have stricken the statute down for "uncertainty of meaning."

Having upheld the law, the court proceeded to overturn Scopes's conviction on the grounds that the one-hundred-dollar fine had been imposed by the judge. This, they said, contravened the Tennessee Constitution, which required that any fine over fifty dollars must be assessed by the jury.[36] The court suggested that the attorney general should drop the case, which he did. Without a defendant, the opponents of the law had no basis on which to continue their challenge to its constitutionality. Although, as Governor Peay had predicted, no further prosecution under the statute was ever attempted, the law remained on the books until it was repealed (under threat of renewed litigation) in 1967.[37]

32. Rhea County Court, *World's Most Famous Court Trial*, 311–12.
33. *Scopes v. State*.
34. *Leeper v. State*, 518.
35. "No preference shall ever be given, by law, to any religious establishment or mode of worship"—Tennessee Constitution, art. I, §3.
36. Tennessee Constitution, art. VI, §14.
37. The fact that no further prosecutions were brought does not, of course, mean that the law had no effect. On this, see below.

What does this episode show us about the relation between science and religion? The case was in fact a conglomerate of several simultaneous confrontations. Two were clearly *not* part of any warfare between science and religion. They must be identified and set aside before we can proceed to analyze the other two, which had some relation to science or to religion.

The first, of course, is the confrontation between prosecutor and defense attorney that is an inherent feature of America's adversarial system of justice. The prosecutor, Tennessee district attorney general Thomas Stewart, was rumored to be an evolutionist.[38] He was in court to prosecute a case and to uphold the state law, as it was his sworn duty to do. Scopes's lawyers, of course, were there to defend the accused. *This* confrontation, which provides much of the drama of the case, was in many respects the same as it would have been had Scopes been charged, not with teaching evolution in the classroom, but with the more common offense in Judge Raulston's courtroom—distilling moonshine up in the hills. It differed only in that only a particular kind of defense would do. There was no point in arguing that Scopes had not *taught evolution*—the defense had to be that the Butler Act was not really a law; that it was unconstitutional. For the purpose of overturning the law, however, a favorable ruling on any of the defense's eleven objections would be sufficient. It would serve their purposes if the court judged the act to be a violation of the defendant's right to "free communication of [his] thoughts and opinions";[39] it would serve those same purposes (though only minimally) if the act were struck down for having a subject other than the one expressed in its title.[40] With regard to *this* confrontation, any relation between the charges or the litigants and science or religion is strictly accidental.

The second of those confrontations was the struggle between two political philosophies—William Jennings Bryan's commitment to majority rule, and the ACLU's commitment to libertarianism.

Bryan was a committed (though not an absolute) majoritarian. His confidence in the ultimate good judgment of the people is all the more admirable in a man three times defeated in a race for the presidency. His political principles can be summarized by quoting two lines drawn from his public addresses. On the basis of his majoritarianism, he argued that "the hand that writes the paycheck rules the school."[41] His second applicable principle was based not on majoritarianism but on fairness: "If the Bible

---

38. Haldeman-Julius, *Clarence Darrow's Two Great Trials*, 13.
39. In violation of Tennessee Constitution, art. I, §19.
40. In violation of Tennessee Constitution, art. II, §17.
41. Bryan, "Science vs. Evolution," 46.

cannot be defended in the schools, it should not be attacked, either directly or under the guise of philosophy or science."[42] Walter Lippmann, who opposed the laws, recognized the importance of this principle and gave Bryan his Jeffersonian due:

> [Bryan] asked whether, if it is wrong to compel people to support a creed they disbelieve, it is not also wrong to compel them to support teaching which impugns the creed in which they do believe. Jefferson had insisted [in his Bill for Establishing Religious Freedom (1779)] that the people should not have to pay for the teaching of Anglicanism. Mr. Bryan asked why they should be made to pay for the teaching of agnosticism.[43]

The ACLU, which had formed a committee on academic freedom in 1924, articulated *its* principles in the following terms:

> 1st. There should be no legislative interference whatever with the school curriculum. The preparation of the curriculum should be left entirely in the hands of professional educators.
>
> 2nd. Teachers should be permitted the same freedom of expression inside the classroom as is demanded by citizens outside the classroom. The free exercise of this right should not be interfered with by the authorities of the institutions which employ them.[44]

That second principle has not, in subsequent years, been maintained by anti-anti-evolutionists. In 1987, the ACLU joined the New Lenox (Illinois) School District in defending the district's right to forbid its teacher Ray Webster from teaching a non-evolutionary theory of creation in the classroom, a view that prevailed in court.[45] Perhaps even in 1924 the operative principle was not free speech for teachers but the normative character of the scientific consensus, despite both popular reservations and the beliefs of individual teachers. That, at least, seems to have been the view of the editors of the *New York World*, who proposed a doctrine of "educational independence" from "untrammeled chance majorities" analogous to the

---

42. Bryan, *Menace of Darwinism*, 51.
43. Lippmann, *American Inquisitors*, 14.
44. American Civil Liberties Union, *Gag on Teaching*, 30–31
45. *Webster v. New Lenox*. See also *Peloza v. Capistrano* (9th Cir. 1994) (affirming that a school district may require a teacher to present evolution as a fact, and may prohibit him from discussing his religious beliefs with students during instructional time) and *LeVake v. School District 656* (Minn. Ct. App., 2001) (denying a high school teacher's right to teach "evidence both for and against the theory" of evolution).

independence of the judiciary, but acknowledging that they were "by no means clear in [their] own minds as to just what that doctrine ought to be."[46]

In this second confrontation also, there is no necessary connection to either science or religion. Scope's Tennessee attorney, John Randolph Neal, said that

> the general public has a wrong impression of the issues at stake in the Scopes case ... We will wage our fight on ... great principles of constitutional law. The evolution and anti-evolution controversy just happens to be involved incidentally.[47]

The same struggle between the ACLU's notion of schoolteachers' rights to say whatever they think in the classroom and the citizens' rights to set limits to what the teachers they hire may say was already occurring in other contexts as well. ACLU statements from the 1920s, even those focused on the Scopes Trial, refer to a diffuse array of educational practices grouped under the heading "Compulsory Patriotism."[48]

There is, to be sure, a second political confrontation underlying the Bryan laws—one between two different views of what constitutes improper (or at least un-American) government education policy on matters affecting or affected by religion. Defenders of the Bryan Laws argued that they were necessary to ensure government neutrality on religious matters. A political advertisement in the *Arkansas Gazette*, as voters faced a referendum on a Bryan law in that state, said simply: "It [sc. the state's proposed Bryan law] does not seek to help the church. It simply forbids the state attacking the church by having evolution taught in the schools at taxpayers' expense."[49] Their opponents argued that the laws constituted impermissible deference to a particular set of religious beliefs. Maynard Shipley complained that "Fundamentalist ... religious dogmas [are] being set up as a bar to freedom of teaching in our legally secular schools."[50] Tennessee's Butler Act was particularly vulnerable on this account as it made specific reference to the Bible. This had served as the basis for objection to the law at trial. The later Mississippi and Arkansas laws made no such reference.

This pair of political confrontations, like the legal one, bore no essential connection to the relation between science and religion. Malone later said:

46. *New York World*, "Strength of Mr. Bryan's Case."
47. Quoted (without citation) in Shipley, *War on Modern Science*, 222.
48. For the ACLU, see American Civil Liberties Union, *Gag on Teaching*, esp. 11–15. For a more general history, see Beale, *Are American Teachers Free?*
49. Anonymous advertisement, "Bible or Atheism."
50. Shipley, "Growth of the Anti-Evolution Movement," 331.

> The issue at Dayton was not Fundamentalism against Modernism, it was not Faith against Agnosticism, it was not Science against Religion. The issue was and is this: Shall the Constitutional guaranty of religious freedom and complete separation of Church and State . . . be violated or narrowed . . . ?[51]

The third confrontation had its origin in Clarence Darrow's hostility to religion. Darrow came to Dayton not as student of science—Larson wrote of him that "he mixed up Darwinian, Lamarckian, and mutation-theory concepts in his arguments, utilizing whichever best served his immediate rhetorical purposes"[52]—but as village atheist.[53] He wrote later that "My object, and my only object, was to focus the attention of the country on the programme of Mr. Bryan and the other fundamentalists in America. I knew that education was in danger from . . . religious fanaticism." Of Bryan, Darrow said that he "represented religion, and in this he was the idol of all Morondom."[54] Darrow's views had nothing in particular to do with science and everything to do with philosophical naturalism (the impossibility of miracles) and secularist politics (the inappropriateness of opening court with a prayer). This confrontation was well illustrated in a single exchange that occurred during the seventh day of the trial. Tom Stewart was trying for the fifth time to put a stop to the Darrow-Bryan debate about the Bible (formally, Darrow claimed he was taking expert testimony from Bryan) and to keep the court on task:

> Gen. Stewart: I want to interpose another objection. What is the purpose of this examination?
>
> Mr. Bryan: The purpose is to cast ridicule on everybody who believes in the Bible . . .
>
> Mr. Darrow: We have the purpose of preventing bigots and ignoramuses from controlling the education of the United States.
>
> . . .
>
> Mr. Bryan: . . . I am simply trying to protect the word of God against the greatest atheist or agnostic in the United States.[55]

---

51. Malone, "Science, Evolution, and Religion," 142.

52. Larson, *Summer for the Gods*, 72.

53. For Darrow's views on God and creation, on immortality, and on teleology in nature (but only by implication on religion), see Darrow, *Story of My Life*, 377–412. Strictly speaking, he was perhaps a militant agnostic rather than an atheist (Rhea County Court, *World's Most Famous Court Trial*, 99).

54. Darrow, *Story of My Life*, 249.

55. Rhea County Court, *World's Most Famous Court Trial*, 299.

It was Scopes's decision (despite the reservations of the ACLU) to accept Darrow's offer to participate in the trial. Scopes himself showed neither interest in nor hostility towards religion. His father, as Scopes later put it, had unorthodox Christian views and had early "broken cleanly with organized religion." Scopes attended church regularly while he lived in Dayton, but for social, not religious, reasons. Some years later, Scopes married a Catholic and apparently entered the Church, but did this, he later said, "simply to please my bride."[56]

So, here is a confrontation with religion, but it is not *science's* confrontation with religion.

The fourth confrontation suggested in the Butler Act, with its opposition between the theory of descent of man from a lower order of animals and "the Story of the Divine Creation of man as taught in the Bible," has the greatest appearance of being a struggle between science and religion. I will argue, however, that, even with respect to this confrontation, *that* characterization of what happened at Dayton distorts history.

The Anti-Evolution Campaign

To understand this fourth confrontation, the Scopes Trial must be placed in a larger historical context. Bryan had first addressed the question of evolution, in his "Prince of Peace" lecture,[57] as early as 1904, but only in 1921 did opposition to evolution become for him a central concern.

To what exactly did Bryan object? What did Bryan mean by evolution? In his 1923 address to the West Virginia legislature he characterized it as the hypothesis that "links all life together and assumes that all species are developed from one or a few germs of life by the operation of resident forces working from within."[58] About common ancestry, by 1925 generally accepted by scientists, Bryan had his doubts.[59] Evolution in general, he thought, was unscientific (it was "hypotheses," i.e., guesses, not classified knowledge), not grounded in any facts (there were no observed instances of one species evolving into another from which one could generalize),[60]

---

56. Scopes, *Center of the Storm*, 22–23, 39, and 258.

57. This, the most famous of his Chautauqua lectures, Bryan delivered hundreds of times over the course of the last twenty years of his life. It was later published as a pamphlet.

58. Bryan, "Science vs. Evolution," 32.

59. Bryan, *Menace of Darwinism*, 32.

60. For a contemporary critique of Bryan's understanding of science, see Rice, "Darwin and Bryan." For the background on Bryan's Baconianism, see Marsden, "Understanding Fundamentalist Views of Science."

and inconsistent with the Bible. His concern, however, was not so much the common ancestry of butterfly and eagle, as it was of man and monkey. He opened a front-page essay in the *New York Times* early in the campaign with the clarification that "the only part of evolution in which any considerable interest is felt is evolution applied to man."[61] In a letter to Howard A. Kelly, a prominent evangelical (and anti-evolutionist) surgeon at Johns Hopkins University, Bryan wrote:

> I would not be concerned about the truth or falsity of evolution below man but for the fact that a concession as to the truth of evolution up to man furnishes our opponents with an argument they are quick to use, namely, if evolution accounts for all the species up to man, does it not raise a presumption of evolution to include man? I see no reason for conceding a change of species until they are able to trace some one species to another.[62]

Its application to human beings, Bryan thought, was not only false, but dangerous. The dangers it posed were two.

First, "religious faith and Christian ideals are being undermined by teachers who believe that man is a descendant from the brutes."[63] Why did he think that this was so? In the chapters she added to the end of his memoirs, his wife, Mary, wrote:

> This is a matter I can easily explain.... [R]epeated indications of unbelief, especially among college students, puzzled him. Upon investigation he became convinced that the teaching of evolution as a fact instead of a theory caused students to lose faith in the Bible[—]first, in the story of creation, and later in other doctrines which underlie the Christian religion.[64]

He was not alone in this worry. Kentucky state representative George Ellis, author of Kentucky's first attempt to pass a Bryan law, brought up his son's experiences at the University of Kentucky in legislative debate on his bill. Butler mentioned a similar incident as the precipitant reason for his decision to introduce a Bryan law in the Tennessee legislature in 1925. Bryan found confirmation of his anecdotal evidence in a statistical study first published by Bryn Mawr College psychologist James H. Leuba in 1916 (and republished in 1921). Leuba's *Belief in God and Immortality* presented data purporting to show that many American students lost their belief in a personal God and

---

61. Bryan, "God and Evolution."
62. Letter to Howard A. Kelly, 22 June 1925, Bryan Papers, Box 47.
63. Bryan, "Science vs. Evolution," 30.
64. Bryan, *Memoirs*, 479.

in the immortality of the soul over the course of their college years. Leuba attributes this loss of religious belief to the "gain in independence which is a normal result of growth and education."[65] Although Leuba does not attempt to determine whether the students who answered his survey had been exposed to evolutionary biology, Bryan placed the blame precisely on Darwinism.[66] Theistic evolution, Bryan repeatedly warned, was a stepping-stone on the way to atheism.

In defense of the causal connection between Darwinism and loss of religious belief, Bryan advanced two lines of argument—case studies and putative logical connections.

As case studies he cited the intellectual biographies (as he understood them) of famous scientists, such as Darwin himself, whose gradual loss of faith over the course of his life Bryan attributed to his adherence to the theory of evolution, and George Romanes, protégé of Darwin and one of the founders of comparative psychology. Leuba may have reinforced Bryan's worries on this point, for he also claimed to have found that belief in the religious tenets mentioned above was much lower among American scientists than most people suspected.

Bryan was correct about Romanes, who does seem to have lost his faith under the influence of Darwinism, regaining it (at least to some extent) only shortly before his death.[67] In the case of Darwin, however, Bryan was mistaken. Loss of faith, in the days of Bishop John William Colenso and of the *Essays and Reviews*, was a Victorian malady the roots of which lay, not in the Galápagos Islands or in Jurassic fossil beds, but in the new biblical scholarship coming out of Tübingen and Oxford.[68] In the case of Darwin, however, the cause was not recent scholarship of any kind, but two other matters. The first was the problem of pain. In a letter to Asa Gray, America's leading botanist, Darwin wrote:

> There seems to me too much misery in the world. I cannot persuade myself that a beneficent and omnipotent God would have designedly created the Ichneumonidae with the express intention of their feeding within the living bodies of caterpillars, or that a cat should play with mice. Not believing this, I see no necessity in the belief that the eye was expressly designed.[69]

---

65. Leuba, *Belief in God* (2nd ed.), 282.

66. Bryan, "God and Evolution," 1.

67. See Turner, *Between Science and Religion*, 134-63, and Chadwick, *Victorian Church*, 2:21-23.

68. See Chadwick, *Victorian Church*, 2:3-4.

69. Letter to Asa Gray, 22 May 1860, in Darwin, *Life and Letters*, 2:312. It is

The second cause was the idea, emphasized by Victorian evangelicals, that Christian belief was necessary to avoid the fires of hell:

> I can indeed hardly see how anyone ought to wish Christianity to be true; for if so the plain language of the text seems to show that the men who do not believe, and this would include my Father, Brother and almost all my best friends, will be everlastingly punished. And this is a damnable doctrine.[70]

Somehow scientists who became committed evolutionists without ceasing to be orthodox Protestants, such as Harvard botanist (and Congregationalist) Asa Gray, Bryan's fellow-Presbyterian James Woodrow, and Bryan's contemporary William Louis Poteat, president of (Baptist) Wake Forest College, seemed to escape Bryan's notice. A similar list of Catholic evolutionists—St. George Mivart, John Zahm, and Erich Wasmann—could also be constructed. Perhaps Bryan did not appreciate the significance of the existence of such men. "Theistic evolution may be described as an anesthetic which deadens the pain while the patient's religion is being gradually removed," Bryan used to say,[71] but these men did not lose their religion. Perhaps he worried about theistic evolution because of what he saw as the *logical* consequences of the theory of evolution, whether Gray and the others saw these consequences or not.

Bryan's second argument for his claims about the effects of Darwinism ran as follows:

> If a man accepts Darwinism, or evolution applied to man, and is consistent, he rejects the miracle and the supernatural as impossible.
>
> [Evolutionists] first discard the Mosaic account of man's creation, and they do it on the ground that there are no miracles ... They reject the supernatural along with the miracle, and with the supernatural the inspiration of the Bible and the authority that rests upon inspiration. If these believers in evolution are consistent and have the courage to carry their doctrine to its

---

important to note, however, that Darwin was still "bewildered" by the theological problem at this point; he went on to write: "I am inclined to look at everything as resulting from designed laws, with the details, whether good or bad, left to the working out of what we may call chance," though he said he was not satisfied with that either.

70. Darwin, *Autobiography*, 87. This passage, having been published only in 1958, was not available to Bryan, but the first one was. For more on Darwin's loss of Christian faith, see Moore, "Of Love and Death." For a collection of other relevant texts, see Frankenberry, ed., *Faith of Scientists*, 122–42.

71. Bryan, *Menace of Darwinism*, 5.

> logical conclusion, they reject the virgin birth of Christ and the resurrection.[72]

There is, of course, nothing in Darwinism, or in any other scientific theory, that could possibly constitute evidence against the occurrence of miracles. Bryan had simply confused Darwinism with theological modernism, which was his real enemy. Bryan went on to say: "[T]he theistic evolutionist puts God so far away that He ceases to be a present influence in the life."[73] There is also nothing in Darwinism, or in any other science, that puts God "far away." Here Bryan has confused Darwinism with some kind of deism.

Bryan would have done well to ponder the warning sounded by Harvard geologist, and lifelong Baptist, Kirtley Mather in the witness statement he prepared at the Scopes Trial:

> When men are offered their choice between science, with its confident and unanimous acceptance of the evolutionary principle, on the one hand, and religion, with its necessary appeal to things unseen and unprovable, on the other, they are much more likely to abandon religion than to abandon science. If such a choice is forced upon us, the churches will lose many of their best educated young people.[74]

How might students have reacted were they to read the compatibilist writings of America's best nineteenth-century botanist instead of listening to the incompatibilist speeches of its best twentieth-century orator?

Bryan, in his public lectures and speeches, also warned of a second danger—that Darwinism undermines Christian moral ideals. Part of Bryan's concern was that "morality is dependent on religion," that religion is "the only basis for morality."[75] So, if Darwinism undermines religion, it undermines morality as well. But Bryan saw special moral problems arising from natural selection (as he understood the concept):

> If hatred is the law of man's development; that is, if man has reached his present perfection by a cruel law under which the strong kill off the weak—then, if there is any logic that can bind

---

72. The first quotation comes from Bryan, "God and Evolution," 1; the second from Bryan, *Menace of Darwinism*, 46–47. For a short overview of his entire argument, see also Bryan, "Fundamentals."

73. Bryan, "God and Evolution," 1.

74. Rhea County Court, *World's Most Famous Court Trial*, 248.

75. Bryan, *Menace of Darwinism*, 15 and 41.

the human mind, we must turn backward toward the brute if we dare to substitute the law of love for the law of hate.[76]

One has only to look at Darwin's own life—a life of generosity, humility, and compassion—to see that Darwin certainly did not draw the conclusions Bryan drew, but one of Bryan's intellectual vices seems to have been a misplaced confidence in his ability to see the conclusions of other men's views better than they could see them themselves.

Bryan was influenced in his view of natural selection and its effects on character by another book published at about the time he began his campaign—Stanford biologist Vernon Kellogg's *Headquarters Nights: A Record of Conversations and Experiences at the Headquarters of the German Army in France and Belgium*. Theodore Roosevelt, in his foreword to the book, calls it an exposition of "the shocking, the unspeakably dreadful moral and intellectual perversion of character which makes Germany at present a menace to the whole civilized world." In 1915, Kellogg, then attached to Herbert Hoover's Commission for Relief in Belgium as assistant director in charge of famine relief for northern France, was stationed at the Great Headquarters of the German Armies in Charleville. Among the officers with whom he spent many evenings in conversation, one, his escort officer, happened to be a biologist he had known while studying at the University of Leipzig some twenty years before. Kellogg was shocked by the views he heard expressed by his German hosts:

> [Theirs] is a point of view that justifies itself by a whole-hearted acceptance of the worst of Neo-Darwinism, the *Allmacht* of natural selection applied rigorously to human life and society and *Kultur* . . . [He] has a logically constructed argument why for the good of the world there should be this war, and why for the good of the world the Germans should win it completely and terribly.[77]

"My 'Headquarters Nights,'" Kellogg concluded, "are the confessions of a converted pacifist." But what Kellogg saw as a perversion of Darwinism,[78] Bryan saw as Darwinism's natural consequence. This interpretation was only reinforced for him by the more theoretical work of British sociologist

---

76. Bryan, *Menace of Darwinism*, 36.

77. Kellogg, *Headquarters Nights*, 20–23. Kellogg does not name this officer.
The Neo-Darwinism referred to by Kellogg is the version of Wallace and Weismann, according to which natural selection is the nearly exclusive mechanism of evolutionary change, not the version of the Mendelian-Darwinian synthesis, which when he wrote was still about two decades in the future.

78. For Kellogg's analysis, see Kellog, "War and Human Evolution."

Benjamin Kidd, whose *Science of Power* traced a line of thought from Darwin through Friedrich Nietzsche to the German militarism that Kellogg had heard defended first-hand at Charleville.

That natural selection might run along entirely different lines Byran did not seem to notice. Mather, in the witness statement he prepared at Dayton, provided the appropriate reply to Bryan's argument:

> At times of crisis in the past, it was rarely selfishness or cruelty or strength of talon or of claw that determined success or failure. Survival values at different times have been measured in different terms. Ability to breathe air by means of lungs rather than to purify the blood by means of gills meant success in escaping from the water to the land. Love of offspring and tender care of the young gave the weak and puny mammals of long ago the ability to triumph over much stronger and more powerful reptiles like the dinosaur. Especially in the strain that leads to man can we note the increasing spread of habits of cooperation, of unselfishness of love. The survival of the "fit" does not necessarily mean either the survival of the "fittest" or of the "fightingest."[79]

One must acknowledge, however, that Bryan was by no means the only one thus to recast Darwin on this point. Darwin's *New York Times* obituarist, to pick just one example, had made the same error many years before: "It is a law and fact in nature that there shall be the weak and the strong. The strong shall triumph and the weak shall go to the wall."[80]

These books—Kidd's and Kellogg's as well as Leuba's—fixed in Bryan's mind the conviction that the theory of the evolutionary origins of man was "the greatest enemy of the Bible."[81] By 1921 Bryan had decided to launch a crusade against evolution. He began by including a lecture on "The Origin of Man" (later retitled "The Menace of Darwinism") in a series he had been invited to give at the Union Theological Seminary in Richmond, Virginia, later that year.[82]

By the end of the year, he had heard from the Baptist State Board of Missions in Kentucky of their proposed law prohibiting the teaching of evolution in government-funded educational institutions. Bryan wrote a letter to Rev. John W. Porter, pastor of Lexington's First Baptist Church and leader

---

79. Rhea County Court, *World's Most Famous Court Trial*, 245.
80. *New York Times*, "Death of Charles Darwin."
81. Bryan, *Bible and Its Enemies*, 19.
82. The entire series was published as in Bryan, *In His Image*.

of the anti-evolution movement in the state, offering his support.[83] Shortly thereafter, Bryan was in the thick of his last political campaign, beginning with a speech to a joint session of the legislature in Frankfort on 19 January 1922.

Several features of Bryan's policy proposal deserve particular notice. Although implicit in his address to the West Virginia legislature, they are stated explicitly in a letter he wrote shortly thereafter to Florida state senator W. J. Singleterry,[84] when Bryan's adopted home state took the matter up.

First, the anti-evolution legislation Bryan proposed concerned (and on his own principles could only apply to) public institutions. "Christians are compelled to build their own schools and colleges in which to teach Christianity; why should not agnostics and atheists be compelled to build their own schools and colleges in which to teach atheism and agnosticism?" It is important to remember that the anti-evolution crusade explicitly included universities.[85] This is easy to forget. It was, after all, precisely high school teachers (John T. Scopes and Gary L. Scott in Tennessee (1925 and 1965, respectively) and Susan Epperson in Arkansas (1965) who challenged these laws. There is some reason to believe that the laws were in fact ignored from the start at the affected universities.[86]

Second, it concerned the evolutionary origins of man only, not of plants or of animals. To whatever extent the campaigners' anti-evolutionary views may have been more comprehensive, Bryan's *policy proposal* was limited to what he perceived as the real harm—the idea of human evolution. The three Bryan laws that actually passed, and most of the proposals in every state, were limited in this way.[87] Despite this fact, one must acknowledge that many partisans on both sides of the issue seemed to pay no attention to the limited nature of the measures themselves. The only newspaper advertisement that supporters of Arkansas's anti-evolution initiative bothered

83. Fortune, "Kentucky Campaign," 227.

84. Bryan, Letter to W. J. Singleterry, 11 April 1923, Bryan Papers, Box 37. The passages quoted in the next four paragraphs all come from that letter.

85. An attempt to exclude them from a proposed Bryan law was voted down by the Arkansas House of Representatives in 1927 (*New York Times*, "Act on Evolution Bills"). For a discussion of anti-evolutionist concerns about higher education in general, see Roberts, "Conservative Evangelicals and Science Education." For a particular incident, see Wyllie, "Wisconsin Evolution Controversy."

86. On Tennessee, see Montgomery, *Threshold of a New Day*, 46–47. More generally, see the American Civil Liberties Union report, *Fight for Civil Liberty*, 27.

87. The sole enacted exception was the first anti-evolution statute, Oklahoma's short-lived restriction on the state purchase of schoolbooks that taught "the 'Materialistic Conception of History' [or] The Darwin Theory of Creation vs. the Bible Account of Creation" (Oklahoma, "Chapter 175: State Text Books" §12).

to place bore the headline "The Bible or Atheism, Which?," and read "All atheists favor evolution. If you agree with atheism, vote against Act No. 1. If you believe in the Bible vote for Act No. 1."[88] Bryan, in his speech to the Dayton Progressive Club shortly before the Scopes Trial, said that "if *evolution* wins in Dayton, Christianity goes."[89] The opponents of the Bryan laws were no more focused. Some of the statements submitted by expert witnesses in Dayton addressed only historical geology or the evolutionary origins of animals despite the fact that neither of these topics was forbidden in any way by the Butler Act.

Third, it forbade only the teaching of the evolutionary origins of man *as an established truth*: "I would put in [the statute] the two words 'as true' ... A book which merely mentions it as an hypothesis can be considered as giving information as to views held, which is very different from teaching it as a fact."[90] The Florida resolution, apparently written by Bryan himself, uses precisely this wording, though no other state's legislation did so. Representative Samuel F. Williamson proposed amending the Mississippi bill to include the phrase "as established fact," but his amendment was tabled (66–41). In Arkansas, however, Rev. Ben M. Bogard, pastor of Little Rock's Antioch Missionary Baptist Church and one of the leaders of the anti-evolution campaign in his state, wrote to the *Arkansas Gazette* that "the law does not prohibit teaching what evolution is.... To tell a student what a theory is is vastly different from telling him that the theory is true."[91]

Finally, Bryan urged that no penalty be attached to the bill. "We are not dealing with a criminal class and a mere declaration of the state's policy is sufficient." Bryan was willing to add penalties to these statutes if it should prove necessary, but the legislators in most states seemed to follow the principle *sine poena nulla lex* and included some combination of fines, imprisonment, and loss of job or even of licensure.

The result of Bryan's crusade was legislative initiatives in some twenty states over the course of the decade.[92]

88. Anonymous advertisement, "Bible or Atheism."

89. *New York Times*, "Bryan in Dayton" (italics added).

90. Bryan, Letter to W. J. Singleterry, 11 April 1923, in Bryan Papers, Box 37.

91. *Arkansas Gazette*, "Meaning of the Anti-Evolution Law." More official answers came only in 1967–68, when the issue came before the courts. The Arkansas Supreme Court refused to address the matter (*Arkansas v. Epperson*). At oral argument before the US Supreme Court, the counsel for the state of Arkansas said that "Arkansas would interpret the statute 'to mean that to make a student aware of the theory ... just to teach that there was such a theory' would be grounds for dismissal and for prosecution under the statute" (*Epperson v. Arkansas*, 102–3).

92. The most convenient summary is provided in Shipley, "Growth of the Anti-Evolution Movement," but a more comprehensive account, together with the texts of

Although there had been a preliminary skirmish in South Carolina,[93] the anti-evolutionists had their first run at a comprehensive ban on teaching human evolution in the public schools in Kentucky in 1922.[94] Shortly after Bryan's speech to a joint session of the state legislature, Representative George Ellis, and then Senator James R. Rash, introduced versions of Bryan laws in the legislature of the Bluegrass State. Prominent among opponents of the bill were University of Kentucky President Frank McVey, Rev. E. L. Powell (pastor of Louisville's First Christian Church), and Rev. Edgar Young Mullins (president of Louisville's Southern Baptist Theological Seminary and of the Southern Baptist Convention itself).[95] The Senate bill died in committee; the Ellis bill, which would have imposed both fine and jail time for teaching "Darwinism, Atheism, Agnosticism, or The Theory of Evolution insofar as it pertains to the origin of man," reached the floor of the House. There, after a roll call vote that would have killed the bill (38–36, with forty votes required for passage), both proponents and opponents scoured the statehouse in search of representatives who had missed the vote. When the smoke began to clear and the vote stood at 41–41, Bryce Cundiff, from rural Breathitt County, sent the bill down to defeat.

The first legislative success of the anti-evolution campaign came in Oklahoma in 1923,[96] but was of more symbolic than practical value. That success came when state Representative J. L. Montgomery proposed to amend an appropriations bill providing free textbooks for children in the first eight grades of school. The Montgomery Amendment added the restriction that "no copyright shall be purchased, nor textbook adopted, that teaches the 'Materialistic Conception of History' (i.e.) the Darwin Theory

---

most of the bills can be found in Wilhelm, *Chronology*, 307–98.

93. In 1922, Senator F. A. Miller proposed amending the general appropriations bill to withhold state funding from any school that taught, "as a creed to be followed, the cult known as 'Darwinism.'" This, its author explained, meant evolution by natural selection, as opposed, say, to the evolutionary theories of Lamarck, Bergson, Osborn, or others. The amendment met no opposition in the Senate, but was removed from the bill in the conference committee. See *Science*, "Proposed Legislation."

94. See Fortune, "Kentucky Campaign"; Miller, "Kentucky and Evolution"; and Halliburton, "Kentucky's Anti-Evolutionary Controversy."

95. For McVey's views on evolution, see his statement to the people of Kentucky (of 12 February 1922), *Gates Open Slowly*, 292–96. His account of the fight constitutes chapter 14 (pages 221–236) of the same book.

Mullins's view was that "Nothing could be more ill-advised than for Americans to attempt to employ legislative coercion in the realm of scientific opinion" (*Christianity at the Crossroads*, 66). See also Ellis, *Man of Books and a Man of the People*," chs. 8 and 10.

96. Oklahoma, Text Books Law, §12. For a history, see Halliburton, "Nation's First Anti-Darwin Law"; Halliburton, "Second Anti-Evolution Law in Oklahoma"; and Watson, "Oklahoma."

of Creation vs. the Bible Account of Creation." The amendment passed the House by a large margin and survived challenge in the Senate. The bill itself, a popular reform measure, was signed into law but proved so expensive that it was repealed two years later.

In the same year, in Bryan's adopted state of Florida, the legislature passed a concurrent resolution stating that

> Whereas, The public schools and colleges of this State... should be... free from teachings designed to attack the religious beliefs of the public... [I]t is improper... for any... teacher... in the public schools and colleges of this State... to teach as true Darwinism, or any other hypothesis that links man in blood relationship to any other form of life.[97]

Most state legislatures met only every other year in the 1920s, so legislative efforts resumed only in 1925, when the issue was raised in North Carolina and Tennessee.

Controversy over evolution had begun in the Tarheel State as early as 1920, when Baptist evangelist T. T. Martin launched in the denomination's press an attack on William Louis Poteat, biologist and president of (Baptist) Wake Forest College, whose teaching of evolution at that college had long been known.[98] The legislative campaign in the General Assembly began, however, only in 1925, when D. Scott Poole introduced a bill modeled closely on Florida's resolution in the state's House of Representatives. The bill evoked intense interest and the galleries were packed both in the committee hearing and in the House session, in which the measure was taken up. On 19 February, the House rejected Poole's bill 67–46.[99]

The case of Tennessee, the first state actually to outlaw the teaching of human evolution in public schools, was discussed above. Governor Peay, who signed the Butler Act into law, seems to have seen it as more symbolic than operational, for he attached a signing statement saying that

> After a careful examination, I can find nothing of consequence in the books now being taught in our schools with which this bill will interfere in the slightest manner. Therefore, it will not put our teachers in jeopardy. Probably the law will never be applied. It may not be sufficiently definite to permit of any specific application.[100]

97. Florida House, Concurrent Resolution № 7.

98. See Linder, "Poteat and the Evolution Controversy"; and Linder, *William Louis Poteat, Prophet of Progress.*

99. See Gatewood, "Evolution Controversy in North Carolina."

100. Peay, Message.

Peay's statement about the state's biology textbooks was arguably incorrect. Evolution does not feature prominently in Hunter's *Civic Biology*, but the book clearly suggests the truth of the evolutionary origins of man.[101] As for its practical effect, the point was not to *prosecute* teachers, but to affect teaching in the classroom and that it seems to have done. It is easy to imagine that, the law being on the books, teachers might have chosen not to address the question, whether from fear of punishment or (as Bryan imagined that they would) out of respect for law. Howard K. Beale, who made a study of freedom of teaching in 1933 (a study not limited to the three states with Bryan laws on the books), reported that "between a third and a half of the teachers are afraid to express acceptance of the theory of evolution, even if they make no effort to persuade their pupils."[102] In 1960, Scopes returned to visit Dayton for the premiere of the film version of *Inherit the Wind*. He reported that "Teachers still had to sign a pledge that they wouldn't teach evolution, . . . [and] because of it, two Memphis teachers had to cancel a debate on evolution."[103]

Bryan died within days of the end of the Scopes Trial, but others took up the cause when the legislative season resumed. The campaign was able to secure passage of anti-evolution legislation in two more states.

The first of those subsequent successes came in Mississippi in 1926. There a bill similar to the Butler Act but differing in several particulars (including lacking any explicit reference to the Bible and restricting not only teaching but also textbook selection) was passed by the legislature 76-32, with thirty-two absent or not voting in the House; and 29-16 in the Senate. It was signed into law by Governor Henry L. Whitfield on 11 March 1926.[104]

Arkansas enacted the last of the Bryan laws in 1928. In 1927, State Representative A. L. Rotenberry had introduced an anti-evolution bill at the beginning of the new legislative session. The bill narrowly passed the House (50-47) but was killed in the Senate, where the final (procedural) vote was 14-17. Rotenberry and his allies then put the matter to the voters by initiative, and the bill was passed by referendum in 1928, with 63 percent of the vote.[105] Efforts to repeal the measure were intermittently introduced

---

101. "The development or evolution of plants and animals from simpler forms to the many and present complex forms of life have a practical bearing on the betterment of plants and animals, including man himself" (Hunter, *Civic Biology*, 404).

102. Beale, *Freedom of Teaching*, 241.

103. Scopes, *Center of the Storm*, 269 and 271.

104. Mississippi, Chapter 311. For the history, see Curtis, "Mississippi's Anti-Evolution Law."

105. Arkansas, Initiated Act № 1. For the history, see Halliburton, "Arkansas Anti-Evolution Law'"; Ledbetter, "Anti-evolution Law"; and Lisenby, "Brough, Baptists, and

(in 1937, in 1959, and in 1965), but in Arkansas legislative repeal of a law passed by referendum requires a two-thirds vote. These efforts, therefore, had little chance of success. The law remained on the books until struck down by the US Supreme Court in 1968, a development that will be discussed in chapter 6 below.

In addition to promoting the Bryan laws, anti-evolutionists sometimes sought to achieve their ends through various state and local agencies, such as state textbook commissions and state or local boards of education. Sometimes these efforts were successful; sometimes they were not. For example, in Texas, after the legislature twice (in 1923 and 1925) refused to pass a Bryan law, Governor Miriam Ferguson, in her capacity as chair of the State Textbook Commission, was able, in October 1925, to ensure that state-approved textbooks did not mention evolution. At least two publishers (Holt and Macmillan) agreed to publish "Texas editions" of their biology textbooks to meet the state's contracting requirements.[106] An attempt was made, with less success, to keep the teaching out of Atlanta schools in 1926.[107]

It was also possible for school officials, even independent of any official policy, to allow an applicant's views on evolution to affect hiring. Such may have happened to Scopes's sister. Shortly after the conclusion of her brother's trial, Lela Scopes was apparently rejected for a teaching position in mathematics at a Paducah, Kentucky, public high school over her refusal to make a public disavowal of her brother's views on evolution.[108] Surely there must have been more such cases, but it is generally difficult to sort out the details nearly a century after the fact. Those who have attempted to identify them—Shipley, Wilhelm, and even Beale—often settle for cases that show far less than they are supposed to show.[109]

Bombast."

106. *New York Times*, "Cuts Evolution from Texas Books"; and *New York Times*, "Texas Schoolbooks Omit Evolution." See also *Literary Digest*, "No Evolution for Texas."

107. Beale, *Are American Teachers Free?*, 235–36; *New York Times*, "Ban Evolution in Atlanta Schools"; and *New York Times*, "Ends Evolution Dispute."

108. Scopes, *Center of the Storm*, 233–34. This is John Scopes's version. Miriam Allen de Ford, the wife of Maynard Shipley (head of the anti–anti-evolutionist Science League of America), has it that Lela Scopes was refused a renewal of her contract ("After Dayton: A Fundamentalist Survey.") See also de Camp, *Monkey Trial*, 135–36.

109. Shipley (*War on Modern Science*, 318), where the case of Henry Noble Sherwood shows hiring policies that may be objectionable, but not a war on modern science; Beale (*Are American Teachers Free?*, 229–32), where the cases of David H. Pierce and George C. Hein are not as focused on evolution as they must be to make his point; Wilhelm (*Chronology*, 122–27), where the account of the firing of three School Sisters of St. Francis at St. Mary of the Assumption School in Staten Island is similarly not a case focused on evolution (as his source—*New York Times*, "School on S.I. Dismisses 3 Nuns in Dispute on Teaching Evolution"—despite its headline, shows).

The ACLU continued for several years to seek plaintiffs with standing to challenge the new Bryan laws. In an Associated Press story that the *Arkansas Gazette* published under the headline "Here's a Chance for an Arkansas Teacher," the ACLU even assured prospective plaintiffs that the case "would not be 'another drama of international notoriety' like the Scopes case."[110] Nevertheless, it was unable to find anyone willing to initiate a second court challenge. By 1928, the anti-evolutionists' zeal for prohibiting the teaching by law had apparently waned. They were able to defeat intermittent efforts to repeal the Bryan laws they had already passed, but they were not able to add any more such laws to the books. And so the First Curriculum War came to an end.

The Identity of the Belligerents

No one can deny that the campaign Bryan launched was a war against evolution, but who were the belligerents? Was it a war between science and religion? The conventional answer—in the affirmative—does not fairly characterize the conflict.

First, although Bryan and his allies had religious motives, they cannot be *identified* with religion—not with Christianity, or even with conservative Protestantism.[111] This was not a battle between science and religion, but

---

110. ACLU, "Here's a Chance." See also ACLU, *Fight for Civil Liberty*, 27.

111. Whether they can be identified with Fundamentalism is a harder question. Bailey has written that "the contradictions between fundamentalism and the theory of evolution were as real and irreconcilable as religious conservatives imagined them to be" (Bailey, *Southern White Protestantism*, 73). On a strict construction of the term, that is not so. The five Christian doctrines identified as Fundamentals by the General Assembly of the (Northern) Presbyterian Church in the USA in 1910 were the inerrancy of Scripture, the Virgin Birth, substitutionary atonement, the bodily Resurrection and Ascension of Our Lord, and the historical reality of the miracles reported in the Bible. This is, for example, Bryan's standard in his "The Fundamentals." Acceptance of the doctrine of inerrancy did not, as the *Scofield Reference Bible*'s comments on Gen 1:2 and 1:5 show, and as Bryan made clear on the witness stand in Dayton (Rhea County Court, *World's Most Famous Court Trial*, 298–99), commit Fundamentalists to a six-day creation. Even the articles that constitute *The Fundamentals* show a range of views on the question of evolution. Contrast the theistic evolutionism of James Orr's "Science and the Christian Faith" (*Fundamentals*, 4:91–104) with Henry H. Beach's "Decadence of Darwinism" (*Fundamentals*, 8:36–48).

The term is not, however, always understood by reference to just those fundamentals. In 1927, for example, William Bell Riley wrote that "when the Fundamentals movement was originally formed it was supposed that our particular foe was the so-called 'higher criticism'; but, in the onward going of affairs, we discovered that basal to the many forms of modern infidelity is the philosophy of evolution" ("Defense of Fundamentalism").

one in which there were conservative Protestants on both sides of the issue. While Presbyterian Bryan led the anti-evolution campaign, John Gresham Machen, one of conservative Presbyterianism's leading theologians, turned down Bryan's invitation to testify for the prosecution at the Scopes Trial,[112] and Hay Watson Smith, pastor of Little Rock's Second Presbyterian Church, worked and preached against passage of a Bryan law in Arkansas. While Baptists William Bell Riley and J. W. Porter promoted Bryan laws, Edgar Young Mullins, president of the Southern Baptist Convention, worked against them. While it was a Primitive Baptist, John Washington Butler, who wrote Tennessee's anti-evolution law, it was another Primitive Baptist, Bryce Cundiff, who cast the deciding vote against Kentucky's in that state's House of Representatives.

Conservative Protestant opposition to the Bryan laws and to the broader themes of the campaign against evolution had various grounds. Some conservative Protestants were evolutionists in some sense of the term. Others, without maintaining the truth of the theory, at least rejected the idea that it was necessarily incompatible with Christian doctrine. Still others, including incompatibilists, opposed the laws on separationist grounds. Separation of church and state has traditionally had an important place in Baptist political philosophy,[113] and some Baptists (Mullins is a leading example) thought the principle told against the anti-evolution bills.[114]

The same struggle between proponents and opponents of the Bryan laws (and for that matter between evolutionists, mere compatibilists, and incompatibilists) surfaced even within the conservative denominations. Among the business items at the 135th General Assembly of the (Northern) Presbyterian Church of the United States of America, meeting in Indianapolis in May 1923, was the election of a moderator for the denomination. Nominees included both Bryan and Charles F. Wishart, president of Wooster College. Wishart was a theistic evolutionist, and the college was well-known for the presence of that idea in its classrooms. Though the vote

---

112. For his refusal of Bryan's invitation, see his letter to Bryan of 2 July 1925, Machen Papers. While Machen says that he is "morally certain of the debasing character of much of the teaching with regard to this subject that has been going on in the public schools," he takes care to specify that it is "the naturalistic doctrine of evolution" that causes his concern. That he distinguishes between that and various theistic doctrines of evolution is clear in his two letters of 18 February 1926 to Rev. George S. Duncan, in the same archive.

113. Article XVIII of the 1925 Baptist Faith & Mission, a confession of faith approved by the Southern Baptist Convention, reads in part: "no ecclesiastical group or denomination should be favored by the state more than others . . . The church should not resort to the civil power to carry on its work."

114. Mullins, *Crossroads*, 66.

was close, Bryan was defeated, as, a few days later, was Bryan's proposal to withhold church funds from any educational institution that "taught as a proven fact, either Darwinism or any other evolutionary hypothesis that links men in blood relationship with any other form of life." The commissioners at the Assembly were not willing to go any further than to "withhold official approval" from institutions where "any teaching . . . is given that seeks to establish a materialistic evolutionary philosophy of life."[115] That the assembly was not one dominated by modernists is shown by the fact that a few days later it removed Harry Emerson Fosdick from his pulpit at the First Presbyterian Church in New York. Fosdick had, the year before, repudiated fundamentalism in his famous sermon "Shall the Fundamentalists Win?"[116]

The Southern Baptist Convention was also divided on the issue of evolution with the anti-anti-evolutionists prevailing at the denominationwide level until about 1926 and the anti-evolutionists thereafter.[117] Two facts illustrate the predominance of the former through the first half of the decade. The first is that Mullins, who, though not an evolutionist, helped lead the fight against Bryan laws in Kentucky, held some of the highest positions in the denomination—the presidency of the Southern Baptist Convention, from 1921 to 1923, and of the Baptist World Alliance between 1923 and 1928. The second was the content of the Statement of Baptist Faith and Message of 1925. In 1924, the denomination, in an attempt to address the issue of evolution more directly, had appointed a committee, under Mullins's chairmanship, to prepare a statement for consideration at the 1925 convention. The resultant document stated only (in Article III) that "Man was created by the special act of God, as recorded in Genesis," in defense of which it quoted Gen 1:27 and 2:7, without further comment. Both in the committee and at the convention meeting itself, Clarence P. Stealey, editor of the *Oklahoma Baptist Messenger*, attempted to secure a more explicit rejection of the theory of evolution. He attempted, for example, to include in the statement an affirmation that "man came into this world by direct creation of God and not by evolution." His effort was rejected by the convention with 2,013 messengers voting against Stealey's proposal, and only 950 voting in favor.[118] The next year, the tide turned in favor of the anti-evolutionists. At

---

115. *New York Times*, "Bryan Loses Fight." For a fuller account, see Tait, "Wishart and Bryan."

116. For a fuller view of Fosdick's theology, however, one must also read his later "Church Must Go beyond Modernism."

117. For a general account, see Thompson, *Tried as by Fire*, 101–36.

118. *Annual of the Southern Baptist Convention, 1925*, 76. Stealey printed the remarks Mullins made to the convention in objection to Stealey's amendment as "President Mullins Address" in the *Baptist Messenger*, of which he was the editor. In 1927,

the convention meeting of 1926, President George W. McDaniel declared in his opening address that "this Convention . . . rejects every theory, evolution or other, which teaches that man originated in, or came by way of, a lower animal ancestry."[119] The meeting went on to endorse McDaniel's address and to demand that all convention institutions make "assurance . . . of a hearty and individual acceptance" of the same.[120] In this case, as in the case of the Northern Presbyterians, the conflict was a one *within* a religious denomination, not one between religion and science.

Protestant colleges and universities, of course, fell outside the scope of the Bryan laws, but anti-evolutionary policies at such institutions are still relevant to the Warfare Thesis. Indeed, Andrew Dickson White himself had cited three such cases from the nineteenth century (all discussed in chapter 4 above). What does a look at Protestant higher educational institutions in the 1920s show? Unsurprisingly, it reveals the same variety of views as one finds in the assemblies and conventions of the denominations themselves. Some denominational colleges expected their faculty not to teach the theory of evolution. In April 1923, Kentucky Wesleyan College suspended Ralph G. Demaree, professor of physics and mathematics, for a chapel talk in which he defended the compatibility of the biblical account of creation and the theory of organic evolution (as well as making disparaging remarks about proponents of the Bryan laws). He was reinstated only on condition that he make no more official or public comments on the topic.[121] In June 1925, the Danish Lutheran Church chose not to reelect Rev. Carl F. Hoiberg as president of its seminary (Grand View College in Des Moines), a choice Hoiberg attributed to the fact that he was an evolutionist.[122] Not all the cases of anti-evolutionary dismissals are quite as reported in the secondary literature, however. Willard B. Gatewood, in his *Controversy in the Twenties*, has five people being dismissed at Kentucky Wesleyan (rather than the one who in fact lost his job); he presents dismissals over other matters (such as Jesse W. Sprowls at Tennessee and Henry Fox at Mercer) as anti-evolution cases,

---

as a result of the anti-evolutionist editorial line he had taken in the Messenger, Stealey was removed from the editorship by the Baptist General Convention of Oklahoma, the paper's owner. See Gaskin, "Baptist Messenger"; and Hebard, "Stealey Controversy."

119. *Annual of the Southern Baptist Convention, 1926*, 18.

120. *Annual of the Southern Baptist Convention, 1926*, 98.

121. *New York Times*, "Evolution Exponent Refuses to Retract"; and *New York Times*, "College Reinstates Evolution Exponent."

122. Associated Press, "Evolutionist Loses Post as College Head"; and United Press, "Loses Job Because of Evolution." Both news services misspelled Hoiberg's name; the AP also misspelled the name of the college.

claims not consistent with the historical record.[123] At Grand View College, both Hoiberg and his conservative theological opponent V. S. Jensen lost their jobs, and Hoiberg's successor, S. V. Rodholm, according to Hoiberg, was also an evolutionist.[124] Meanwhile, the theory of evolution continued, despite the protests of the anti-evolutionists, to be taught at some denominational colleges, including Baptist Wake Forest and Presbyterian Wooster. Some, for example Baptist Baylor, remained battlegrounds.[125]

It is undeniable that the passage of Bryan laws was a project grounded in the religious belief of the campaigners and their supporters. What is deniable is that it was precisely Bryan, Riley, and Porter, rather than, say, Wishart, Smith, Mullins, and Poteat, who constituted religion's contribution to the fight between evolutionists and anti-evolutionists. Even many of those who doubted the truth of the theory of evolution, as most Southern Baptists at the time apparently did, refused in state after state to pass Bryan laws. James J. Thompson summarized his history of that denomination by commenting that "Baptists played a significant role in maintaining freedom of teaching in many Southern states."[126]

If the first objection to the claim that the anti-evolution campaign of the 1920s was a war of religion against science is that the claim mischaracterizes one belligerent as religion, the second objection is that the notion of a war between religion and science partially mischaracterizes the idea against which anti-evolutionists were waging war as science.

The anti-evolution campaign had two targets. The broader campaign *can* fairly be characterized as a campaign against science. Although Bryan and his allies insisted that they were not opposed to science—Bryan, as noted earlier, denied that evolution was science—his grasp both of evolution and of science in general was weak. It is, however, also true that evolutionary

---

123. Sprowls was told by the university administration not to teach Robinson, *Mind in the Making* in his adolescent psychology course, lest the book's approach to evolution come to the attention of the state legislature. But the American Association of University Professors committee that investigated the matter concluded that "Professor Sprowls'a views on evolution were not one of the reasons ... which led to the decision of the authorities to discontinue his services" (Garner et al., "Report on the University of Tennessee," 217).

Fox's problems at Mercer University were the result of theological views too modernist for Mercer. Numbers wrote that "although his views on evolution inevitably clouded the picture, it was his refusal unequivocally to affirm his belief in the deity of Christ, the divine inspiration of the Bible, and of the Virgin Birth lead to his termination" (*Creationists*, 48). See also Dowell, *History of Mercer*, 281–82.

124. United Press Association, "Loses Job Because of Evolution"; Hansen, "Carl Peter Hoiberg," 19.

125. See Brown, "Brooks and the Evolution Controversy at Baylor."

126. Thompson, *Tried as by Fire*, 135.

theory was sometimes the object of exaggerated enthusiasm. The council of the American Association for the Advancement of Science (AAAS), for example, said in 1922 that

> the theory of evolution is one of the most potent of the great influences for good that have thus far entered into human experience; it has promoted the progress of knowledge, it has fostered unprejudiced inquiry, and it has served as an invaluable aid in humanity's search for truth in many fields.[127]

Worse, evolutionary biology had sometimes been appropriated by metaphysical naturalists and atheists and put to use in their own philosophical projects. Nevertheless, a more modest claim for the theory can surely be made: that it (common ancestry, but not the mechanism of evolutionary change) had, by 1925, become the scientific consensus. The general critique of evolution did, therefore, surely constitute a war waged by one particular interdenominational group of Christians against a major scientific theory. It did not, however, thereby constitute warfare between theology and religion (or even Christianity) on the one hand and science on the other.

The campaign's narrower, *legislative*, target was not the general theory of the evolutionary origin of species, but only evolutionary anthropogenesis. Statutory language, almost without exception, was limited to opposing the idea that "man [is linked] in blood relationship to any other form of life" or that "man has descended from a lower order of animals."[128] Bryan was explicit about the *tactical* purpose of the broader campaign in the letter to a supporter quoted above:

> I would not be concerned about the truth or falsity of evolution below man but for the fact that a concession as to the truth of evolution up to man furnishes our opponents with an argument ... [that it] raise[s] a presumption in behalf of evolution to include man ...[129]

This difference between the rhetorical and the legislative target was often missed entirely. In 1929, immediately after passage of Arkansas's anti-evolution referendum, Orland Kay Armstrong, back to reporting after having established the department of journalism at the University of Florida, decided to take a look at what effect the Butler Act had had on education in

---

127. American Association for the Advancement of Science, Resolution.

128. The former language, presumably Bryan's, comes from Florida; the latter (Butler's, see Haldeman-Julius, *Clarence Darrow's Two Great Trials*, 18) from Tennessee (though it was also the language of the Mississippi and Arkansas statutes).

129. Bryan, Letter to Howard A. Kelly, 22 June 1925, Bryan Papers, Box 47.

Tennessee. To the point here is a comment made by an unnamed "ranking member of the State Normal School," one that "summarized the sentiment of about fifty other educators whom [Armstrong] interviewed": "It is impossible to teach biology, psychology, sociology or even physical geography without using the most fundamental fact in science, that of the evolutionary development of organic life."[130] But of course there was nothing illegal about teaching the evolutionary development of organic life in Tennessee. The *significance* of the restricted focus of the Bryan laws was often missed even by those who did acknowledge the *fact*. The editors of the modernist *Christian Century* took a swipe at their fundamentalist rivals on the occasion of an Arkansas attorney general's opinion about the exact content of that state's recently enacted Bryan law:

> it is perfectly lawful to teach the theory of evolution from . . . primordial slime up to . . . the highest anthropoid apes, and beginning again with the lowest form of man . . . [to] proceed with the story of human development from that point to the present . . . But if so much of evolution can be taught under the law, it would seem that the imagination of the students ought to be able to supply the rest.[131]

Imagination can, of course, do a lot, as Aesop showed us long ago, but human exceptionalism is a philosophical thesis that stands or falls not on the basis of mere imaginability, but of argument.

The question of whether the narrower, legislative campaign was, like the broader one, a war on science requires a more elaborate and nuanced answer. The AAAS had surely been correct in asserting that "evidences in favor of the evolution of man . . . are increasing in number and importance every year."[132] There were, however, two religious questions that no amount of progress in the study of bones and behavior could answer—one was historical and one anthropological.

---

130. Armstrong, "Bootleg Science," 139.

131. *Christian Century*, "Interpreting the Anti-Evolution Law." The attorney general's office had been asked whether using Katharine Elizabeth Dopp's *Tree Dwellers* would violate the law. Dr. Dopp, an early disciple of Dewey, was an instructor at the University of Chicago; the book was one of a series she had written to introduce grade-school children to the industrial and social history of the human race and was in use around the country. For an understanding of what its opponents did not like about the book, see the review by Thomas Edward Shields, "Note on Education." The opinion of the attorney general's office was that the book did not violate the law (*Arkansas Gazette*, "Evolution Law Held Not Violated").

132. American Association for the Advancement of Science, Resolution.

First, the historical question: Was the body of the first man the product of an immediate divine act? J. Gresham Machen raised this objection to the possibility of a decisive scientific resolution of the question:

> What was the origin of the human life of ... Jesus? Was he descended from previous men by ordinary generation? ... [I]f we had only the kind of evidence that is relied upon to establish the doctrine of evolution with regard to the origin of the first man, we should certainly answer that question in the affirmative ... Yet despite all the evidence, we hold, on the testimony of the first chapter of Matthew and the first chapter of Luke, that Jesus was not as a matter of fact descended from previous men by ordinary generation, but that at the beginning of His life upon this earth there was a creative act of God, the supernatural conception in the womb of the virgin Mary.[133]

The fact that something *could have* been produced by natural processes does not show that it *was* so produced. It is possible to ask whether processes *sufficient* to produce a certain effect did *actually* produce that effect in a given case, as the continuing problem of trilobite forgeries in the commercial fossil market reminds us. Imperfections give many forgeries away, but when we have an eyewitness to the forgery (or a confession), the absence of imperfections in the product is irrelevant. Similarly with supernatural action, nothing in the wine served last at Cana suggested its supernatural origin. The steward could only tell that it was good. No doubt he supposed that it had come from the vintner, and there is no reason to think that a modern laboratory would have found anything that would have cast doubt on such a supposition. We know of its miraculous origin only by testimony, as we do in the case of the Virgin Birth. And so it is, Bryan and his allies could have argued, with the origin of Adam. They may have been wrong, as I believe that they were (in part) about just *what* God revealed. Still, the argument to *that* conclusion requires theological, not just scientific, work.

There is also a more general question, grounded more in philosophical and theological anthropology than in history—one that turns on the nature of man and the reach of science. If man is a purely material being, then the origin of man (barring revealed truths to the contrary) is no less a scientific question than is the origin of squirrels and oak trees. If, however, man is a composite of material body and immaterial soul, then it is not just a scientific question. As one of Scopes's expert witnesses, Harvard geologist Kirtley

---

133. Machen, *Christian View of Man*, 137–38.

Mather, rightly said, "It is the business of the theologian, not of the scientist, to state just when and how man gained a soul."[134]

The conflict over the Bryan laws became a fight between anti-evolutionist Christians and evolutionist science educators in part because of the failure of both sides to formulate precisely the thesis in contention.

What was the exact meaning of the *sententia prohibita*—that the origin of man is one of descent (or ascent) from lower animals? The general idea that the human race arose as a result of the evolutionary transformation of pre-human animal species covers a range of more particular views, distinguished in the diagram.

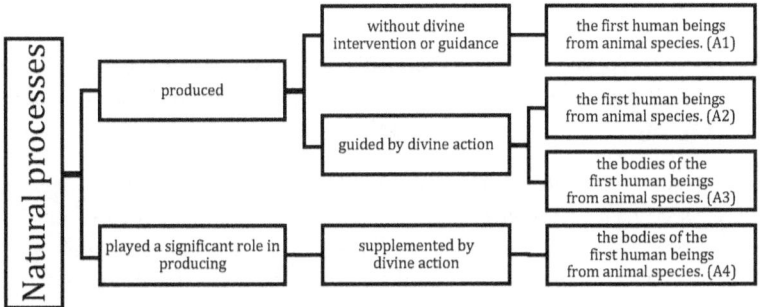

None of these four views is necessarily atheistic; none is even generally non-creationist. B. B. Warfield, the conservative Presbyterian theologian who died just as the First Curriculum War was beginning, identified, among a range of possible views on the relation between evolution and creation, one (not his) which: "confines the creative operations of God to the origination of the primal world-stuff. Everything subsequent to that . . . is explained as a mere modification of the primal world-stuff by means of its intrinsic forces."[135] Such a view, he acknowledged, could (though it would not have to) include a role for "the providential guidance of God." He called this view, which covers A1–A2, "theistic evolution." However, in light of the fact that most people now use that term somewhat differently, we might better call nonatheistic versions of A1 deistic evolution and A2 minimally theistic evolution.

---

134. Rhea County Court, *World's Most Famous Court Trial*, 250. For more on Mather's views, see Mather, *Science in Search of God*. Mather's formulation is, to be sure, peculiar: Did *man* gain a soul or did man come into existence only once the first soul was created?

135. Warfield, "Creation, Evolution, and Mediate Creation," 202.

Warfield and his contemporaries found a version of A1 in Otto Pfleiderer's "Evolution and Theology." There Pfleiderer defends the view that "every moment [in the course of life] is to be regarded as the effect of the causes lying in the preceding condition."[136] What happens in the world may be a "progressive realization of the divine purpose,"[137] but this is less than divine guidance.

A2, like A1, maintains that natural evolutionary processes are sufficient to produce human beings. Evolutionary processes operate under providential guidance, but no immediate act of divine *production* is necessary. Warfield characterized the view as follows: "A governing God may be acknowledged, provided only that he governs in, with and through natural causes only, so that all that comes to pass finds its entire account in the secondary causes operative in its production."[138] What would the noncreative providential guidance that distinguishes A2 from A1 look like? Warfield suggested the answer in his minimalist defense of providentialism against A1:

> Why should the evolutionist insist that the ascent to man must have been accomplished by the blind action of natural forces to the exclusion of all oversight and direction of a higher power? ... Even though the evolutionist had before him the whole series of generations through which he supposes man to have risen to humanity, he would be as little justified in asserting that this series of steps was accomplished apart from the directing hand of God as would a lover of domestic animals be justified in excluding the breeder as a factor in producing a pen of ... prime Berkshire pigs ... because ... he could trace their descent through generations, given which the result could not fail to follow.[139]

The analogy to animal breeding does not provide an argument for the *operation* of providence in anthropogenesis, but it does show that the sufficiency (in some sense) of natural causes does not *exclude* the operation of providence. Animal breeding programs can limit themselves to the use of processes that are (in a meaningful sense) natural; they do not have to resort to genetic engineering. Providence can limit itself to natural processes, A2 asserts; it does not have to step outside those processes to accomplish its ends.

---

136. Pfleiderer, "Evolution and Theology," 2–3. See also p. 9.
137. Pfleiderer, "Evolution and Theology," 19.
138. Warfield, "Creation, Evolution, and Mediate Creation," 200.
139. Warfield, "Manner and Time of Man's Origin," 213–14.

A3–A4 share with the deistic and minimally theistic evolutionisms of A1–A2 the idea that evolution has a role in anthropogenesis, but differ with them over whether evolutionary processes are sufficient to account for the origin of the human race. Underlying that difference is a distinction between the production of the human body and the production of the human person, a distinction that Christianity's nonmaterialist anthropology makes possible, and one that allows for divine creation (of the soul) in anthropogenesis. How can a coherent composite account be constructed? There are two ways in which such a mixed account of anthropogenesis can be elaborated.

The first, A3, asserts that evolutionary processes are sufficient to explain the origin of the human body, divine action being operative only in the production of the human soul, where, philosophical anthropologists have argued, it is necessary for other reasons. Erich Wasmann, SJ, writing in 1909, put the latter point as follows: "the human soul could not have been derived through natural evolution from that of the brute, since it is of a spiritual nature; for which reason we must refer its origin to a creative act on the part of God."[140] The idea that the human soul was (or at least could have been) directly created by God even though the human body was the product of natural evolutionary processes had been articulated in England by William Henry Flower and by St. George Mivart,[141] and in the American South by James Woodrow.[142]

Defenders of A3 thought that the creation of the human soul was sufficient to make true the revealed doctrine that man was directly created by God. Other Christians, for various reasons, thought that it was not and argued instead for immediate divine action in the origin of the human body as well. For some, that led to endorsement of the kind of comprehensive anti-evolutionism articulated by the 1924 General Assembly of the (Southern) Presbyterian Church in the United States: "Adam and Eve were created body and soul by immediate acts of almighty power ... Adam's body was directly fashioned by Almighty God without any natural animal parentage."[143] Others thought that went too far. Warfield asked: "Why should the Biblicist assert that the creation of man by the divine fiat must have been immediate in such a sense as to exclude all process, all interaction of natural forces?"[144] and laid the conceptual foundations for A4 as an alternative to

---

140. Wasmann, "Evolution," 655.
141. Flower, *Introductory Lecture*, 20–21; Mivart, *Genesis of Species*, 300–305.
142. Woodrow, *Evolution*, 17.
143. Presbyterian General Assembly, *Minutes* for 1924, 64.
144. Warfield, "Manner and Time of Man's Origin," 213.

anti-evolutionist anthropogenesis. He emphasized the difference between creation and evolution as one between a process of origination (producing something that did not exist before) and a process of modification (implying pre-existence and yielding only a difference of state). Then, relying on seventeenth-century Swiss Reformed theologian Johannes Wolleb's observation that creation was *partim ex nihilo, partim ex materia non habili*,[145] he proposed the terms "absolute creation" for creation *ex nihilo* and "mediate creation" for creation *ex materia inhabili supra naturae vires*, the production "out of ... inapt material [of] something above what the powers intrinsic in it are capable of producing."[146]

Of those four theses, which did the Bryan laws prohibit teachers from teaching?

The language of Florida's resolution ("no blood relationship") would seem to prohibit even A4, but the language of the three Bryan *laws* ("no descent") was different language and might have been interpreted as prohibiting only A1 and A2. Tennessee Supreme Court Justice Alexander W. Chambliss, in his concurring opinion in *Scopes*, thought that it did not prohibit more than materialistic evolution, "which denies that God created man."[147] On that construction of the statute, perhaps even the minimally theistic evolutionism of A2 would pass muster. That reading, however, was not crucial to the outcome of the case and, as *obiter dictum* in a concurrent opinion, it was in any case not law. Those who were trying to apply the law—school principals, for example—might well give the language of the Butler Act a broader reach.

The proponents of the Bryan laws clearly wanted to prohibit A1 and probably A2 as well. About whether they wanted to prohibit A3 or A4 as well they are simply not clear. They never addressed that question. Perhaps they never considered it. Perhaps they would not have agreed among themselves about it if they had considered it. With respect to the non-theological parts of the theses, science educators and their allies, the opponents of the Bryant laws, clearly wanted to keep at least A4 *in* the classroom. Did they want to be free to teach A3 as well? What about A1 or A2? They never addressed these questions. Perhaps they never considered them. Perhaps they would not have agreed among themselves about the matter if they had considered it.

---

145. Wolleb, *Compendium Theologiae Christianae*, I.V.

146. Warfield, "Creation, Evolution, and Mediate Creation," 204.

147. *Scopes v. State*, 368. Tennessee's Butler Act made explicit reference to "Divine Creation of man as taught in the Bible" in a way that the Mississippi and Arkansas Bryan laws did not (Tennessee, Chapter № 27 [Butler Act]).

What ideas were actually being presented to students about evolution in general and the evolution of man in particular?[148]

Evolutionary biology made its appearance in American high school textbooks in the last quarter of the nineteenth century. Asa Gray's *Elements of Botany for Beginners and for Schools* concentrated, of course, on the structure and function of plants, but, in a discussion of classification near the end of the book, Gray made a passing mention of evolution:

> varieties may be incipient species; and nearly related species probably came from the same stock in earlier times. For there is every reason to believe that existing vegetation came from the more or less changed vegetation of a preceding geological age.[149]

Yale's James Dwight Dana, who had rejected evolution in the first (1863) edition of his *Text-book of Geology*, revised his judgment in the second (1874) edition: "The evolution of the system of life went forward through the derivation of species from species, according to natural methods not yet clearly understood, and with few occasions for supernatural intervention."[150] The University of California's Joseph Le Conte's *Compend of Geology* (1884) defined geology as "a history of the *evolution* of the earth and its inhabitants."[151] Only in zoology did the leading schoolbook (written as it was by Louis Agassiz, one of the most prominent American biologists in his day, but also America's leading anti-Darwinist)[152] continue to take an anti-evolutionist line even late in the century. Some late nineteenth-century textbooks avoided the question of the origin of species altogether.

The possibility of the evolution of man was first appraised negatively. In 1874, Dana had written that "for the development of Man, gifted with high reason and will, and thus made a power above Nature, there was required, as Wallace has urged, the special act of a Being above Nature."[153]

---

148. For earlier accounts, see Larson, *Trial and Error*, 7–27; and Skoog, *Topic of Evolution, 1900–1968*, 151–55, as well as Skoog, "Topic of Evolution: 1900–1977."

149. Gray, *Elements of Botany*, 177.

150. Dana, *Text-book of Geology* (2nd ed.), 263. This represents a conversion from the anti-evolutionist views he had advanced in the first (1863) edition of the book. Dana, it should be noted, was deeply religious. For more on Dana, see Sanford, "Dana and Darwinism."

151. Le Conte, *Compend of Geology*, 242 (italics original). Le Conte had offered a compatibilist account of evolution and Christian theology in Le Conte, *Religion and Science*; and in Le Conte, *Evolution and Its Relation to Religious Thought*. For more on Le Conte, see Stephens, *Joseph LeConte*.

152. Agassiz, *Principles of Zoology*.

153. Dana, *Text-book of Geology* (2nd ed.), 263.

When William North Rice revised Dana's textbook in 1897, two years after Dana's death, he wrote that

> the upward progress, from Protozoan simplicity, through Fish and Amphibian and Reptile and Mammal, has culminated at last in Man himself, the crown of creation, sharing with the animal kingdom a place in nature, but asserting by his intellectual and spiritual endowments a place above nature.[154]

"The whole process of the evolution of Man," Rice added, "has been guided by infinite Wisdom." At the same time, however, a more fully naturalist approach was already beginning to emerge. Albert P. Brigham, while acknowledging the fully human character of all human fossils so far found, wrote in 1900:

> In this, as in all questions, the truth should be sought without prejudice or fear. The antiquity of man and his possible evolution from lower forms of life are questions of science. No answer which science may render is inconsistent with the highest views of our origin and destiny.[155]

Evolution does not figure prominently in the biology textbooks of the first two decades of the twentieth century. There are several possible explanations for this, including the emphasis on practical matters ("biology directed civic betterment" as Hunter put it[156]) and a concern that evolution was a topic too abstract for inclusion in a high-school course.[157] Coverage increased somewhat in textbooks published during the 1920s although books published before 1925 (the year the Butler Act passed) were more likely to suggest that the theory was true than were those published later in the decade. Of the fourteen textbooks from the 1920s reviewed by Gerald Skoog,[158] only five mentioned the evolution of man (the only topic proscribed by the Bryan laws); eleven discussed human uniqueness; three included an explicit discussion of religion and science. To take some concrete examples, Truman J. Moon's *Biology for Beginners* asserted that "not only man but all living things, both plant and animal, are not only related, but actually descend from common ancestors."[159] Hunter's *Civic Biology* was vaguer: "[The *evolutionary series*] begin[s] with very simple one-celled

---

154. Rice, *Revised Text-book of Geology*, 464.
155. Brigham, *Textbook of Geology*, 460.
156. Hunter, *Civic Biology*, 10.
157. See, for example, Peabody and Hunt, *Biology for Human Welfare*, vi.
158. Skoog, "Topic of Evolution, 1900–1968," 157–75.
159. Moon, *Biology for Beginners*, 321.

forms and culminate[s] with a group which contains man himself."[160] Moon rejected human exceptionalism—"certainly man is an animal just as truly as the beast of the field."[161] Henry R. Linville's *Biology of Man and Other Organisms* acknowledged that human brains are much larger than are those of gorillas, but then went on to emphasize that "this should be taken to mean that we are different from the gorilla more particularly in degree than in kind."[162] Hunter made no stronger a claim for exceptionalism when he said that "man is separated mentally by a wide gap from all other animals."[163] As for the significance of evolution for religion, Moon denied that evolutionary biology has antireligious implications: "Evolution does not teach . . . that God can be left out of the scheme of Creation . . . [R]est assured that in the minds of the greatest scientists and philosophers there is no conflict between the conclusions of Science and Religion."[164] Linville said that "with the progress of general understanding, the leaders of the Church for the greater part . . . now teach evolution as a proved law of life, applying even to religion itself."[165] That last remark seems almost custom-made to reinforce all of William Bell Riley's worst fears—that "basal to the many forms of modern infidelity is the philosophy of evolution."[166] It also gave justification to the more restrained concerns expressed by Mullins, who still worried that "science is engaged in an effort to remake religion," though he immediately went on to concede that "it is not so much science itself as the theologians of science who have put their hands to this plow."[167]

And the teachers? Certainly they varied, both in their views about evolution and in their approach to the subject. One must, however, take note of Beale's observation that

> one basic cause of fundamentalist attacks on the schools is the fact that hundreds of poorly-trained teachers of science, with a desire to shock people with their new information and no adequate training in their subject, have been sent out into the schools with exactly this attitude that science is a body of indisputably 'proved facts.'[168]

160. Hunter, *Civic Biology*, 194.
161. Moon, *Biology for Beginners*, 321.
162. Linville, *Biology of Man*, 155.
163. Hunter, *Civic Biology*, 195.
164. Moon, *Biology for Beginners*, 329–32.
165. Linville, *Biology of Man*, 465.
166. Riley, "Defense of Fundamentalism," 8.
167. Mullins, *Christianity at the Crossroads*, 74.
168. Beale, *Are American Teachers Free?*, 252.

All this is important. To the extent that the controversy between the proponents of the Bryan laws and their critics is over the exclusion of A1 from the school curriculum, then, offensive to scientific ears as it may be to say so, the controversy was not over science at all. A1 is not a purely scientific thesis, as Machen's analogy to the virgin birth and Mather's comments about who is competent to address the question of the origin of the human soul (both cited above) show.

For those who hold a materialist anthropology, the question of the origins of man will be no less a scientific issue than is the question of the origin of butterflies and slime mold, but the soundness of the materialist anthropology which that answer presupposes is not itself a purely scientific issue. For Christians, and for others whose anthropology includes the thesis that man has an immaterial soul the origin of which cannot be established by scientific methods, a complete account of the origin of man would be beyond the reach of science.

The controversy of the 1920s, then, is not a case of the friends of science thwarted in their attempts to teach scientific theories by uncomprehending and retrograde Christian anti-evolutionists. Part of the cause of conflict was the anti-evolutionists' determination to keep at least A1 out of the science classrooms of what were supposed to be religiously neutral public schools. Some anti-evolutionists, to be sure, would have opposed even A3 and A4 by an extension of the argument from Machen cited above. Another part of the cause, however, was science educators' use of evidence that supported only A4 as an argument for A3 or even for A2,[169] and their silence about the distinction between A2 and A1.

So does the controversy of the 1920s show the illicit and harmful interference of theologians, preachers, and religious laity in the good work of scientists? The anti-evolution campaign, and the laws it produced, were a clumsy response to a legitimate problem. Since the question of the origins of man is not a purely scientific problem, the religious resistance that occurred was not precisely the kind of "interference" that Warfare Theorists would need in order to support their thesis. The *clumsiness* of the interference may have done harm both to religion and to science, but it was the clumsiness, not theology or religion themselves, that caused the problem. The carelessness of science educators in their formulation of evolutionary accounts of anthropogenesis was as much at fault as was the language of the statutes.

Does this in any larger way illustrate a conflict between theology or religion and science? It was a conflict created by a theological mistake (bad hermeneutics) on one side, but it was caused no less by scientific overreach

---

169. This was implicit in the AAAS resolution cited above.

on the part of some evolutionists and culpable imprecision on the part of others. It was a conflict exacerbated by the words and actions of some of the friends of science, who, according to Beale, "share . . . with [their] opponents responsibility for the passage of these . . . laws . . . They . . . substituted epithets for arguments. 'Ignorance,' 'fanaticism,' 'bigotry,' 'imbecility' were hurled at fundamentalists."[170] The conceptual resources necessary for a *modus vivendi* accommodating the legitimate concerns of both sides were available in the 1920s. Unfortunately, too few of the principals on either side seemed able to articulate either the theory of evolution or the Christian requirement of a nonmaterialist anthropology in a way clear enough to avoid social conflict.

Conclusion

So what do the events of the 1920s show us about religion in its relation to science? That some religious groups broadened a legitimate concern about a mixed question into a broader attack on some legitimate scientific work. That is to their discredit, of course, but even if it were an example of a recurrent phenomenon it would hardly be a sign of the great war that the Warfare Theorists claim to have identified, and about which antireligious secularists warn us. Other religious denominations did not participate in the broadening. Even among the members of those denominations that did participate, there were opponents as well as supporters of the endeavor.

This battle between evolutionists and anti-evolutionists (even if we restrict our focus to religiously motivated anti-evolutionists) is not brought into focus by thinking of it as a war between science and theology or religion. Since it was fought at the same time as the three-way conflict between fundamentalism, modernism, and skepticism, of which Frederick Lewis Allen said that it reverberated all through the decade and reached its climax in the Scopes case of 1925,[171] confusion of the two conflicts is easy. But the fact that anti-evolutionists played a significant role in the establishment of such major interdenominational associations as the World Christian Fundamentals Association (WCFA), and the fact that they were sometimes even able to recruit major denominational organizations to their cause (e.g., the Southern Baptist Convention after 1926) says at most something about those denominations. Other conservative Protestants, as I emphasized above, opposed the laws; some remained neutral. Catholics stayed out of the

---

170. Beale, *Are American Teachers Free?*, 249.
171. Allen, *Only Yesterday*, 195 and 201.

fight altogether.[172] It certainly cannot, therefore, provide any general insight into the relationship between science and Christianity, or religion.

---

172. See Morrison, "American Catholics."

CHAPTER 6

Creation Science, Intelligent-Design Theory, & the Second Curriculum War

THERE WAS A KIND of armistice between the end of the campaign for Bryan laws, in about 1928, and the resumption of the fight over evolution in the 1960s. This is suggested, for example, by a review of coverage by the *New York Times*. Richard D. Wilhelm found many articles on the topic in the 1920s and again many starting in the 1960s, but few before the 1920s and few in the intervening decades.[1] Some historians have suggested that the Bryan campaign was triggered, in significant part, by the spread of high school education, with concomitant exposure of more and more students to the theory of evolution. The outbreak of a second curriculum war occurred against a background of renewed Protestant evangelical political activism. Mark A. Noll notes that such activism "was standard in the nineteenth century, but . . . had largely diminished after the 1930s."[2] Its reappearance in the 1970s was probably caused by a variety of factors—events and trends ranging from constitutional law (e.g., the prohibition of officially composed prayers in public schools in 1962 and the establishment of a legal right to abortion in 1973[3]) to increasingly permissive attitudes about sexuality. Resumption of hostilities on the curricular front can be attributed to three, more particular, causes—the publication of new textbooks, developments in American first-amendment law, and the emergence of two new strains of anti-evolutionism—Creation Science and Intelligent-Design Theory.

---

1. Wilhelm, *Chronology*, 26.
2. Noll, *History of Christianity*, 445.
3. The cases, of course, are *Engel v. Vitale* and *Roe v. Wade*.

Biology Textbooks

The first new feature of the 1960s was increased attention to the concept of evolution in high school biology textbooks. Anti-evolutionists have always exerted what pressure they could on textbook publishers, with some success. Where they were not strong enough to secure the passage of Bryan laws (as for example in Texas), they were sometimes able to influence textbook selection, which in turn gave publishers an incentive to downplay the concept of evolution, or even to omit it altogether. Texas Tech education professor Gerald Skoog, one of the leading researchers into textbook history, wrote that "prior to 1960, evolution was treated in a cursory and generally non-controversial way. However, there was a continued increase in the emphasis on evolution in the textbooks from 1900 to 1950 when the concept was deemphasized slightly."[4]

This was not, to be sure, true of every textbook on the market. Ella Thea Smith's *Exploring Biology*, one the most explicitly evolution-attentive textbooks of the period, devoted seventy-five pages to the topic and was quite clear about the soundness of the theory:

> That living things have undergone vast changes in the past no one can deny.
>
> The fossil evidence is conclusive that man himself did not appear suddenly on the earth in his present form, but has gradually developed from a much more primitive species.[5]

Nor did it always shy away from controversy. Although most of its treatment of evolution is philosophically neutral, Smith does say that "We may continue to call ourselves the highest animals as often as we wish, since there is no other animal able to speak to dispute our claim. But biologists know that we are only 'highest' in some respects and quite primitive in others."[6] One would think that the fact that no other animals are able to dispute the claim would count as evidence for superiority in a singularly important respect, and not just as an explanation of how we can get away with asserting it, but Smith's philosophical remark received no elaboration. The book did well

---

4. Skoog, "Topic of Evolution: 1900–1977," 622. Skoog analyzed both changes in the textbook market (the variety of books available for adoption at any particular time) and of particular textbooks from one edition to another.
 Skoog later extended this study in Skoog, "Coverage of Evolution in the 1980s." He discussed textbooks' treatments of human evolution, in Skoog, "Coverage of Human Evolution in the 20th Century."

5. Smith, *Exploring Biology*, 520 and 528. See also her remarks on p. 541.

6. Smith, *Exploring Biology*, 114.

through the 1950s,[7] second on the market only to Truman J. Moon's *Modern Biology*,[8] which became rather less attentive to the theory of evolution from edition to edition between 1921 and the 1950s.

Many educators felt that the theory of evolution did not get the attention it deserved. Writing in 1950, Newark high school teachers Estelle R. Laba and Eugene W. Gross complained in a journal on high-school pedagogy that "many textbooks used here [sc. in northern New Jersey] are inadequate and evasive in their treatment of organic evolution."[9] According to three scholars who studied the issue, the situation only got worse during the decade that followed.[10] Skoog attributed this lack of emphasis on evolution, in significant part, to "pressures exerted by organized religious groups."[11]

In the 1960s, however, as Skoog's research shows, all this changed, and "several textbooks gave unprecedented emphasis to evolution."[12] In 1958, in the wake of the Soviet launch of Sputnik, the American Institute of Biological Sciences had established (and the National Science Foundation had funded) the Biological Sciences Curriculum Study (BSCS), whose task was to prepare a new set of biology textbooks for American high schools. These books were explicitly evolutionistic (one version of the books included a full column of entries under *evolution* in the index) but not dogmatically so:

> The kinds of variation that we see in existing populations plus the types of evolutionary trends deduced from the most complete series of fossils, provide strong evidence for the belief that the ... evolutionary forces we see in operation today have guided evolution in the past.
>
> There is every reason to believe that the evolution of man is a result of the contemporary action of [evolutionary] forces.[13]

They do not deny human exceptionalism, even though the evidence they cite (tool use and brain size) is not quite the thought and choice that have been the foundation of more traditional accounts of the idea. The new

---

7. For her Harcourt editor's account of the publication of Smith's book, see his memoirs, Reid, *Adventure in Textbooks*, 69–72.

8. This was a revision of a book that had first appeared as *Biology for Beginners* in 1921.

9. Laba and Gross, "Evolution Slighted," 398.

10. Skoog, "Topic of Evolution: 1900–1977," and, using a different methodology, Grabiner and Miller, "Effects of the Scopes Trial."

11. Skoog, "Topic of Evolution, 1900–1977," 635. For a challenge to this conclusion, see Ladouceur, "Ella Thea Smith."

12. Skoog, "Topic of Evolution, 1900–1977," 622.

13. Biological Sciences Curriculum Study, *Biological Science*, 630 and 662.

textbooks soon accounted for half of national sales for high-school biology textbooks. In response, other publishers seem to have increased their attention to evolution as well. Some have questioned whether this change in emphasis was quite as great as is generally claimed. G. G. Simpson, for example, complained in a letter to the editors of *Science* that "there is what I believe to be a self-serving legend that the bold introduction of modern evolutionary biology into high-school texts was the ... work of the [BSCS]" and emphasized the role of evolution in Smith's *Exploring Biology*.[14] In any case, anti-evolutionists objected strongly to the adoption of the BSCS textbooks,[15] and coverage of evolution was somewhat muted in the 1970s and 1980s, though it remained more prominent than it had generally been earlier in the century.[16]

At the same time there was even more-widespread public objection to another project funded by the National Science Foundation. *Man: A Course of Study* (MACOS), developed in the mid-1960s, was an attempt to introduce a new social-science curriculum into fifth- and sixth-grade classrooms. Sociologist Dorothy Nelkin, who seems to be sympathetic to the project, said of it that "the course is not only built on evolutionary assumptions, but denies the existence of absolute values."[17] While on the one hand the contrasts between man and, for example, baboons, emphasized human exceptionalism based on the role of culture in human life, on the other hand the authors wrote, "we hope that through this course children will come to understand that what we regard as acceptable behavior is a product of our culture."[18] Whether a ten-year-old child can really catch the distinction between "what we regard as acceptable behavior is a product of our culture" and "what is morally right is a product of our culture," indeed whether the authors themselves even intended such a distinction, is open to doubt. In any case, the book's invitation to ten-year-olds to think about infanticide and senilicide among the Netsilik Inuit displayed, in the minds of many parents, not only bad judgment, but a general philosophy very different from their own and one that did not belong in the public schools.

The increased emphasis on evolution in the biology classroom, and the publication of MACOS, may well have played some role in the outbreak of the Second Curriculum War. It is no doubt difficult for the authors of

14. Simpson, "Evolution and Education."

15. For examples, see Nelkin, *Creation Controversy*, 46–47; and Grabiner and Miller, "Effects of the Scopes Trial," 836.

16. Skoog, "Topic of Evolution, 1900–1977," 633–35; and Skoog, "Coverage of Evolution."

17. Nelkin, *Creation Controversy*, 51.

18. Dow, "*Man: A Course of Study*," 6.

high-school textbooks to write to the satisfaction of all concerned on issues as controversial as evolutionary biology. Nevertheless, high-school biology textbooks were sometimes unnecessarily dogmatic and scientistic, as even their defenders have conceded.[19] For example, a 1972 California Board of Education review of thirty textbooks found one (unnamed) textbook that said: "Science is the total knowledge of facts and principles that govern our lives, the world, and everything in it, and the universe of which the world is just a part."[20] Two other factors, however, may have played an even more important role in the resumption of hostilities.

Delineating the "Wall of Separation": Evolution, School Curricula, and the First Amendment from Little Rock to Dover

As part of the fulfillment of the Federalist promise to add a bill of rights to the Constitution of 1787, the first Congress proposed, and the states ratified, an amendment prohibiting Congress from making any law "respecting an establishment of religion, or prohibiting the free exercise thereof." The Bill of Rights, having been enacted as a restriction on the powers of the new federal government, did not limit the powers of state governments.[21] Indeed two of the eleven states that ratified this first amendment to the Constitution maintained established churches until the early nineteenth century. However, in the 1920s, the Supreme Court began to incorporate the rights the Bill guarantees piecemeal into the Fourteenth Amendment. That process began with the free speech cases (in the wake of the First World War)[22] and reached the religion clauses of the First Amendment only in 1934.

---

19. See, for example, Nelkin, *Creation Controversy*, 116; and Nelkin, "Science-Textbook Controversies."

20. Quoted in Nelkin, *Creation Controversy*, 114.

21. *Barron v. Baltimore* and, in response to the claim that the Fourteenth Amendment makes the rights mentioned in the Bill rights against the states, the *Slaughterhouse Cases*. As Justice David Brewer, speaking for the Court, put it in a slightly later case: "The first ten Amendments to the federal Constitution contain no restrictions on the powers of the state, but were intended to operate solely on the federal government" (*Brown v. New Jersey*).

There is, nevertheless, a long-running debate among historians and legal scholars over precisely this question. For an overview, see Abraham and Perry, *Freedom and the Court*, 30–91.

22. *Gitlow v. New York* and *Fiske v. Kansas*, in which the Supreme Court asserted (in *Gitlow*), and then exercised (in *Fiske*), its right to overturn state criminal syndicalism statutes that, in its judgment, ran afoul of the First Amendment.

The first of the religion clauses was judged binding on the states for the first time in *Hamilton v. Regents of the University of California.* In 1933, Albert Hamilton and several other Methodist students at the University of California refused, on the basis of a religiously-informed conscience, to complete the course in military science and tactics required of them by the university. The Supreme Court recognized the applicability of the Free Exercise Clause to the states, but denied that the right was violated by a requirement that students who enroll in the state's university undergo military training.

The other of the religion clauses, the Establishment Clause, was first explicitly applied to the states in the 1947 New Jersey school bus case, *Everson v. Board of Education.* In that case, the Supreme Court, while upholding a New Jersey law that provided free transportation to *all* school children (including those attending parochial schools) clearly asserted that the Establishment Clause applied to the states. The case also gave prominence to Thomas Jefferson's interpretation of the First Amendment as "building a wall of separation between Church & State."[23] That metaphor was turned into a rule in 1963, when Justice Thomas Clark, writing for the Court in the Pennsylvania Bible-reading Case, *Abington v. Schempp,* ruled that "to withstand the strictures of the Establishment Clause, there must be a secular legislative purpose and a primary effect that neither advances nor inhibits religion."[24]

---

23. The phrase comes from Jefferson's 1802 letter to the Danbury Baptists. The letter had previously been cited by Chief Justice Waite in the Mormon polygamy case (*Reynolds v. United States*, 164), but that case was decided on free exercise, not on establishment, grounds.

24. *Abington v. Schempp*, 222. A tax case (*Walz v. Tax Commission of the City of New York*) later added a third, entanglement, test. This prong came too late to apply to the Bryan-law cases discussed below, but was available for use in later evolution cases. The integrated rule (the Lemon test) was articulated by Chief Justice Warren Burger, speaking for the court in a set of three school-aid cases:

> Three such tests may be gleaned from our cases. First, the statute must have a secular legislative purpose; second, its principal or primary effect must be one that neither advances nor inhibits religion; finally, the statute must not foster "an excessive government entanglement with religion." (*Lemon v. Kurtzman*, 612–13)

The soundness of the Lemon test remains controversial. Antonin Scalia, for one, would abandon it (see, for example, his comments in two other evolution-law cases, *Freiler v. Tangipahoa* II and *Edwards v. Aguillard*, 636–40—or, more colorfully, in *Lamb's Chapel v. Center Moriches*, 398–400). Sandra Day O'Connor's alternative endorsement test, in a Christmas display case (*Lynch v. Donnelly*, 674–76) will be mentioned below.

Those cases laid the foundation for a renewed legal attack on the Bryan laws in Arkansas, Tennessee, and Mississippi, laws that, though not actively enforced in the courts, remained on the books.

The Fall of the Bryan Laws

The first such attack came in Arkansas in 1965 when, after a third failed attempt to repeal Arkansas's Bryan law,[25] the Arkansas Educational Association (AEA) had decided to challenge Initiated Act № 1 in federal court. The challenge came out of Little Rock's Central High School, the same school where the 101st Airborne Division had enforced federal integration law at bayonet point less than a decade before. This more peaceful controversy over the content and reach of federal law began when a committee of biology teachers at the school selected James H. Otto and Albert Towle's *Modern Biology*[26] for use in school biology classrooms. Selection of the book had itself been a violation of state law, but the AEA chose to challenge the law on the point of teaching. Susan Epperson, a biology teacher at the school with Arkansas roots and an undergraduate degree from (Presbyterian) College of the Ozarks, along with Howard H. Blanchard Jr., Assistant Executive Secretary of the AEA and a parent of children in the Little Rock public schools, filed their complaint in Pulaski County chancery court shortly before the teachers were to reach the chapter discussing the evolution of man.

Chancellor Murray O. Reed scheduled the case for a one-day hearing on 1 April 1966. The issues were more or less those of *Scopes*. Plaintiffs' attorney asserted the free speech rights of Epperson and the right to learn of Blanchard's son. The attorney general asserted the state's right to establish the curriculum of its schools. The state wanted to introduce expert testimony critical of the theory of evolution, but Reed, like Raulston before him, insisted on sticking to more narrowly legal issues. On 27 May, Reed declared the law unconstitutional because it "tends to hinder the quest for knowledge, restrict the freedom to learn, and restrain the freedom to teach" in violation of the Fourteenth Amendment.[27] The state filed an appeal.

---

25. The previous attempts had come in 1937 and 1959, but legislative repeal of a law passed by referendum requires a two-thirds vote in Arkansas.

26. This book was the latest version of Moon's popular textbook. Moon had removed references to the evolution of man from his textbook in 1926. Otto and Towle's 1965 edition, the first to appear without Moon's name, was also the first to restore discussion of this topic to the book.

27. Quoted in *Epperson v. Arkansas*, 100. The opinion of the Chancery Court was not officially reported.

The state supreme court gave the case short shrift, announcing (in a two-sentence opinion) that the statute was "a valid exercise of the state's power to specify the curriculum in its public schools" and withholding judgment on "whether the Act prohibits any explanation of the theory of evolution or merely prohibits teaching that the theory is true."[28] Epperson filed an appeal with the US Supreme Court. The state gave what Justice Hugo Black described as a "pallid, unenthusiastic, even apologetic defense of the Act,"[29] practically ensuring that the statute would fall. And indeed all nine justices judged the statute unconstitutional, though for different reasons. Justice Potter Stewart thought that the state could not make it a criminal offense "for a public school teacher so much as to mention the very existence of an entire system of respected human thought,"[30] the interpretation that the Arkansas attorney general's office had put upon the statute at oral argument. Justice Hugo Black thought that the law was "too vague to enforce."[31] The majority, with Black explicitly dissenting on this point, found the law inconsistent with the Establishment Clause. Justice Abe Fortas, who had been a high-school student in Tennessee when the Butler Act was passed, wrote for the court that

> Government in our democracy, state and national, must be neutral in matters of religious theory, doctrine, and practice . . . Arkansas's law cannot be defended as an act of religious neutrality. Arkansas did not seek to excise from the curricula of its schools and universities all discussion of the origin of man. The law's effort was confined to an attempt to blot out a particular theory because of its supposed conflict with the Biblical account, literally read.[32]

Justice Black, in his rejection of the Establishment Clause argument used by the majority in *Epperson*, expressed his concern about "whether this Court's decision forbidding a State to exclude the subject of evolution from its schools infringes the religious freedom of those who consider evolution an anti-religious doctrine."[33] Black had merely gone on to ask: "If the theory is considered anti-religious, as the Court indicates, how can the State be bound by the Federal Constitution to permit its teachers to advocate such an 'anti-religious' doctrine to school children?" Anti-evolutionists put a

28. *Arkansas v. Epperson*.
29. *Epperson v. Arkansas*, 97.
30. *Epperson v. Arkansas*, 116
31. *Epperson v. Arkansas*, 112
32. *Epperson v. Arkansas*, 103–4 and 109.
33. *Epperson v. Arkansas*, 113.

more demanding question—whether the state would even be permitted to present the theory (see below), but they never got the answer they sought.

Meanwhile, as the *Epperson* case was still working its way through the state and federal courts, a multifront attack on the Butler Act had opened in Tennessee.[34] The opening salvo was fired by Knoxville lawyer Martin Southern in early 1967. Southern filed suit with the state on behalf of his son, whose education, Southern claimed, would suffer were the act not declared unconstitutional.[35] As the judge was preparing to hear the case, bills to repeal the Butler Act were filed in both houses of the Tennessee General Assembly. The chancellor, Len G. Broughton, put Southern's suit on hold in the hopes of a legislative resolution of the matter.

Meanwhile, two days after the House of Representatives passed a repeal bill (by a vote of 59–30) and with favorable Senate action expected,[36] a third front arose in Jacksboro, a mere sixty miles from Dayton. There, science teacher Gary L. Scott was fired by the Campbell County School Board for remarks he had made about evolution and the Bible.[37] Scott had originally intended to seek reconciliation with the school board and to ensure payment of his salary, which he was, with the threat of a lawsuit, able to obtain. Nevertheless, as the National Education Association and others rallied to his support, he decided to broaden his focus of his efforts.

In the interim between his dismissal and his settlement with the school board, the state Senate first voted down (16–16), and then scheduled a reconsideration of, the repeal bill.[38] To put pressure on the Senate, Scott and his supporters filed a class action suit on behalf of all teachers, with a promise to seek dismissal of the suit if the Butler Act was repealed. The Senate voted 20–13 for repeal, and the bill was quickly signed into law by Governor Buford Ellington.[39]

34. See Webb, "Repeal of the Butler Act."

35. *Southern v. McCanless.*

36. *New York Times*, "Tennessee Takes Step to Repeal Its 42-Year-Old 'Monkey Law,'" and (for the vote total) Tennessee House of Representatives, House Bill № 48, *House Journal*, 554.

37. Students had complained that Scott characterized the Bible as "a bunch of fairy tales." Scott denied this (and denied that he had taught the evolutionary origins of man), saying that he had said only that "many things in the Bible were explained in the form of parables and that some of those cannot be taken literally" (*Louisville Courier-Journal*. "Tennessee Teacher Fired"). See the reporting on the issue in the *New York Times*: "'Monkey Law' Ousts Tennessee Teacher"; "Full Pay Is Asked in Evolution Case"; "Tennessee Teacher Wins Support in Evolution Case"; "Tennessee Teacher Is Rehired but Vows 'Monkey Law' Fight."

38. *New York Times*, "Tennessee Keeps its 'Monkey Law.'"

39. *New York Times*, "Tennessee Ending Its 'Monkey Law.'"

That left only Mississippi with a Bryan law still more or less on the books. In late 1969, Mrs. Arthur G. Smith (on behalf of her school-age daughter) asked the Mississippi courts to declare the state's Bryan law unconstitutional. At about the same time some Mississippi legislators sought repeal of the statute, but the repeal bill failed to pass the House by a vote of 42–70. Back in the courts, although the Chancellor's Court tried to distinguish that state's law from the Arkansas law that had fallen in *Epperson*, the Mississippi Supreme Court unanimously denied the relevance of any difference between the two laws and applied *Epperson*, on 21 December 1970.[40] With that decision, the Bryan laws were gone.

The anti-evolutionism that provided support for such legislation was still alive, however, and the next forty years saw a variety of new laws, policies, and lawsuits designed to blunt the impact of *Epperson*.

The Legislative and Policy Counter-attack

In response to their defeat at the hands of the Warren court, anti-evolutionists took two basic approaches at the political level. The first was to demand that the teaching of evolution be balanced by the presentation of both a critique of evolutionary theory and a non-evolutionary (if not explicitly creationist) alternative. The second was some kind of announcement to students acknowledging, if not raising, questions about the epistemological status of the theory of evolution.

Both approaches were taken by the Tennessee General Assembly, which enacted a new law on the topic in 1973.[41] Public schools, if they used biology textbooks that discussed the "origins or creation of man and his world"[42] at all, would be required by law to choose textbooks that met two conditions. First, the textbooks would have to state specifically that the

---

40. *Smith v. Mississippi*. See also Associated Press, "Mississippi Voids Evolution Curb."

41. Tennessee, Chapter № 377 (Textbook Selection Act).

42. The addition of the phrase "and his world" is an expansion of anti-evolutionist legislative efforts beyond the evolution of man (the explicit target of the Bryan laws). Unfortunately, legislators, courts, and commentators seem unable to keep distinct the questions of the origins of matter (or of the universe), of the earth, of life, of species, and of man. In resolving a Louisiana case (concerning a law that referred to all of the above), the opinions sometimes referred to the origins of life, and sometimes to the origins of man, without any apparent reason for varying from one phrase to the other. The Dover (Pennsylvania) School Board, in an important incident discussed below, wanted students to be told that "Intelligent design is an explanation of the origin of life that differs from Darwin's view." Darwin, of course, offered no explanation of the origin of life at all.

account they presented was "a theory and not a scientific fact." Second, they would have to place "an equal amount of emphasis on the origins and creation of man and his world as the same is recorded in other theories, including, but not limited to, the Genesis account in the Bible."[43]

Opponents of the new law filed suit in both state and federal courts. The federal courts acted more quickly, the Sixth Circuit Court of Appeals striking the act down 2–1 as an establishment of religion.[44] Writing for the court, Judge George Edwards (applying *Epperson*) argued that the preferential treatment afforded to the book of Genesis[45] constituted an establishment of religion and (applying *Lemon*) argued that the express exclusion of "all occult or satanical beliefs of human origin" from the scope of the act would improperly entangle the state in theological disputes.[46] The state chose not to appeal the case. The clauses on the basis of which Tennessee's new law was struck down, however, were not essential to the aims of the anti-evolutionists; the law had been carelessly drafted.

The equal-time strategy had to wait until anti-evolutionists could offer a nonreligious alternative to evolution, an attempt that will be discussed below. Meanwhile, while California was able to forge a compromise by promulgating an antidogmatism policy,[47] two local efforts to acknowledge the controversy were challenged in the courts.

Those challenges came when two school boards attempted to work out a compromise between evolutionists and anti-evolutionists by acknowledging the controversy in a formal statement to students. Some local anti-anti-evolutionists (with outside help) took aggressive steps to keep the school boards from implementing any such compromise. Both cases reached the courts.

The first case arose in Tangipahoa Parish, Louisiana, where the parish school board, on 19 April 1994 by a vote of 5–4, instructed teachers to read the following "disclaimer" at the beginning of each relevant unit of instruction:

> It is hereby recognized by the Tangipahoa Parish Board of Education, that the lesson to be presented, regarding the origin of life and matter, is known as the Scientific Theory of Evolution

---

43. Tennessee, Chapter № 377 (Textbook Selection Act).

44. *Daniel v. Waters*.

45. *Daniel v. Waters*, 489–91. The Genesis account not only had to be included but, unlike textbooks, the book of Genesis (usable as a reference) was exempted from the requirement that it be labeled as theory rather than fact.

46. *Daniel v. Waters*, 491.

47. Larson, *Trial and Error*, 140.

> and should be presented to inform students of the scientific concept and not intended to influence or dissuade the Biblical version of Creation or any other concept.
>
> It is further recognized by the Board of Education that it is the basic right and privilege of each student to form his/her own opinion or maintain beliefs taught by parents on this very important matter of the origin of life and matter. Students are urged to exercise critical thinking and gather all information possible and closely examine each alternative toward forming an opinion.[48]

Shortly after the school board acted, but before the policy was implemented, several parents of children in the affected schools challenged the measure in federal court as an establishment of religion in violation of both the federal and the state constitutions.[49] District court judge Marcel Livaudais said that, try as he might, he could discern no secular purpose for the disclaimer. Without such a purpose, the measure failed the first prong of the Lemon test.[50] Although a three-judge panel of the Fifth Circuit Court of Appeals identified two secular purposes, it judged the disclaimer unconstitutional on the basis of its primary effect (or, more or less equivalently, for failing the endorsement test):

> The primary effect of the disclaimer is to protect and maintain a particular religious viewpoint, namely belief in the Biblical version of creation . . .
>
> The disclaimer, taken as a whole, encourages students to read and meditate upon religion in general and the 'Biblical version of Creation' in particular.[51]

The school board petitioned for a rehearing *en banc*, but the petition was denied, a decision from which seven of the circuit's judges dissented. Judge Rhesa Hawkins Barksdale, writing for the dissenters, argued:

> the primary effect of the disclaimer is . . . to advance tolerance and respect for diverse viewpoints . . . [T]o the overwhelming majority of the parish students, the scientific concept of evolution conflicts with their (or their parents') beliefs about the

---

48. *Freiler v. Tangipahoa Parish* (5th Cir. 2000), 603. The disclaimer was misquoted in lower court decisions.

49. *Freiler v. Tangipahoa Parish* (5th Cir. 1999).

50. *Freiler v. Tangipahoa Parish* (E.D. La. 1997), 828–30.

51. *Freiler v. Tangipahoa Parish*, (5th Cir. 1999), 346.

origin of life and matter; and its exclusive place in the curriculum had caused concern among students and parents. The disclaimer's message is one of respect for diverse viewpoints, informing students that teaching evolution as the sole concept for the origin of life and matter is not intended to influence or dissuade them from forming their own opinions about the subject or from maintaining beliefs taught by their parents.[52]

The US Supreme Court refused to hear the case, prompting Justice Antonin Scalia to add: "We stand by in silence while a deeply divided Fifth Circuit bars a school district from even suggesting to students that other theories besides evolution—including, but not limited to, the Biblical theory of creation—are worthy of their consideration."[53]

The second case arose in Cobb County, Georgia, where, in 2001–2, the school board was in the process of revising the curriculum in a way that would give the theory of evolution more prominence than it had hitherto received in the county's schools. Although this would bring the curriculum into compliance with state guidelines, it would certainly be unpopular with the county's many anti-evolutionist parents. In order to effect a compromise, the school board proposed to paste onto all relevant textbooks a sticker that stated, "This textbook contains material on evolution. Evolution is a theory, not a fact, regarding the origin of living things. This material should be approached with an open mind, studied carefully, and critically considered."[54]

Again, evolutionist intransigents challenged the compromise in court as an establishment of religion.[55] In 2004, the district court ruled in favor of the plaintiffs and ordered the school board to remove the offending stickers as impermissible under the effect prong of the Lemon test and the endorsement test: "The Sticker sends a message to those who oppose evolution for religious reasons that they are favored members of the political community, while the Sticker sends a message to those who believe in evolution that they are political outsiders."[56] One might have thought that it would have been the school board's selection of a textbook that included a 101-page defense of evolution that constituted an endorsement, and not the thirty-word concession to the anti-evolutionist losers in the fight over curriculum, but federal district court judge Clarence Cooper saw it differently. The school board took the case to the Eleventh Circuit Court of Appeals, but so much

52. *Freiler v. Tangipahoa Parish* (5th Cir. 2000), 603–8.
53. *Tangipahoa Parish v. Freiler*, II.
54. Reproduced in Hart, "Anti-Evolution Stickers."
55. *Selman v. Cobb County* (N.D. Ga. 2005).
56. *Selman v. Cobb County* (N.D. Ga. 2005), 1306.

of the crucial evidence had in the interim gone inexplicably missing that the appellate judges saw no alternative but to vacate the decision and to remand the case to the district court for rehearing. Shortly thereafter, the school board, while continuing to maintain the constitutionality of the stickers, decided that the distraction and expense involved made continued litigation unwise. The stickers having already been removed, the school board agreed not to replace them with any similar stickers and to pay a portion of plaintiff's legal fees.[57]

Statements to students of the kind proposed in Tangipahoa Parish and Cobb County have so far been declared unconstitutional only with reference to the wording and context of the particular cases. As Judge Ed Carnes put it: "factual context is everything."[58] Although the warnings strategy has not fared well in the courts in which it has been challenged, these decisions have little precedential value—one was vacated by a higher court; the other explicitly stated that it did not "confront the broader issue of whether the reading of any disclaimer before the teaching of evolution would amount to an unconstitutional establishment of religion."[59] A more carefully written disclaimer might still pass legal muster.

Nevertheless, the aggressive measures taken by anti-anti-evolutionist organizations such as the ACLU and the National Center for Science Education remind school boards of the costs of trying to defuse local controversy in this way. The idea that freedom of religion must accommodate religion those organizations do not like is apparently not a principle that the organizations recognize.

Counterattack in the Courts

While some anti-evolutionists were appealing to legislatures and school boards for protection against the teaching of evolution in the public schools, others sought relief in the courts. There were three basic ways this was done—by appeals to the Establishment Clause, to the Free Exercise Clause, and to the Free Speech Clause of the First Amendment.[60]

The first claim—that the teaching of (or other government support for) the theory of evolution itself constituted an establishment of religion—came in Houston in 1970, when Leona Weber filed a case in federal district

---

57. Cobb County (Georgia), "Agreement."
58. *Selman v. Cobb County* (11th Cir. 2006), 1338.
59. *Freiler v. Tangipahoa Parish* (5th Cir. 1999), 342.
60. Some plaintiffs, of course, asserted multiple claims simultaneously, but the claims will be discussed separately here.

court as first friend of minor Rita Wright.[61] There she argued that in teaching the theory of evolution, Houston's public schools violated *Epperson*'s requirement that the state maintain neutrality with respect to competing religious beliefs, in effect "lending official support to [and thereby 'establishing'] a 'religion of secularism.'"[62] Extending the holding of *Burstyn v. Wilson* (that "it is not the business of government in our nation to suppress real or imagined attacks upon a particular religious doctrine")[63] from the publications, speeches, or motion pictures of private parties at issue in *Burstyn* to government-sponsored speech in the schools, district court judge Woodrow B. Seals asserted that in this case

> the offending material is peripheral to the matter of religion. Science and religion necessarily deal with many of the same questions, and they may frequently provide conflicting answers ... Teachers of science in the public schools should not be expected to avoid the discussion of every scientific issue on which some religion claims expertise.[64]

His further references to totalitarianism, book-burning, and taboo subjects[65] are implausible characterizations of the complaint before his court—surely he would have prevented the schools from, say, defending the divinity of Christ without thinking of himself as engaged in book-burning—but his dismissal of the case for failure to state a claim can be sustained without these extravagances, as indeed it was by the Fifth Circuit Court of Appeals.[66]

William Willoughby, religion editor of the *Washington Star-News*, met with similar failure in his 1972–1975 Establishment Clause challenge to the National Science Foundation's use of government funds in preparing the evolution-friendly textbooks of the Biological Sciences Curriculum Study mentioned above.[67]

The second line of attack was to claim that a positive presentation of the theory of evolution violated the free-exercise rights of students.[68] This

---

61. *Wright v. Houston* (S.D. Texas 1972).

62. Weber also asserted free-exercise claims on behalf of Wright.

63. *Burstyn v. Wilson* (striking down a New York attempt to forbid the showing of Rosselini's sacrilegious film *The Miracle*); quoted in *Wright v. Houston* (S.D. Texas 1972), 1211.

64. *Wright v. Houston* (S.D. Texas 1972), 1211.

65. *Wrigh v. Houston* (S.D. Texas 1972), 1211.

66. *Wright v. Houston* (5th Cir. 1973). Despite this decision, establishment claims were also advanced in *Peloza* and *LeVake*, cases discussed as free-speech cases below.

67. *Willoughby v. Stever*.

68. Or teachers (as in the *LeVake* case mentioned below) or even museum-goers

claim was made by Wright, but Judge Seals, emphasizing the State Board of Education's expressed willingness to excuse students from the classes in question without penalty, dismissed the claim.[69] The same claim was made by Kelly Segraves, cofounder and director of the Creation-Science Research Center, on behalf of his children in California in 1979. In that case, superior court judge Irving Perluss thought that the state's 1972 antidogmatism policy represented sufficient protection for the free-exercise rights of anti-evolutionists and emphasized to the state the importance of thorough dissemination of that policy throughout the schools.[70]

The third line of attack was to claim that the free speech rights of teachers are violated when they are forbidden from expressing their own anti-evolutionist views or are required to teach the theory of evolution.

The first such free speech complaint was brought by Ray Webster, a social science teacher at Oster-Oakview Junior High School in New Lenox, Illinois. Webster's problems began with a student complaint that his teaching practice violated the principle of separation of church and state. To resolve the problem, Alex Martino, the district superintendent, cautioned Webster, in writing, against "advocacy of a Christian viewpoint" in general and against teaching "creation science" in particular. Webster then sued the school district, claiming that it had violated his rights of free speech. The ACLU, which now thought that teachers' free speech rights were less comprehensive than it had claimed in *Scopes*, joined in the complaint. Webster's case was dismissed by the district court for failing to state a claim, a judgment that was affirmed by the Seventh Circuit Court of Appeals in 1990.[71] The reasoning of the two courts was essentially the same. Judge Kenneth F. Ripple put the key points as follows:

> A school board generally has wide latitude in setting the curriculum.
>
> The school board had the responsibility to ensure that the establishment clause was not violated.
>
> Webster has not been prohibited from teaching any nonevolutionary theories.

(*Crowley v. Smithsonian Institution*).

69. *Wright v. Houston* (S.D. Texas 1972), 1211–12. A student's constitutional *right* to such an exemption has not been upheld and indeed was denied in *Mozert v. Hawkins* in 1987.

70. *Segraves v. California*.

71. *Webster v. New Lenox*.

The religious advocacy of Webster's teaching is prohibited and nothing else.[72]

A similar claim was made, and also dismissed for failure to state a claim, by John E. Peloza, a high-school biology teacher at Capistrano Valley High School, in California.[73] Peloza's case differed from Webster's primarily in its explicit extension to Peloza's speech outside the classroom. In a *per curiam* decision, the Ninth Circuit Court of Appeals said:

> While at the high school, whether he is in the classroom or outside of it during contract time, Peloza is not just any ordinary citizen. He is a teacher.

and

> The school district's interest in avoiding an Establishment Clause violation trumps Peloza's right to free speech.[74]

A slightly different claim was made some years later by Rodney LeVake, a biology teacher at Faribault High School in Faribault, Minnesota.[75] LeVake was removed from his biology classroom (and assigned to teach another science class instead) because his expressed doubts about the truth of the theory of evolution raised questions in the minds of school officials about his willingness to teach the school's curriculum in the way that they expected him to do. More explicitly than had judges in the earlier cases, appellate court judge Daniel F. Foley emphasized that

> Determining a public employee's free speech rights is a difficult task. A reviewing court must analyze the "balance between the interests of the [public employee], as a citizen, in commenting upon matters of public concern and the interests of the State, as an employer, in promoting the efficiency of the public services it performs through its employees."[76]

---

72. *Webster v. New Lenox* (7th Cir. 1990), 1006, with the third and fourth sentences quoted from the opinion of the district court (*Mem. op.*, 4–5).

73. *Peloza v. Capistrano* (C.D. Cal. 1992) and (9th Cir. 1994) Peloza also made Establishment Clause claims.

74. *Peloza v. Capistrano* (9th Cir. 1994), 522.

75. See *LeVake v. Independent School District #656* (Minn. Ct. App. 2001), 504–6, which provides a detailed history of the incident.

76. *LeVake v. Independent School District #656* (Minn. Ct. App. 2001), 508. The embedded quotation is from *Pickering v. Board of Education*, 568.

Again, the court recognized no free speech right in this case. The key to district court judge Bernard Borene's summary judgment against LeVake is found in his observation that

> Plaintiff's classroom at the high school is a nonpublic forum, and the District has the right to limit the speech in that classroom to the teaching of the designated curriculum,[77]

a point reiterated by Judge Foley on appeal.

Developments in Anti-Evolutionist Thought I: Creation Science

Simultaneous, and intertwined, with the suits just mentioned, was anti-evolutionist work on a more radical strategy—the attempt to articulate a nonreligious alternative to evolutionary biology (and, sometimes, to the paleoetiological sciences *in toto*). Anti-evolutionists were looking for an idea that would meet their criteria of being

(AE1) A scientific theory, and

(AE2) A theory that, in William Whewell's phrase, "points upwards."[78]

Meeting these two criteria would require a broad account of what counts as science. At the same time, the account would have to be

(AE3) A nonreligious account

if it were to pass muster with respect to recently developed establishment law. Meeting both AE2 and AE3 would require a distinction between theology and religion, or between belief (that a creator exists) and practice (worship). Some anti-evolutionists, to be sure, characterize the task somewhat differently, arguing for what might be called the Parity Thesis. In Duane Gish's words:[79]

(P1) Neither creation science nor evolution is a scientific theory

(P2) Creation science and evolution are equally religious.

---

77. *LeVake v. Independent School District #656* (Minn. Dist. Ct. 2000), 20–21, (order granting summary judgment).

78. "The mystery of creation is not within her [sc., geology's] legitimate territory; she says nothing but she points upwards" (Whewell, *History*, 2:573).

79. Gish, Letter to the Editor of *Discover* magazine. See also Gish, *Fossils Say No!*, chap. 1.

In a seminal note in the *Yale Law Journal*, Wendell Bird argued that balanced treatment of evolution and an alternative view meeting AE1-3 specified above would be the best way to maintain the religious neutrality mandated by *Everson* in the public schools.[80]

There have been two distinct attempts to construct such an alternative to evolution—Creation Science and Intelligent-Design Theory.

The first of these two ideas was developed by Henry Morris, fundamentalist in religion and hydraulic engineer by profession. Morris was for many years a professor of engineering at Virginia Polytechnic Institute and was author of a textbook, *Applied Hydraulics in Engineering*. Morris had chosen to study hydraulics precisely in order to develop "a sound system of deluge geology."[81]

At the time of the Scopes Trial, most fundamentalist anti-evolutionists held one of two other views on the early history of the earth.

The first, the idea that the "days" of Genesis were actually geological ages, was defended by prominent conservative Christian geologists in the nineteenth century (notably, Arnold Guyot,[82] John William Dawson,[83] and George Friedrich Wright) and by some of the leading anti-evolutionists of the 1920s, including both William Bell Riley and William Jennings Bryan. Wright had written, in his contribution to *The Fundamentals*, "The world was not made in an instant, or even in one day (whatever period day may signify) but in six days."[84] Bryan expressed his support for this view in his testimony at the Scopes Trial.[85]

The second view current among fundamentalists during the 1920s was that the creation of the world described in Gen 1:1–2 occurred long before the events of the six days described in the rest of the chapter. The early history of the world included an initial creation and then a subsequent ruin and restoration, the description of the latter constituting the Hexaëmeron. Into the gap between verses 2 and 3 of Genesis 1, proponents of this view asserted, there is room for all the dinosaurs, all the geological transformations, and all the fossil formation to which empirical work points. This was

---

80. Bird, "Freedom of Religion."
81. Morris, *History*, 147.
82. Guyot, *Creation*.
83. Dawson, *Archaia*, and many later works.
84. Wright, "Passing of Evolution," 5.
85. Rhea County Court, *World's Most Famous Court Trial*, 298–99.

the view defended by Harry Rimmer,[86] another of the leading Christian anti-evolutionists.

The views are compatible with each other, and both are advanced by C. I. Scofield in the *Scofield Reference Bible*, which fundamentalists so highly respected:

> [On Gen 1:2]: the earth had undergone a cataclysmic change as the result of divine judgment. The face of the earth bears everywhere the marks of such a catastrophe. There are not wanting intimations which connect it with a previous testing and fall of angels.[87]

> [On Gen 1:5]: The word "day" is used in Scripture in three ways [one of which is] a period of time, long or short, during which certain revealed purposes of God are to be accomplished ... The frequent parabolic use of natural phenomena may warrant the conclusion that each creative "day" was a period of time marked off by a beginning and ending.[88]

The view that the world was only about six thousand years old was, by contrast, the view of very few Christian anti-evolutionists. One of those few was George McCready Price, a Seventh-day Adventist, self-taught in science, who spent most of his life trying to put into scientific terms the events suggested by a literalistic reading of Gen 1 and reported by Adventist prophet Ellen G. White on the basis, she said, of a vision.[89]

Price's young-earth creationism, and the flood geology that it needed in order to account for fossils and strata, was able to break out of the narrow Adventist circles to which it had, until then, largely been confined with the publication of *The Genesis Flood: The Biblical Record and its Scientific Implications*, by John C. Whitcomb and Henry Morris, in 1961. Whitcomb was an Old Testament scholar whose recently published dissertation formed the nucleus for the first four chapters (the chapters on Scripture), while Morris was finally able to bring his long-standing interest in the Flood to fruition by writing the final three chapters (the chapters on geology).

Out of that work developed a project that came to be known as "Scientific Creationism" or "Creation Science." The project had both a substantive and a methodological component. Substantively, it maintained in general

---

86. See Rimmer, *Modern Science*.
87. Scofield, ed., *Scofield Reference Bible*, Gen 1:2n3.
88. Scofield, ed., *Scofield Reference Bible*, Gen 1:5n1.

89. Price wrote many books on his subject over the course of nearly sixty years. A classical exposition of his views is *The New Geology*. For White, see *Patriarchs and Prophets*.

that "the account of origins in Genesis is a factual presentation of simple historical truths." On their account, that included the following theses:

(CS1) The world is relatively young (created 6,000–10,000 years ago);

(CS2) The world was created over the course of a six-day creation week;

(CS3) All basic types of living things (including man) were directly created by God;

(CS4) Biological "kinds" are fixed, with biological changes since creation week occurring only within those original kinds; and

(CS5) There was a great flood worldwide in its extent and in its effect.

It is, of course, possible to accept these theses just because one thinks that they are found in the Bible; surely most creation scientists do accept them for that reason.[90] The idea behind the term *"scientific* creationism," however, is that the theses could *also* be defended by a scientific argument, or at least by an argument that is as scientific as are arguments for historical geology and evolutionary biology. Morris maintained that only two accounts of "origins" are worthy of serious consideration—his own Scientific Creationism and atheistic evolutionism (a combination of uniformitarian geology, a naturalistic account of the origins of life, and a neo-Darwinian biology combining natural selection and random mutations, and the evolutionary origins of mankind). Theistic evolutionism, as well as the varieties of old-earth creationism found in the *Scofield Reference Bible*, or in the thought of William Jennings Bryan, are, in his framing of the question, not on the table.

Anti-evolutionists hoped that Scientific Creationism would provide them with a set of ideas that could be presented in public school classrooms. If (per *Epperson*) evolution could not be excluded from the curriculum of the school to which they had to send their children, perhaps at least these ideas could be presented as well, both as a bulwark against evolutionary ideas and as a pointer from natural phenomena to the existence of God.

Morris repeatedly emphasized the preferability of a persuasive and exhortatory rather than a coercive approach—resolutions rather than bills or judicial orders.[91] Other proponents of Scientific Creationism, however,

---

90. The first point in the Creation Research Society's Statement of Belief requires members to believe that

> The Bible is the written Word of God, and because it is inspired throughout, all its assertions are historically and scientifically true in the original autographs. To the student of nature this means that the account of origins in Genesis is a factual presentation of simple historical truths.

91. See, for example, Morris, *History of Modern Creationism*, 244.

chose to take the legislative route and the early 1980s twice succeeded in adding it to the state curriculum.

Their first success came in Arkansas in 1981. Bird's idea about how the teaching of the theory of evolution in the public schools could be neutralized had reached Paul Ellwanger, a South Carolina anti-evolution activist, who cast it into a form suitable for legislation. This he distributed to various like-minded colleagues and it eventually reached the desk of Arkansas state senator James L. Holsted, who introduced it as Senate Bill 482, later to become Arkansas's famous Act 590, the Balanced Treatment for Creation-Science and Evolution-Science Act. There, with only minimal hearings or debate, it was passed (69–18 in the House; 20–2 in the Senate), and on 19 March, within a week of its Senate passage, Governor Frank White signed it into law.

The act required that "Public schools . . . give balanced treatment to creation-science and to evolution-science," which the bill defined in the following terms:

> Creation-science includes the scientific evidences and related inferences that indicate:
>
> (1) Sudden creation of the universe, energy, and life from nothing;
>
> (2) The insufficiency of mutation and natural selection in bringing about development of all living kinds from a single organism;
>
> (3) Changes only within fixed limits of originally created kinds of plants and animals;
>
> (4) Separate ancestry for man and apes;
>
> (5) Explanation of the earth's geology by catastrophism, including the occurrence of a worldwide flood; and
>
> (6) A relatively recent inception of the earth and living kinds.
>
> Evolution-science includes the scientific evidences and related inferences that indicate:
>
> (1) Emergence by naturalistic processes of the universe from disordered matter and emergence of life from nonlife;
>
> (2) The sufficiency of mutation and natural selection in bringing about development of present living kinds from simple earlier kinds;

(3) Emergence by mutation and natural selection of present living kinds from simple earlier kinds;

(4) Emergence of man from a common ancestor with apes;

(5) Explanation of the earth's geology and the evolutionary sequence by uniformitarianism; and

(6) An inception several billion years ago of the earth and somewhat later of life.[92]

Act 590 was promptly challenged in the federal courts. The ACLU, which organized the case, arranged as primary plaintiff Methodist minister William McLean. McLean was joined in the suit by the Catholic bishop of Little Rock, three other bishops (two Methodist and one Episcopalian), and seven other Methodist and Presbyterian ministers.

The case was put on the docket of Judge William R. Overton, who held a two-week trial in December 1981. In contrast to Raulston and Reed, Overton allowed both plaintiffs and the state to submit expert testimony to the court.[93] The plaintiffs had no trouble securing the testimony of leading scholars—scientists Steven Jay Gould (from Harvard University) and Francisco Ayala (from the University of California, Davis), philosopher of science Michael Ruse (from the University of Guelph), historian George Marsden (from Calvin College), sociologist Dorothy Nelkin (from Cornell University), and theologian Langdon Gilkey (from the University of Chicago).[94] The defense was not able to match this list, and indeed some of the witnesses it *was* able to bring to Little Rock contradicted key elements in the state's defense of the law. Two witnesses with advanced degrees in science, Harold Coffin and Ariel Roth (both of the Geosciences Research Institute at Loma Linda University), denied that creation science was testable. Another, Chandra Wickramasinghe (from the University of Cardiff), said that no rational scientist could believe that the earth is less than a million years old or that its geology could be explained by a single catastrophe.[95]

On 5 January 1982, Judge Overton issued his decision: "the evidence is overwhelming that both the purpose and effect of Act 590 is the advancement of religion in the public schools."[96] The act was, as a matter of

---

92. Arkansas, Act 590: Balanced Treatment, 1232–33.

93. A full record of the trial has never been published, but some transcripts of depositions and testimony has been gathered by the McLean v. Arkansas Documentation Project and made available on their website.

94. At least two have provided personal recollections of the trial. See Ruse, "Philosopher's Day in Court"; and Gilkey, *Creationism on Trial*.

95. Lewin, "Where Is the Science in Creation Science?"

96. *McLean v. Arkansas*, 1264. Plaintiffs also asserted that Act 590 violated their

historical fact, "simply and purely an effort to introduce the Biblical version of creation into the public school curricula."[97] On the basis of the text of the statute alone, independent of the circumstances of its passage, Creation Science was "unquestionably a statement of religion"[98] and lacked any scientific merit.

Overton based his judgment about the religious character of Creation Science not only on its relation to Genesis but on the more general concern that creation points to a creator (i.e., to God) and thereby to religion. Defense witness Norman Geisler raised at trial the obvious objection that religion is a matter of commitment, not one of bare belief (or, as justice Antonin Scalia put it in a later, related, case, "to posit a past creator is not to posit the eternal and personal God who is the object of religious veneration"[99]). Legally, however, Overton was here on relatively solid ground. He cited an earlier case in which an elective course in transcendental meditation offered by five New Jersey public schools had been held to violate the Establishment Clause: "Concepts concerning . . . a supreme being of some sort are manifestly religious . . . . These concepts do not shed that religiosity merely because they are presented as philosophy or as a science."[100] If the purpose of the Establishment Clause is to prevent political fights over religious matters, perhaps prudence requires an expansive legal understanding of the term *religion*. There are good reasons for keeping the public-school classroom as far as possible away from theology and not just from religion. Silence will preserve the peace at school board meetings better than will unorthodoxy. Whether in the final analysis those are just policy judgments best made by the nation's elected officials, or whether they are reasonable applications of the Establishment Clause itself, can be left for final resolution to judges and legal scholars.

Overton also objected to the act's "contrived dualism" between "the literal interpretation of Genesis" and "the godless system of evolution," a dualism that had "no scientific factual basis or legitimate educational purpose."[101] Taken on its own, Creation Science was "a hodgepodge of

---

free-speech rights, but the court announced that it was "not prepared to adopt such a broad view of academic freedom in the public schools" (1273).

97. *McLean v. Arkansas*, 1264.

98. *McLean v. Arkansas*, 1265.

99. *Edwards v. Aguillard*, 629.

100. *Malnak v. Yogi*, 1322. The district court added (1315) that "Religion, as comprehended by the first amendment now includes mere affirmation of belief in a supreme being." Being from another circuit, this case provides merely persuasive, not binding, precedent.

101. *McLean v. Arkansas*, 1266.

limited assertions"[102] whose unity came from its status as its proponents' understanding of the book of Genesis. Worse, the act gave one theistic account of origins a privileged position over other widely held theistic accounts. Surely that is part of the reason why Methodist and Catholic bishops showed up in Judge Overton's courtroom. Teaching Creation Science, with its young earth and its flood geology, would create the same problems for most Catholics and Methodists as teaching historical geology did for many fundamentalists. It was to avoid that kind of fight, as the Catholics and Methodists realized, but Bird and his allies apparently did not, that the Establishment Clause was written in the first place.

In his evaluation of the scientific merits of Creation Science, Overton, following philosopher of science and plaintiff witness Michael Ruse, characterized science as having as essential features methodological naturalism, testability, and tentativeness.[103] He measured Creation Science against these criteria and found it wanting.

In the end, Overton declared the act unconstitutional and Arkansas's attorney general Steve Clark chose not to file an appeal. The law's defenders, disappointed with Clark's handling of the case, decided to concentrate their efforts on Louisiana, which had passed a more carefully worded statute and where another judicial showdown was in the offing.

The first version of the Balanced Treatment for Creation-Science and Evolution-Science Act was introduced in the Louisiana state legislature by Senator Bill Keith in June 1980. A year later, after seven legislative committee hearings and floor debate in both houses, an amended bill passed both houses (26-12 in the Senate; 71-19 in the House) and was signed into law by governor David Treen. The law, which required that if the subject of "the origin of man, life, the earth, or the universe" were taught at all, it be treated in a balanced way, with both evolutionary and Creation Science models presented and both presented as theories.[104] The key terms were defined without any reference to the content of Genesis in an attempt to immunize the measure against some of the constitutional objections that had been made against Arkansas's Act 590 by Judge Overton:

> "Creation-science" means the scientific evidences for creation and inferences from those scientific evidences.

---

102. *McLean v. Arkansas*, 1267.

103. The opinion itself named five such features (*McLean v. Arkansas*, 1267), but in my judgment some of the criteria can be combined without loss of meaning.

104. Louisiana, Act № 685: Balanced Treatment.

"Evolution-science" means the scientific evidences for evolution and inferences from those scientific evidences.

As had happened in Arkansas, the constitutionality of the statute was challenged in federal court. This time the primary plaintiff was a schoolteacher, but he was joined in the suit by a Catholic priest, a rabbi, and ministers from five different Protestant denominations. The defense was conducted by Bird, whom the state had deputized as special assistant attorney general for the purpose.

The case was decided against the state at summary judgment by district court judge Adrian Duplantier, and that decision was upheld by a three-judge appellate panel. Bird's request for rehearing *en banc* was denied by the narrowest of margins, and the case went to the Supreme Court, where it was heard on 10 December 1987.[105] The court declared the act unconstitutional by a vote of 7–2. Justice William Brennan, writing for the court, saw a violation of the Establishment Clause: "it seeks to employ the symbolic and financial support of government to achieve a religious purpose."[106] Justice Scalia, joined by Chief Justice William Rehnquist, wrote a spirited dissent in which he argued that the act did, *pace* Brennan, articulate a secular purpose—namely, ensuring "*students*' freedom from *indoctrination*." "What is crucial [to ascertaining the purpose of a piece of legislation]," he went on to say, "is not [the legislators'] *wisdom* in believing that purpose would be achieved by the bill, but their *sincerity* in believing it would be," and "the legislative history gives ample evidence of the sincerity of the Balanced Treatment Act's articulated purpose."[107] The complaint against the act never having gone to trial, Brennan's opinion does not go beyond Overton's on the points most relevant to our primary interest.

Developments in Anti-Evolutionist Thought II: Intelligent-Design Theory

The second attempt at constructing an anti-evolutionary idea that would meet criteria AE1–3—an account that was scientific, and pointed upwards without being religious—its proponents call Intelligent-Design Theory. The goal of the developers of this second theory was to identify some feature of the world that would allow them to flesh out this argument scheme:

(ID1) The natural world includes X.

---

105. *Aguillard v. Treen*, which later became *Aguillard v. Edwards*.
106. *Edwards v. Aguillard*, 597.
107. *Edwards v. Aguillard*, 610, 627, 631, and 621 (italics original).

(ID2) Anything that contains X, must have been designed.

So,

(ID3) the natural world must have been designed.

From that, the argument proceeds to the existence of an (intelligent) designer. ID2 is broad enough to include several distinct kinds of argument, including St. Thomas Aquinas's Fifth Way to prove the existence of God[108] and arguments based on the anthropic principle,[109] but the project at the heart of the second campaign of the Second Curriculum War was narrower, in a way that will be specified shortly. In any case, Intelligent-Design Theory must be distinguished from Creation Science, despite the practice of many of its friends and foes, who seem not to care about the details of an idea as long as the idea is in some sense anti-evolutionist.[110] Its proponents seem to have realized that Intelligent-Design Theory met criteria AE1–2 (mentioned above) as well as Creation Science had done and, shorn of the earlier theory's young-earth and flood-geology baggage, at less cost. Its opponents erred when they took this point of commonality to be a proof of identity. The differences are as follows:

First, this theory, unlike Creation Science, is centered on a single coherent idea. There is no logical connection uniting the fundamental tenets of Creation Science—a young earth, a six-day creation week, and a geologically important great flood. It is not, that is to say, a *unified* scientific theory. What holds those theses together at all is the Scientific Creationists' theological commitment to a certain interpretation of Genesis.

Second, it is not explicitly biblical. This helped proponents keep their focus on the critique of Darwinism without risking internecine struggles over the meaning of Genesis. This also helped its proponents deny that theirs was a religious account, a denial necessary to secure the theory a place in the curriculum of American public schools. Although this may have made the

---

108. Thomas Aquinas, *Summa theologica*, Ia, Q. 2, a. 3.

109. See Leslie, "Fine-Tuned Cosmos"; Manson, ed., *God and Design*.

110. Judge John C. Jones (in the *Kitzmiller* case discussed below), and others, have placed great weight on the historical links between the two movements. Some Scientific Creationists, in the wake of their legal defeat in the *Aguillard* case, retreated to the more modest goal of attempting to secure a place for Intelligent-Design Theory in the public schools. That retreat is a sufficient explanation for the fact, discovered by plaintiffs in *Kitzmiller*, that early drafts of the Intelligent Design school textbook Percival Davis's *Pandas and People* had emphasized the concept of creation, but had replaced that concept with "intelligent design" in the wake of the *Aguillard* decision (see Forrest, "My Role in *Kitzmiller*"). That is not, however, sufficient to show that the two ideas are the same. It only shows that anti-evolutionists were willing to settle for asserting less than they had originally hoped to be able to assert in public-school classrooms.

movement more appealing to old-earth ("progressive") creationists without explicitly excluding young-earth creationists, it was also (not surprisingly) the cause of some criticism from many of the (in fact Bible-centered) Scientific Creationists.[111]

Third, the theory is purely biological, with no relevance to geology. Again, it is not committed to a young earth, to a six-day creation week, or to a worldwide flood: none of these play any role in Intelligent-Design Theory in the strict sense of the term.

Fourth, within biology, it is a critique precisely of the power of the natural selection of random mutations to do all the work required to form new species (or, more precisely, to produce complex new structures and processes). It is not even properly a critique of common ancestry. Indeed, Michael Behe, one of the leading proponents of Intelligent-Design Theory, accepts the Common Ancestry Thesis,[112] though some other proponents (e.g., Phillip Johnson[113]) do not. The theory itself is neutral on this point.

Finally, Intelligent-Design Theory is not *per se* a form of creationism at all. The Demiurge of Plato's *Timaeus* imposed order and beauty on pre-existent matter; he designed the world (i.e., effected a "purposeful arrangement of parts"[114]), but he did not bring it into being out of nothing. He did not, that is to say, create it.[115] A designer need not be a creator. The core argument of Intelligent-Design Theorists, if they can get it to work at all, will get us to the former, but not to the latter. Although Intelligent-Design Theory is sometimes called neocreationism, it would be more accurate to call it, at best, ersatz creationism, since it does not really focus on the classical understanding of the concept of creation (as exnihilation) at all, even though its proponents surely do *also* accept that doctrine.

Intelligent-Design Theory has its deep roots in William Paley's *Natural Theology*, the book that so impressed Darwin in his early Cambridge years,[116]

---

111. Morris, "Intelligent Design."

112. Behe,. *Darwin's Black Box*, 5; and Behe, *Edge of Evolution*, 64–83. Behe explicitly includes common ancestry for man and chimpanzee (Behe, *Edge of Evolution*, 71–72).

113. For example, in Johnson, *Darwin on Trial*, 45–85.

114. The definition is Behe's (Behe, *Darwin's Black Box*, 193). But can simple objects, such as electrons, not also be designed? Perhaps "purposeful assignment of properties"—mass, charge, spin, and so forth—should also be counted as design.

115. Plato, *Timaeus*, 28a.

116. "The logic of... [Paley's] *Natural Theology* gave me as much delight as did Euclid. The careful study of [Paley's] works... was the only part of the Academical Course which, as I then felt and as I still believe, was of the least use to me in the education of

but also the book of which his own work *On the Origin of Species* was the refutation. Paley's subtitle summarized his project: *Evidences of the Existence and Attributes of the Deity Collected from the Appearances of Nature.* His opening paragraph gives the flavor of the whole:

> suppose I had found a *watch* upon the ground, and it should be enquired how the watch happened to be in that place.... [W]hy should not this answer [sc., the watch might have always been there] serve for [a] watch as well as for [a] stone? ... For this reason, and for no other, viz. that, when we come to inspect the watch, we perceive ... that its several parts are framed and put together for a purpose ... [T]he inference, we think, is inevitable, that the watch must have had a maker ...[117]

Historian Ronald Numbers has suggested that the more immediate intellectual roots of this movement can be traced to two books, both of which appeared in the mid-1980s. The first, *The Mystery of Life's Origin*, was written by a chemist, a geochemist, and an engineer and featured an introduction by Dean H. Kenyon, a biologist who had coauthored a major textbook on the origins of life. All of the authors are Protestants. It was focused exclusively on the question of the origin of life and did not address the origin of species. Darwin is mentioned only in passing. The second, Michael Denton's *Evolution: A Theory in Crisis*, was written by a geneticist. Unlike the authors of the other book, Denton had no religious affiliation. This work is an attack on Darwin's common ancestry thesis, although it includes a critique of natural selection as well.

The current Intelligent Design movement really developed, however, from three other books published between 1991 and 1998, each of which articulated, in its own way, a central idea of the movement's core argument.

The first of those books was Phillip E. Johnson's *Darwin on Trial*. Johnson, a professor of law at the University of California, Berkeley, took an interest in evolution when he read Richard Dawkins's anti-religious defense of evolution (and attack on theism), *The Blind Watchmaker: Why the Evidence of Evolution Reveals a Universe without Design*. Johnson began his book by explicitly distinguishing creationism from Creation Science. "Creationism," he said, is not only broader than Creation Science but is even compatible with the evolutionary origin of species, requiring only that "a supernatural Creator not only initiated this process but in some meaningful sense *controls* it in furtherance of a purpose."[118] The book makes explicit mention

---

my mind" (Darwin, *Autobiography*, 59).

117. Paley, *Natural Theology*, 1–3.
118. Johnson, *Darwin on Trial*, 4.

of the concepts of intelligent design and of complexity,[119] concepts which would figure more prominently in the work of other authors a few years later. It includes a long critique of the arguments for biological evolution but none of arguments for historical geology. Against the former, he repeated the usual objections—"survival of the fittest" as a tautology, the imperfections of the fossil record, and the like.[120] His presentation suffers from the usual defects. It says, for example, that it is a problem for Darwinism that "species that were once thought to have turned into others overlap in time with their alleged descendants."[121] He misses completely the significance of Darwin's argument about the geographical collocation of related fossil and living organisms.

Johnson's contribution to this new wave of anti-evolutionism was the argument (in the final four chapters of his book) that evolution is improperly naturalistic, a topic I have addressed elsewhere.[122]

The second of the seminal books is Michael Behe's *Darwin's Black Box: The Biochemical Challenge to Evolution*.[123] Behe is a Catholic biochemist who teaches at Lehigh University. With reference to his theory of natural selection, Darwin had said in *The Origin of Species* that "if it could be demonstrated that any complex organ existed, which could not possibly have been formed by numerous, successive, slight modifications, my theory would absolutely break down." Darwin added that he could find no such case and that in general "we should be extremely cautious in concluding that an organ could not have been formed by transitional gradations of some kind."[124] Behe thinks that "Darwin's black box" (the cell) contains exactly the kind of complexity that Darwin acknowledged would be fatal to his theory of natural selection. Behe's central thesis is that

---

119. Johnson, *Darwin on Trial*, 117 and 32, respectively.

120. Johnson, *Darwin on Trial*, 57 and 51.

121. Johnson, *Darwin on Trial*, 73.

122. Kemp, "Scientific Method and Appeal to Supernatural Agency." See also Plantinga, *Where the Conflict Really Lies*.

123. See also Behe, "Reply to My Critics." Behe followed this book with a second, Behe, *Edge of Evolution*.

124. Darwin, *Origin*, 189–90, quoted by Behe, *Darwin's Black Box*, 39. Darwin means, of course, that his theory of natural selection (not his common ancestry thesis) would absolutely break down. Even that is an exaggeration, as Darwin never claimed (and indeed denied) that natural selection was the exclusive cause of evolutionary change. He must have meant only that his theory would break down as an explanation of that organ.

(B1) Darwinian processes (i.e., the natural selection of small, random mutations) are incapable of producing some of the systems (e.g., structures and processes) found in living things.

From this he inferred that

(B2) Some of the systems found in living things were produced by intelligent design.

How did Behe argue for B1?

First, he tried to make the concept of complexity more precise. That idea is not, of course, entirely new; it is found already in Paley's *Natural Theology*, and Darwin addressed, as he knew that he had to do, "organs of extreme perfection and complication."[125] Behe defined an *irreducibly* complex system as "a single system necessarily composed of several well-matched, interacting parts that contribute to the basic function, wherein the removal of any one of the parts causes the system to effectively cease functioning."[126]

Second, Behe applied the concept at the cellular and biochemical level, which, he says, is necessary to its proper evaluation.[127] Behe's argument can be put as follows:

(B3) Some biological organisms include irreducibly complex systems.

So,

(B4a) No biological organisms including irreducibly complex systems could have been formed by Darwinian processes.

So,

(B1) Some biological organisms could not have been formed by Darwinian processes.

B3 is defended by his examples—cilia (in particular, bacterial flagella), blood clotting, vesicular transport, cellular defense mechanisms, and metabolic pathways—to which he devoted five chapters of *Darwin's Black Box*, but B4 also needs defense. His argument for that thesis (or, strictly, for a thesis to which B4a is practically equivalent) runs as follows:[128]

---

125. Darwin, *Origin*, 186–90.

126. Behe, "Reply to My Critics," 693–95. Behe's original definition (Behe, *Darwin's Black Box*, 39) did not include the word "necessarily."

127. Behe, *Edge of Evolution*, 10.

128. See Behe, *Darwin's Black Box*, 43.

(B5) All systems formed by Darwinian processes have functional physical precursors.

(B6) No irreducibly complex system has a functional physical precursor.

So,

(B4b) No irreducibly complex system could be formed by Darwinian processes.

B6 follows from the definition of irreducible complexity—if the system had a functional physical precursor, then it would be able to function without *all* of its parts, in which case it would not be *irreducibly* complex. B5 comes from the idea that "natural selection [Darwinian processes] can only choose systems that are already working." It is important to note that Behe explicitly acknowledges that Darwinian processes played some role in the history of life and that species in whose origin intelligent design played a role may nevertheless have a measure of common ancestry.[129] He denies only that Darwinian processes were fully responsible for all the complex systems that characterize living organisms.

Next, how did Behe make the positive case for the Intelligent-Design Thesis (B2)? How does he get from B1 to B2? Defining design as "purposeful arrangement of parts,"[130] he argued as follows:

(B3) Some of the systems found in living things are irreducibly complex.

(B7) The best explanation of that irreducible complexity is intelligent design.

So,

(B2) Some of the systems found in living things were produced by intelligent design.

The argument for B7 is that we know from our own productive activity that intelligent designers can produce irreducibly complex systems (including perhaps, in the case of genetic engineering, biological ones) and that (so it seems) neither Darwinian processes nor any other known natural process can do so. Behe claims that this argument for B2 is a scientific argument.[131]

Behe is quite explicit that his version of intelligent design is an attack on natural selection, not on common ancestry, for which Behe thinks that the evidence is very good. Combining the part of evolutionary biology which he

---

129. Behe, *Darwin's Box*, 229–30; and Behe, *Edge of Evolution*, 68.
130. Behe, *Darwin's Black Box*, 193–94.
131. E.g., Behe, *Darwin's Black Box*, 194. He does, briefly, consider two alternatives.

accepts with his substitute for the part he rejects, one would get this: species originate by descent, with some modification by means of intelligent design, from one or a few first kinds. He in fact proposes a neo-saltationist theory of evolution reminiscent of Richard Goldschmidt's "hopeful monster" theory.[132] Goldschmidt, however, offered a naturalistic theory; Behe has offered a providentialist one. The fact that Behe (though not all of his views) has been embraced by anti-Darwinist Christians suggests that perhaps the heart of the issue, for at least some of them, is providentialist antinaturalism and not anti-evolutionism (i.e., separate ancestry) per se.

It is important to add that Behe is remarkably silent about details here.[133] Presumably, the designer changes the genotype of an individual conceptum (or some analogue, in the case of organisms that reproduce asexually), replacing some of the bases in its DNA or even inserting entirely new base sequences (new genes) in a way that will produce in the developed organism systems absent in its progenitors. That preserves common ancestry (just as does allowing at least a modest amount of horizontal, or interspecific, gene transfer) while denying the random character of the most interesting mutations[134] and thus diminishing the importance of Darwinian processes in the emergence of the complex structures and processes that characterize living things.

The third book, William A. Dembski's *The Design Inference: Eliminating Chance through Small Probabilities*,[135] is intended as a more abstract defense of arguments for design as operative cause. It is, in effect, an alternative to B7 (the warrant for Behe's argument to the best explanation), though Dembski and Behe never suggest that they differ on exactly what justifies the argument from B3 (irreducible complexity) to B2 (intelligent design). Dembski, a Christian mathematician and philosopher, was finishing his doctoral dissertation at the University of Chicago as Behe was writing his own book and was already far enough along in the development of his ideas that Behe was able to cite his work in *Darwin's Black Box*.

---

132. See Goldschmidt, *Material Basis of Evolution*; Gould, "Return of Hopeful Monsters."

133. His "speculative scenario" that "the first cell already contain[ed] all of the irreducibly complex biochemical systems discussed here and many others" (*Darwin's Box*, 227–28) is possible only because miracles are possible. Otherwise, the genes for these complex systems would be destroyed by random mutations millions of years before the organisms which needed them came into being, as many of his critics have pointed out.

134. The mutations are nonrandom in the sense that they are explainable by reference to the benefit they bring to the mutated organisms.

135. See also, for the larger context and significance of his argument, Dembski, *Intelligent Design*.

Dembski's ultimate goal is clear from the opening page of his book, where he promises to "breathe new life into classic design arguments" by showing when chance constitutes a good explanation of a low-probability event and when it does not. He used this distinction to argue that Darwinian processes (on his view, "chance") do not constitute a good explanation of the origin of species (and that analogous theories will not do so for the origin of life).

He illustrates his question by reference to the case of one Nicholas Caputo, the "man with the golden arm," and the history of elections in Essex County, New Jersey. In 1984, Senate candidate Mary Mochary and two local Republican Party officials brought suit against Caputo, the clerk responsible for determining the order in which candidates for public office would be placed on the county ballot, alleging that he was not conducting the drawing for positions fairly. State law required that the order be determined by lot, and although Caputo appeared to have followed the statutorily specified procedures, forty of the last forty-one drawings in the county had given the (preferred) top position on the ballot to the candidates of Caputo's own Democratic Party. The chances of such a result are about one in fifty billion. As the New Jersey Supreme Court observed, "few persons of reason will accept the explanation of blind chance."[136] But the same calculation would show those to be the odds of the actual outcome of the last forty-one drawings in every county in the state—even those in which each party got the top position about half the time. Each possible sequence is just one of fifty billion possible outcomes, and each has an equal chance of occurring. So why was Caputo in court? What makes chance any worse as an explanation of what happened in Essex County than it would have been in explanation of the results in any of New Jersey's twenty other counties? That is the problem that Dembski undertook to address.

Nineteenth-century American philosopher C. S. Peirce had already identified one feature that would convince us that the results of a seemingly random process (like drawing a lot or flipping a coin) were not in fact due to chance—predesignation.[137] If Caputo had regularly printed Essex County ballots (with any candidate order whatever) before conducting each year's drawing for the determination of ballot positions, and had only once had to reprint them after the drawing had been made, we would conclude that he was not conducting a random drawing. Predesignated patterns are not, however, the only ones for which we can rule out chance as a possible explanation. A match with Caputo's (presumed) preferences is as hard to attribute

---

136. *Mochary v. Caputo*, 122–23.
137. Peirce, "Probable Inference," 206–11.

to chance as a match with preprinted ballots would have been. Dembski calls suspicion-generating patterns "specifications."

That concept having been introduced, Dembski proposed his concept of an Explanatory Filter as key to inferring that something was brought about by design (the Design Inference). There are, he went on to argue, "many professions whose livelihood depends on drawing design inferences." His list ranges from the fields of forensic science and cryptography to archeology and the search for artificial intelligence.[138]

The Explanatory Filter, the use of which is at the heart of the Design Inference, is built on two basic principles.

The first is the Trichotomy Principle: "Whenever explaining an event, we must choose from three competing modes of explanation[—]regularity, chance, and design."[139] Regularity and chance are perhaps clear enough, but a word needs to be said about Dembski's definition of *design*, for he abandons the ordinary meaning of the term. *The Oxford English Dictionary* has "a plan or scheme conceived in the mind and intended for subsequent execution";[140] Del Ratzsch, in a careful philosophical analysis of the concept defines design as "deliberate agent activity intentionally aimed at generating particular ... structures ... which correlate to mind."[141] Dembski proposes to mean by it instead merely "patterned improbability," "the set-theoretic complement of the disjunction regularity-or-chance."[142] This definition has the advantage (as he sees it) of making the Trichotomy Principle true by definition of the word "design", but, it being psychologically impossible to detach the word from the mind-to-matter component that everyone else includes in the idea, this advantage is purchased at some cost. It is, we should keep in mind, design in the ordinary sense that Dembski really wants as the conclusion of his argument. To avoid perpetuating the confusion created by his definition, I will, when necessary, refer to what Dembski calls design as "Type-D" causality, events, and so forth.

Dembski must effect a *logical* reconnection of the concepts of Type-D causality and of intelligent design if he is to achieve the objective he specifies before he even gets to his title page: to present a reliable method for detecting intelligent causes.[143] His argument is that the contingency, complexity,

138. Dembski and Will, *Intelligent Design Uncensored*, 62. See also Dembski, *Design Inference*, 20 and, in particular, 47.
139. Dembski, *Design Inference*, 36.
140. Simpson and Weiner, preparers, *Oxford English Dictionary*, s.v. "design."
141. Ratzsch, *Nature, Design, and Science*, 15–16.
142. Dembski, *Design Inference*, xii.
143. "The Explanatory Filter pinpoints how we recognize intelligent design" (Dembski, *Design Inference*, 66).

and specification that rule out regularity and chance (that lead him to invoke Type-D causality) are also the distinguishing characteristics of choice (or equivalently, of intelligent agency).[144]

The second foundation of the Explanatory Filter is the Priority Principle: "There is . . . an order of priority to explanation. Within this order, regularity has top priority, chance second, design last."[145] Events that occur with a high degree of probability (e.g., a coin falling when it is dropped) can be attributed to laws of nature ("regularity"). For other, "contingent," events we can eliminate regularity as the explanation. Intermediate-probability events can be attributed to chance. Caputo is on hand to provide us with another example. On 12 August 1985, just a month after the New Jersey Supreme Court had suggested that he adopt new procedures to reassure voters of the fairness of ballot-position drawings, Caputo's office conducted another drawing—to determine ballot position for that fall's elections. For the forty-first time in forty-two drawings, the Democratic candidate was placed at the top of the ballot.[146] The chances of this outcome in a fair drawing were 1:2; chance cannot be ruled out, even in Newark. Even some low-probability events can be so explained. Every major win in a lottery is an example. Nevertheless, Dembski argues, while some low-probability events can be attributed to chance, others cannot and must be classified as Type-D events. This, he went on to say, "faithfully represents our ordinary human practice of sorting through events we alternatively attribute to regularity, chance, or design [i.e., neither regularity or chance]."[147] It is, he asserts, an application of Occam's razor—regularity is the simplest of these explanatory options; chance is the next simplest.[148]

Dembski applied his Explanatory Filter to the origin of life and of species (or of their parts—e.g., hemoglobin), L in the schema below, with the following argument:

(D1) All events must be explained by regularity, chance, or design.

(D2) No low-probability event is explained by regularity.

(D3) No specified, low-probability event is explained by chance.

(D4) L is a low-probability event.

So,

---

144. Dembski, *Design Inference*, 62–66.
145. Dembski, *Design Inference*, 38.
146. Associated Press, "Essex Democrats Stay Lucky."
147. Dembski, *Design Inference*, 47.
148. Dembski, *Design Inference*, 38–40. See also p. 45.

(D5) *L* is not explained by regularity.

(D6) *L* is a specified event.

So,

(D7) *L* is not explained by chance.

So,

(D8) *L* is explained by design (i.e., classified as a Type-D event).[149]

Of course Dembski still needs to get from Type-D causality to intelligent design in the ordinary sense of the term.

The ideas of Behe and Dembski can be integrated into the following set of theses:

(ID4) The origin of biological species (and of life) is beyond the reach of Darwinian processes.

(ID5) Certain features of biological organisms can only be attributed to intelligent design.

(ID6) Arguments to intelligent design are sometimes good arguments even without any independent evidence of the existence of a possible designer.

Unfortunately, there are problems with all three of these ideas. Behe's claim that Darwinian processes cannot produce the kind of complexity that exists in biological species has found little support among biologists. Dembski's philosophical claims about the Design Inference have also been widely criticized.

The problems with Behe's ideas are as follows:

First, we do not yet understand well enough the structures and processes he cites to make the strong claims he makes about them. For example, although much is known about how blood-clotting cascades work, much remains to be learned, as Behe himself acknowledges:

> Many experiments on blood clotting are hard to do; some of the proteins . . . are found in only minute quantities in blood . . . Furthermore, because the initial stages of clotting feed back to generate more of the initial activating proteins, it's often quite difficult to sort out just who is activating whom.[150]

---

149. Dembski, *Design Inference*, 56, but the exact formulation is mine.
150. Behe, *Darwin's Black Box*, 85.

Similarly in the case of the bacterial flagellum. Progress in understanding them began only in the late 1960s.[151] In 2003, Harvard biologist Howard C. Berg said, "We know a great deal about motor structure, genetics, assembly, and function, but we do not really understand how it works."[152] A few years later, Mark Pallen and Nicholas Matzke wrote:

> the flagella research community has scarcely begun to consider how these systems have evolved. This neglect probably stems from a reluctance to engage in the 'armchair speculation' inherent in building evolutionary models, and from a desire to determine how a system works before wondering how it got to be that way.[153]

Behe himself has acknowledged that the "exact roles of most of the proteins [in the flagellum] are not known."[154]

Second, we do know enough about these structures and processes to realize that at least some of them are not, in fact, irreducibly complex. The blood-clotting cascade found in human beings, for example, despite what Behe suggests, is more complex than bare functionality requires. Parahemophiliacs lack proaccelerin (one of the enzymes involved in the allegedly irreducibly complex blood-clotting cascade), and the patient in whom the disorder was discovered lived to be eighty-eight.[155] Whales and other sea mammals also lack some parts of the human blood-clotting cascade, which Behe claims is irreducibly complex.[156]

Third, Behe too hastily rejects the resources available to Darwinians. He underestimates the theory's reach. H. Allen Orr has offered an outline of how Darwinian processes can produce irreducible complexity:

> An irreducibly complex system can be built gradually by adding parts that, while initially just advantageous, become—because of *later* changes—essential. The logic is very simple. Some part (A) initially does some job (and not very well, perhaps). Another part (B) later gets added because it helps A. This new part isn't essential, it merely improves things. But later on, A (or something else) may change in such a way that *B now becomes*

---

151. See Macnab, "Bacterial Flagellum," for a brief history.

152. Berg, "Rotary Motor of Bacterial Flagella," 19.

153. Pallen and Matzke, "From *The Origin of Species* to the Origin of Bacterial Flagella," 788.

154. Behe, *Darwin's Black Box*, 73.

155. Owren, "Parahaemophilia"; and Stormorken, "Discovery of Factor V."

156. Robinson et al., "Hageman Factor (Factor XII) Deficiency in Marine Mammals." See also Semba et al., "Whale Hageman Factor (Factor XII)."

indispensable. This process continues as further parts get folded into the system. And at the end of the day, many parts may *all* be required.[157]

More recently, in response to Behe's work, Richard H. Thornhill and David W. Ussery[158] distinguished four "routes" of Darwinian evolution, two of which, they argued, can produce precisely the kind of complexity that Behe has argued is beyond the reach of Darwinian processes altogether. Those routes are elimination of functional redundancy and adoption from a different function.

Are these abstract possibilities applicable to real systems? Can we determine (or even imagine) how Darwinian processes could create the blood-clotting cascade? The answer is that in general terms we can. Coagulation might be a useful (but not strictly necessary) process in an organism with a low-pressure circulatory system. Introduction of coagulation into such an organism would allow an increase in pressure in the system or the atrophy of the other defenses against rupture (e.g., blood-vessel constriction or platelet aggregation) on which it previously relied. If any of those three subsequent changes occurred, the once merely useful coagulation process would become necessary. Similarly, coagulation accelerants (such as Factors V and VIII), which might only have been useful when coagulation was only a supplement to other effective processes in a low-pressure system, might become necessary when the pressure increased or the earlier systems atrophied.

What about Dembski? Dembski's Explanatory Filter does not formalize the pattern of reasoning we do, or should, use in reasoning about this problem. Indeed the examples of reasoning he used to justify the Filter are better understood as cases of argument to the best explanation,[159] which differs from Dembski's Design Inference in not being limited to the categories of Dembski's Trichotomy Principle or to the presumptions of the Priority Principle.

Dembski and Behe both argue that the argument for the intelligent design of the complex features of living organisms can be made without raising the question of the existence of God. Behe wrote:

> Thus while I argue for design, the question of the identity of the designer is left open. Possible candidates for the role of designer include: the God of Christianity; an angel—fallen or not; Plato's

157. Orr, "Darwin v. Intelligent Design," 29 (italics original).

158. Thornhill and Ussery, "Classification of Possible Routes."

159. See Harman, "Inference to the Best Explanation"; McMullin, *Inference That Makes Science*; Lipton, *Inference to the Best Explanation*.

demi-urge; some mystical new age force; space aliens from Alpha Centauri; time travelers; or some utterly unknown intelligent being. Of course, some of these possibilities may seem more plausible than others based on information from fields other than science.[160]

But this argument also fails. The judgment that intelligent design is the best explanation of the existence of something depends in part on whether there is a likely candidate for inventor and executor of that design.

Unfortunately, further elaboration of those objections would take us too far from our question of whether the promotion of these ideas constitutes a war of religion against science.

Unlike Scientific Creationists, the proponents of Intelligent-Design Theory never attained for their idea any legislative mandate for its inclusion in the public school curriculum. Nevertheless, like Creation Science, it had, in *Kitzmiller v. Dover*, its day in federal court. The incident that precipitated that day happened on 18 October 2004, when the Dover (Pennsylvania) Area School Board first passed a resolution requiring that "Students . . . be made aware of the gaps/problems in Darwin's theory and of other theories of evolution including, but not limited to, intelligent design." The next month, it went on to prepare a statement to be read to students warning them about parts of Darwin's theory for which there was allegedly insufficient evidence and pointing them to Intelligent-Design Theory in general, and to Percival Davis's *Pandas and People*[161] in particular, as an alternative explanation of the origin of life and of biological species. Some sixty copies of that book were put in the high-school library, though not at taxpayers' expense. In December, Tammy Kitzmiller and ten other parents, with the help of the ACLU, brought suit against the school district, asserting that the school board's new policies constituted an establishment of religion.

Judge John E. Jones III, a political and judicial conservative, and a Lutheran, presided over a six-week trial of the case from September to November of 2005. For the second time, expert testimony was admitted at trial. Michael Behe and others testified for the school district, while Brown University biologist Kenneth Miller, author of *Finding Darwin's God* and a prominent critic of Intelligent-Design Theory, was among those who testified for the plaintiffs. Four days after the conclusion of the trial, but before the judge had announced a decision in the case, the citizens of Dover voted

160. Behe, "Modern Intelligent Design Hypothesis."
161. This was a textbook prepared for high-school students.

most of the members of the old school board (and all those up for reelection) out of office.[162] On 20 December, Judge Jones ruled that the school district's policy failed both the endorsement and the Lemon tests of constitutionality. Having been elected to put a stop to the inclusion of Intelligent-Design Theory in the district's science curriculum, the school board did not appeal the decision. Unfortunately for the taxpayers of the city of Dover, the school district still had to pay the plaintiffs' million-dollar legal bill.

The National Association of Biology Teachers and the Definition of *Evolution*

I want to conclude with an incident of a different sort. In March 1995, as it drafted a definition of evolution for inclusion in a larger "Statement on the Teaching of Evolution," the National Association of Biology Teachers (NABT) chose to put, not a textbook definition such as "the theory that living things, and the populations of which they form a part, change gradually over the course of their history, and that all living things are, to some extent, genetically related to one another"[163] or "a change in the frequencies of genes in a population of individuals from one generation to the next,"[164] but something startlingly different: "an unsupervised, impersonal, unpredictable and natural process of temporal descent with genetic modification that is affected by natural selection, chance, historical contingencies and changing environments."[165] Predictably, this definition generated objections. In September 1997, University of Notre Dame philosopher of religion Alvin Plantinga and Sycracuse University religious studies scholar Huston Smith, wrote a joint letter to the NABT, arguing that the question of whether evolution is or is not directed by God is a theological one, and therefore not one that empirical sciences such as biology were capable of answering. The NABT Board of Directors took the matter up at its next meeting (on 8 and 11 October 1997), at first refusing to change the language of the definition, but three days later reconsidering and dropping the offending words, "unsupervised" and "impersonal."

Why does this matter? It did not attain the public notice of the trials at Little Rock or Dover. It does, however, show that the mistakes are not all on the side of those whose concerns are primarily religious. Anti-evolutionists

162. Goodstein, "School Board."
163. Davis and Solomon, *World of Biology*, 686.
164. Pagel, "Evolution," 330.
165. National Association of Biology Teachers, "NABT Unveils New Statement." For the larger history, see Religion News Service. "Evolution Statement Altered."

are indeed often (if not generally) improperly dismissive of the empirical evidence scientists work so hard to produce. But evolutionists can sometimes have (to put the point as charitably as possible) a tin ear with respect to the philosophical and theological aspects of what they say. These were not, it is important to note, Beale's "poorly-trained teachers of science, with . . . no adequate training in their subject." This was the leadership of the National Association of Biology Teachers. To their credit, the NABT did finally correct their 1995 statement. The incident should, however, remind us that Andrew Dickson White was simply wrong when he said that "interferences with science in the supposed interests of religion, no matter how conscientious such interferences may have been, have resulted in the direst evils both to religion and to science, and invariably."[166]

Concluding Remarks on the Second Curriculum War

It is a curious fact that as scientists have made progress in understanding the history of life, Christian anti-evolutionism (in both its Creation Science and its Intelligent-Design formulations) has become more comprehensive in its rejection of the scientific consensus on questions of paleoetiology. While the *legislative* efforts of the 1920s at least (in contrast to the broader rhetorical campaign) were limited to keeping *evolutionary anthropogenesis* out of the schools, Intelligent-Design Theorists have broadened their attack to a focus on the evolution (at least by natural selection) of any biological kinds; Creation Scientists also reject evolutionary cosmology and historical geology. Does this Second Curriculum War constitute a war *between science and religion*? Is religion continuing to do harm to science?

In answer to the first question, the loudest voices continue to say yes. Both anti-evolutionist Christians and the New Atheists—Henry Morris and Richard Dawkins, William Dembski and Daniel Dennett—claim that evolutionary biology (science) is inconsistent with the Christian doctrines of creation and providence. Too many journalists and other outsiders echo that view. The Pew Research Center, for example, stated, in a press release written to interpret its polling on the issue, that "since creationism and evolution are incompatible as explanations, some portion of the public [who, polls showed, agreed with both] is clearly confused about the meaning of the terms." The center calls anti-evolutionism "the biblical account of creation,"[167] seeming to force poll respondents to choose between science and the Bible.

166. White, *History*, 1:viii.
167. Pew Research Center, "Reading the Polls."

The Second Curriculum War

To be sure, the Second Curriculum War was a war, though, as in the cases discussed above, more a continuation of two other wars (evolutionist vs. anti-evolutionist and atheist vs. Christian) than a war between science and religion.

First, it was a resumption of the long-running war between evolutionists and die-hard anti-evolutionists after a kind of armistice on the curricular front between about 1930 and the early 1960s. Although by mid-century most anti-evolutionists were motivated by religious beliefs, it is not so clear that this is universally the case. It is, in any case clear that many Christians see in theistic evolution none of the dangers that have so worried anti-evolutionists from Bryan to Morris and Johnson. The Second Curriculum War between evolutionists and anti-evolutionists is, like the previous wars, a war that has found Christians on both sides. The *McLean* plaintiffs, for example, included a Catholic bishop and bishops and ministers from three Protestant denominations; the *Aguillard* plaintiffs included a Catholic priest, a rabbi, and ministers from five different Protestant denominations. A fight over the California curriculum a decade earlier had found both Catholic and Protestant (as well as Jewish and Buddhist) clergy opposing anti-evolutionist attempts to introduce (a fundamentalist version of) creationism into the science classrooms of that state.[168] We should also note that Theodosius Dobzhansky, one of the founders of the "new synthesis" of Darwinian evolutionary theory and Mendelian genetics, in the very essay that evolutionary biologists love for its title, "Nothing in Biology Makes Sense Except in the Light of Evolution," also wrote "I am a creationist *and* an evolutionist."[169] That is surely also the view of Pope John Paul II and of Józef Życiński, scientist-theologian and former archbishop of Lublin.[170]

To be sure, some Christian anti-anti-evolutionists have been theologically liberal. Rev. C. Julian Bartlett, Dean of the Episcopal Church's Grace Cathedral in San Francisco, was reported to have said, "If at any time, *any* theological doctrine should be proven incorrect under the impact of *scientific* knowledge, I shall discard that theological doctrine."[171] One can hear the voice of William Jennings Bryan from beyond the grave reminding us of what he had said already in 1922: "Theistic evolution may be described as an anesthetic which deadens the pain while the patient's religion is being

---

168. See Moore, "Creationism in California." See also McCurdy, "Evolution or Creation?"

169. Dobzhansky, "Nothing in Biology Makes Sense," 127.

170. Pope John Paul II, "Message on Evolution," and Życiński, *God and Evolution*.

171. Quoted in Moore, "Creationism in California," 182.

gradually removed,"[172] but not all Christian anti-anti-evolutionists were (or are) as liberal as Bartlett seems to have been. Is there any way to determine who "speaks for religion" (or even for Christianity) on the question of evolution?

Would it be the largest single denomination? That would be, even in the United States, the Catholic Church, whose doctrinal statements have been compatibilist, as have been those of a number of Protestant denominations. Although some churches have endorsed various forms of anti-evolutionism, others have not. In 1982, the Southern Baptist Convention endorsed the teaching of Creation Science in public schools. In 1972, by contrast, the Christian Reformed Church explicitly declined to prepare a statement on theistic evolution, noting that "while our creeds clearly affirm the creation of all things by God, neither our creeds nor any official synodical decisions have led our churches to an official position, for example, on the length of the days of creation. Within the Reformed churches ... there has long been toleration of certain alternative views of the length of the creation days so long as these positions affirm God's creation and do not conflict with Scripture and confession."[173]

Should we poll individual believers? Gallup and Pew have been polling on this issue for over thirty years, and have found opinions fairly stable. What do they show? A 2011 Fox News Poll conducted by Anderson Robbins Research and Shaw & Company Research yielded the following results:

> 21 percent of respondents thought that "the explanation for the origin of human life on Earth" was more likely to be "the theory of evolution as outlined by Darwin and other scientists;"
>
> 45 percent thought it to be "the Biblical account of creation as told in the Bible;" and
>
> 27 percent thought that both were true.[174]

Researchers at the Pew Research Center suggest that this indicates "some confusion about the meaning of these terms."[175] I am not so certain. Any attempt to interpret these results is complicated by two factors.

---

172. Bryan, *Menace of Darwinism*, 5.

173. Christian Reformed Church in North America, "Report 44," 530.

174. Fox News announced the results in a press release dated 7 September 2011, which I have seen, but which is no longer generally available. A summary of the results is available online from the National Center for Science Education (www.ncse.ngo/). See National Center for Science Education, "New Fox News Poll."

175. Rosentiel et al., "On Darwin's 200th Birthday." Their comment related directly to an earlier Fox News Poll that yielded similar results.

First, the concepts sometimes seem to be confusing to the pollsters themselves. Does "Darwin's theory of evolution" or "the scientific theory of evolution" (both phrases have been used by Pew and Gallup) include the animalist anthropology of *The Descent of Man*? Does it leave room for the idea that all human beings have immaterial souls and that they are *human* beings only once that human soul was created by God, or does it exclude that idea (as some scientists, though certainly not all, claim)?

In a more recent poll, conducted in May 2012, Gallup asked respondents to indicate which of the following views "comes closest to" their views on the origin and development of human beings":

(G1) Human beings have developed over millions of years from less advanced forms of life, but God guided this process.

(G2) Human beings have developed over millions of years from less advanced forms of life, but God had no part in this process.

(G3) God created human beings pretty much in their present form at one time within the last 10,000 years or so.[176]

Among those who might reasonably be classified as religious respondents (those who said they attended church at least monthly), the results were as follows:

31 percent chose G1;
10 percent chose G2; and
55 percent chose G3.

Suppose someone believes, as the Catholic Church teaches, that God *created* the first human soul (and *a fortiori* the first human being). Suppose they also believe, as Pope John Paul II believed, though the Church does not officially teach, that the human *body* evolved and that the first human being was created much earlier than G3 states. How are they to answer? Which Gallup answer is closer to the standard Catholic view (a view that is probably shared by many Protestants)? Is there any way to measure the distance between views? How many who chose G3 might have chosen "God creates the first human being, since God creates human souls, though the human body may have evolved over millions of years"? Gallup did not ask, so we do not know. It is not unreasonable to think that for many people, the idea that human souls are created is important and the date on which He first did so is not. Is that reason enough to choose G3?

Second, respondents seem not to listen very carefully to the exact wording of the questions in any case. For example, in a 2006 poll, Pew asked

176. Newport, "Creationist View."

respondents whether they thought that living things had "evolved over time" or had "existed in their present form since the beginning of time."[177] Surely all Creation Scientists should answer that they think neither since "In the beginning . . . the earth was void and empty" (Gen 1:1–2), but one can hardly doubt that the 42 percent of respondents who answered that the second was their view agree with the Creation Scientists on the origins of species and of man. I do not think (and surely the pollsters do not think) that that means that the wording of the question does not matter. It might mean that polling on this question is impracticable, if not impossible.[178] In any case a more careful formulation of the choices may not help.

Perhaps more relevant to the question of the identity of the belligerents in the Curriculum War is a Pew finding (from 2005) that "35% . . . of those who accept creationist accounts of life's origins nonetheless oppose removing the teaching of evolution in public schools in favor of teaching creationism."[179] In light of the substantial numbers of Christians who accept some form of biological evolution and the even greater numbers who believe that the theory should be included in the school curriculum, one cannot say that religion (or Christianity) itself is one of the belligerents.

The Second Curriculum War is also the continuation of another long-running war, that waged by militant atheists against religion. Darwinism has, from the first years of its existence, been used by some atheists as a weapon against Christian theology, as I have argued at several points above. The fact that a former professor for the public understanding of science at Oxford University focused much of his efforts on the denunciation of religion as "the God delusion," can serve as symbol of this war.[180] Nevertheless, the old adage still holds—*ab abusu ad usum non valet consequentia* (it does not follow from the misuse of the theory that the theory is not true).

The attempt to interpret the Second Curriculum War as part of a larger war of religion against science is to mischaracterize it.

Does this war against the paleoetiological sciences even do the harm to science which is sometimes attributed to it? Many scientists are by now quite

---

177. Pew Research Center, "July 2006 Survey," 9. Also reported in Pew Research Center, "Evolution of Pew Research Center's Survey Questions."

178. The Pew Research Center has acknowledged these difficulties in "The Evolution of Survey Questions."

179. Rosentiel et al., "On Darwin's 200th Birthday.".

180. See Dawkins, *God Delusion*.

frustrated by continued anti-evolutionist resistance to the scientific consensus and are convinced that this opposition, whether religious or not, does constitute a harm to science. On that point they might do well to reread John Stuart Mill's essay *On Liberty*. There he emphasized "the clearer perception and livelier impression of truth, produced by its collision with error":

> Even in natural philosophy . . . it has to be shown why [some] other theory cannot be the true one: and until this is shown, and until we know how it is shown, we do not understand the grounds of our opinion.
>
> [H]owever true [an opinion] may be, if it is not fully, frequently, and fearlessly discussed, it will be held as a dead dogma, not a living truth.[181]

One does not have to endorse Mill's strongly libertarian thesis to acknowledge that some benefit accrues from the continuation of the controversy (even if one sees one side as nothing more than the determined promulgation of error). This was evident even in Dayton, where the Scopes Trial stimulated general public interest in the theory of evolution. The *New York Times* reported mid-trial that some of the libraries in the state experienced such a demand for books on evolution that they had to order additional copies.[182] Even John Washington Butler, author of the law under which Scopes was tried, commented that he was looking forward to having the issue debated at trial.[183] It is evident today. The attacks on evolutionary geology and biology have generated a large popular-science literature devoted precisely to answering these objections to evolution. While this work varies greatly in quality, much of it is very good and contributes to the public's understanding of science.

It should also be acknowledged that Christian anti-evolutionists are not completely mistaken in their concerns. The line of demarcation between the scientific results of evolutionary biology and the philosophical (typically naturalistic if not atheistic) theses with which they are too often associated seems like a line which should not be so very difficult to draw. Nevertheless, not only the New Atheists, but at one point even the NABT, seem unwilling or unable to draw it.

This war between evolutionists and anti-evolutionists does, however, seem to be doing its share of harm to *religion*. St. Augustine long ago warned that:

---

181. Mill, *On Liberty*, 66 and 64.
182. *New York Times*, "Rush for Evolution Books."
183. *New York Times*, "Author of the Law Surprised."

> Usually even a non-Christian knows something about the earth, the heavens, and the other elements of this world . . . and this knowledge he holds to be certain from reason and experience . . . If [non-Christians] find a Christian mistaken in a field that they themselves know well and hear him maintaining foolish opinions about our books, how are they going to believe those books concerning the resurrection of the dead, the hope of eternal life and the kingdom of heaven, when they think that their pages are full of falsehoods on facts which they themselves have learnt from experience and the light of reason?[184]

Andrew Dickson White, to be fair, warned of this danger as well, though his warning is too sweeping in its condemnation. The warning was repeated by Kirtley Mather at Dayton, in a passage quoted above. The warning is still applicable today.

---

184. Augustine, *De Genesi ad Litteram*, I.19.

CHAPTER 7

Conclusion

Pope St. John Paul II once said about the Galileo case:

> From the beginning of the Age of Enlightenment down to our own day, the Galileo case has been a sort of "myth," in which the image fabricated out of the events was quite far removed from reality ... This myth has played a considerable cultural role ... The clarifications furnished by recent historical studies enable us to state that this sad misunderstanding now belongs to the past.[185]

What he said about the Galileo case applies also to the case of Christian reaction to, and reception of, the paleoetiological sciences in general, and evolutionary biology's answer to the question of the origin of species in particular. In the case that has been the subject of this book, the attempt to interpret that encounter through the lens of the Warfare Thesis fails for three reasons.

First, the thesis presupposes that the line between scientific matters and theological matters is fairly clear. In fact, the lines were not clear; they needed to be drawn, and sometimes redrawn in light of new concepts and new knowledge.

Second, the Warfare Thesis suggests that the controversies (whether over substantive matters or over the exact location of lines of demarcation) saw scientists arrayed on one side of the issue and theologians arrayed on the other. The warfare, when that is the correct term at all, was often driven as much by the clash between new ideas and old ideas as it was by any clash

---

185. Pope John Paul II, "Message on Evolution," §10.

between the defenders of scientific ideas and the defenders of theological ones.

Finally, the thesis suggests that what conflict there was was always due to the unreasoning resistance of theologians to new ideas. In fact, irenicists and polemicists, moderates and over-reachers, can be found among evolutionists and among anti-evolutionists, among scientists and among theologians. Aggressors, when the term is appropriate at all, can never be identified with science or theology generally. At most, the aggressors are particular segments of the scientific or theological community.

The Warfare Thesis both oversimplifies and distorts the relations between science and theology on questions of the origins of the world, of biological species, and of man. Nevertheless, it would be folly to deny that there have been, and continue to be, tensions over these issues. If one is not to understand these tensions as the product of "the conflict of two contending powers,"[186] how is one to explain them?

Tension between science and religion generally arise as a result of the necessity of rethinking and adjusting the frontier between the science and theology. The attempt to make some kind of synthesis of what we learn from the scientific method and what we learn from revelation (and from philosophical theology) is natural and proper. Sometimes, however, new scientific ideas require a rethinking of a well-established synthesis. Rethinking is never easy and meets naturally with resistance on the part of those confident in the value of the old synthesis, suspicious of the new, and, often, not much worried about the scientific results that seem to make revision advisable. This is all made particularly difficult by the fact that each of the primary participants in the discussion of whether a new synthesis is necessary and, if so, what it should look like—the scientists and the theologians—will generally have real expertise only in their own field and thus will fail to appreciate the complexities on the other side of the frontier. In addition, there are often differences in (and differences in the assessment of) the risks of being wrong in each direction. Will greater harm be done by false (paleoetiological) scientific theories or by false religious doctrines?

Sometimes, to be sure, the source of the problem is the unreflective conservatism of theologians (or other religious believers) who, as their fellow-believers often point out to them, have mistaken theological opinions about the truths of revelation. This unreflective conservatism has sometimes included intemperate attacks, both rhetorical and political, on science. At other times, however, the source of the problem is rather the aggressive scientism, agnosticism, or atheism of scientists (or of science-enthusiasts)

---

186. Draper, *History*, vi.

who fail to distinguish between the genuine fruit of scientific inquiry and the naturalistic or atheistic philosophy in which they manage to entangle it. This entanglement often leads to scientistic or otherwise uninformed attacks on religious doctrines or even on religion itself.

The use of the Warfare Thesis as a lens through which to view the relation between science and theology or religion invites its adherents to see as confirmations of the thesis incidents that are not that at all. It does not bring the history of science (or the nature of theology or religion) into focus. Indeed it often distorts each of these subjects. One can only hope that it will soon cease to be a theme in popular intellectual culture.

Bibliography

Abington v. Schempp, 374 U.S. 203 (1963).
Abraham, Harry J., and Barbara A. Perry. *Freedom and the Court: Civil Rights and Liberties in the United States.* 6th ed. Oxford: Oxford University Press, 1994.
Acosta, José de. *Historia Natural y Moral de las Indias.* Seville: Léon, 1590. Translation: *Natural and Moral History of the Indies,* by Frances López-Morillas. Edited by Jane E. Mangan, with an introduction and commentary by Walter Mignolo. Chronicles of the New World Order. Durham: Duke University Press, 2002.
Adams, Frank Dawson. *The Birth and Development of the Geological Sciences.* Baltimore: Williams & Wilkins, 1938.
Adger, John B. "A Calm and Candid Review of Some Speeches on Evolution." *Southern Presbyterian Review* 36 (1885) 377–400.
———. *My Life and Times, 1810–1899.* Richmond, VA: Presbyterian Committee of Publications, 1899.
Agassiz, Louis, with Augustus A. Gould. *Principles of Zoology: Touching the Structure, Development, Distribution, and Natural Arrangement of the Races of Animals, Living and Extinct.* New, rev. ed. Boston: Gould & Lincoln, 1873.
Aguillard v. Edwards, 765 F.2d 1251 (5th Cir. 1985). Rehearing *en banc* denied, 778 F.2d 225 (5th Cir. 1985).
Aguillard v. Treen, 634 F. Supp. 426 (E.D. La. 1985).
Albert the Great. *Commentarii in Secundum Sententiarum.* In *Opera omnia,* vol. 15. 21 vols. Lyon: Prost, 1651.
Allen, Frederick Lewis. *Only Yesterday: An Informal History of the Nineteen-Twenties.* New York: Harper, 1931.
American Association for the Advancement of Science. Resolution of 26 December 1922. *Science* N.S. 57 № 1465 (1923) 103–4.
American Civil Liberties Union (ACLU). *The Fight for Civil Liberty, 1930–1931.* New York City: American Civil Liberties Union, 1931.
———. "Here's a Chance for an Arkansas Teacher." *Arkansas Gazette* (11 November 1928) Page 1.
American Civil Liberties Union (ACLU) Committee on Academic Freedom. *The Gag on Teaching.* New York: American Civil Liberties Union, 1931.
Annual of the Southern Baptist Convention, 1925. Nashville: Marshall & Bruce, 1925.
Annual of the Southern Baptist Convention, 1926. Nashville: Marshall & Bruce, 1926.
Anonymous advertisement. "The Bible or Atheism, Which?" *Arkansas Gazette* (4 November 1928) Page 4.

Arduino, Giovanni. "Saggio Fisico-Mineralogico di Lythogonia, e Orognosia." *Atti della Accademia delle Scienze di Siena* 5 (1774) 228–300.

Aristotle. *Meteorologica*. Translation by H. D. P. Lee. Loeb Classical Library 397. Cambridge: Harvard University Press, 2004.

Arkansas Gazette. "Evolution Law Held not Violated." 11 July 1929. Page 11.

———. "The Meaning of the Anti-Evolution Law." 21 November 1928. Page 8.

Arkansas v. Epperson, 242 Ark. 922, 416 S.W.2d 322, reversed.

Arkansas. Initiated Act № 1. In *Acts, Concurrent Resolutions, Memorials, and Proposed Constitutional Amendments of the Forty-Seventh General Assembly of the State of Arkansas* (1929) 2:1518–19.

———. Act 590: Balanced Treatment for Creation-Science and Evolution-Science Act. *General Acts of the Seventy-Third General Assembly of the State of Arkansas (1981)* 2:2:1231–37.

Armogathe, Jean-Robert, and Vincent Carraud. "La Première Condamnation des Œuvres de Descartes, d'après des Documents Inédits aux Archives du Saint-Office." *Nouvelles de la République des Lettres* 2 (2001) 103–37.

Armstrong, Orland Kay. "Bootleg Science in Tennessee." *North American Review* 227/2 (1929) 138–42.

Ashwell, A. R. *Life of the Right Reverend Samuel Wilberforce*. London: Murray, 1880.

Associated Press. "Essex Democrats Stay Lucky." *New York Times* (13 Aug 1985) B4.

———. "Evolutionist Loses Post as College Head." 14 June 1925. *New York Times* (15 June 1925) 15.

———. "Mississippi Voids Evolution Curb." *New York Times* (22 Dec 1970) 13.

Athenaeum: Journal of English and Foreign Literature, Science, and the Fine Arts. "Science: British Association." № 1706 (7 July 1860) 18–32.

———. "Science: British Association." № 1707 (14 July 1860) 59–69.

Augustine. *De Genesi ad Litteram*. Translation: *The Literal Meaning of Genesis*, by John Hammond Taylor. 2 vols. Ancient Christian Writers 41–42. New York: Newman, 1982.

Bailey, Kenneth K. *Southern White Protestantism in the Twentieth Century*. London: Harper & Row, 1964.

Barbour, Ian. *Religion and Science: Historical and Contemporary Issues*. New York: HarperCollins, 1997.

Barr, James. "Why the World Was Created in 4004 BC: Archbishop Ussher and Biblical Chronology." *Bulletin of the John Rylands University Library of Manchester* 67 (1984–85) 575–608.

Barron v. Baltimore, 32 U.S. 243 (1833).

Barthélemy, Charles. "La Religion de Buffon." In *Erreurs et Mensonges Historiques, Sixième Série*, 94–117. Paris: Blériot, 1881.

Bartholomew the Englishman. *De Proprietatibus Rerum*. Partial translation: *Mediaeval Lore from Bartholomew Anglicus*, by Robert Steele. London: De la More, 1905.

Beach, Henry H. "Decadence of Darwinism." In *The Fundamentals: A Testimony to the Truth*, edited by A. C. Dixon et al., 8:36–48. 12 vols. Chicago: Testimony, 1910–15.

Beale, Howard K. *Are American Teachers Free?* New York: Scribner, 1936.

———. *A History of Freedom of Teaching in American Schools*. Report of the Commission on the Social Studies, American Historical Association, pt. 16. New York: Scribner, 1941.

Beaumont, Léonce Élie de. "Recherches sur Quelques-unes des Révolutions de la Surface du Globe." *Annales des Sciences Naturelles* 18 (1829) 5–25 & 284–415 and 19 (1830) 5–99 & 177–240.

———. "Researches on Some of the Revolutions which Have Taken Place on the Surface of the Globe." *Philosophical Magazine and Annals of Philosophy* N.S. 10 (1831) 241–64.

Beck, H. P., et al. "Finding Little Albert: A Journey to John B. Watson's Infant Laboratory." *American Psychologist* 64 (2009) 605–14.

Bede the Venerable. *De Temporibus, sive de Sex Aetatibus Huius Seculi*. Translation: Calvin B. Kendall and Faith Wallace, *Bede: "On the Nature of Things," and "On Times."* Translated Texts for Historians 56. Liverpool: Liverpool University Press, 2010.

Behe, Michael J. *Darwin's Black Box: The Biochemical Challenge to Evolution*. New York: Free Press, 1996.

———. *The Edge of Evolution: The Search for the Limits of Darwinism*. New York: Free Press, 2007.

———. "The Modern Intelligent Design Hypothesis: Breaking Rules." In *God and Design: The Teleological Argument and Modern Science*, edited by Neil A. Manson, 277–91. London: Routledge, 2003.

———. "Reply to My Critics: A Response to Reviews of *Darwin's Black Box: The Biochemical Challenge to Evolution*." *Biology and Philosophy* 16 (2001) 685–709.

Bell, G. K. A. *Randall Davidson, Archbishop of Canterbury*. 2 vols. Oxford: Oxford University Press, 1935.

Benedict XIV, Pope. *De Nova Martyrologii Romani Editione (Postquam Intelleximus)* (1748). In *Benedicti Papae XIV Opera Omnia*, 16:562–94. 17 vols. in 18 bks. Prati: Aldina, 1846.

———. *De Servorum Dei Beatificatione et Beatorum Canonizatione*. Bologna: Longhi, 1734–38.

Berg, Howard C. "The Rotary Motor of Bacterial Flagella." *Annual Review of Biochemistry* 72 (2003) 19–54.

Biological Sciences Curriculum Study. *Biological Science: An Inquiry into Life*. New York: Harcourt, 1963.

Bird, Wendell. "Freedom of Religion and Science Instruction in Public Schools." *Yale Law Journal* 87 (1978) 515–70.

Blount, Charles. *The Oracles of Reason*. London: n.p., 1693.

Bonaventure. *Commentaria in Quattuor Libros Sententiarum*. In *Opera Omnia*, vol. 1–4. Quaracchi: Typographia Collegii S. Bonaventurae, 1882–89.

Bowler, Peter J. *The Non-Darwinian Revolution: Reinterpreting a Historical Myth*. Baltimore: Johns Hopkins University Press, 1988.

Brigham, Albert P. *Textbook of Geology*. New York: Appleton, 1900.

Brooke, John Hedley. *Science and Religion: Some Historical Perspectives*. Cambridge History of Science. Cambridge: Cambridge University Press, 1991.

———. "Science, Religion, and Historical Complexity." In *Recent Themes in the History of Science and Religion: Historians in Conversation*, edited by Donald A. Yerxa, 37–46. Columbia: University of South Carolina Press, 2009.

Brown v. New Jersey, 175 U.S. 172 (1899).

Brown, Andrew James. "A History of the Christian Interpretation of the Days of Creation in Genesis 1:1—2:3: From the Apostolic Fathers to Essays and Reviews (1860)." PhD diss., University of Queensland, 2010.

Brown, Ellen Kuniyuki. "Samuel Palmer Brooks and the Evolution Controversy at Baylor University, 1921–1923." *Texas Baptist History* 1 (1981) 39–47.

Browne, Thomas. *Religio Medici*. London: Crooke, 1642.

Bryan, William Jennings. *The Bible and Its Enemies: An Address Delivered at the Moody Bible Institute of Chicago*. 3rd ed. Chicago: Bible Institute Colportage Association, 1921.

———. "The Fundamentals." *Forum* 70 (1923) 1665–80. Reprinted in *Orthodox Christianity versus Modernism*, 21–28. New York: Revell, 1923.

———. "God and Evolution." *New York Times* (26 February 1922) Pages 1 and 10.

———. *In His Image*. New York: Revell, 1922.

———. *The Menace of Darwinism*. New York: Revell, 1922.

———. *Orthodox Christianity versus Modernism*. New York: Revell, 1923.

———. *The Prince of Peace*. New York: Revell, n.d.

———. "Science vs. Evolution:" Abstract of an Address delivered at Charleston, West Virginia, before the State Legislature, April 13, 1923. In *Orthodox Christianity versus Modernism*, 29–48. New York: Revell, 1923.

———. William Jennings Bryan Papers. Manuscript Division, Library of Congress, Washington, DC.

Bryan, William Jennings, and Mary Baird Bryan. *The Memoirs of William Jennings Bryan*. Chicago: Winston, 1925.

Buck v. Bell, 274 U.S. 200 (1927).

Buckland, William. "Description of the Quartz Rock of the Lickey Hill in Worcestershire . . . : With Considerations on the Evidences of a Recent Deluge Afforded by the Gravel Beds of Warwickshire and Oxfordshire . . ." *Transactions of the Geological Society of London* 5 (1821) 506–44.

———. *Vindiciae Geologicae, or the Connexion of Geology with Religion Explained*. Oxford: Oxford University Press, 1820.

Buffon, Georges-Louis Leclerc, Comte de. *Époques de la Nature*. Paris: Imprimerie Royale, 1778. Translation: Jan Zalasiewicz et al., *Epochs of Nature*. Chicago: University of Chicago Press, 2018.

———. *Histoire Naturelle: Générale et Particulière*. Paris: Imprimerie Royale, 1749–1788. 29 vols. Partial translation in *From Natural History to the History of Nature: Readings from Buffon and His Critics*, edited by John Lyon and Phillip R. Sloan, 89–209. Notre Dame, IN: University of Notre Dame Press, 1981.

———. Letter to Abbé Jean-Baptiste Corgne de Launay, 4 June 1773. *Revue d'Histoire Littéraire de la France*. 42/1 (1935) 150.

———. *Théorie de la Terre*. Paris: Imprimerie Royale, 1749.

Bulmer, Michael. "Did Jenkin's Swamping Argument Invalidate Darwin's Theory of Natural Selection?" *British Journal for the History of Science* 37/3 (2004) 281–97.

Bultmann, Christoph. "Early Rationalism and Biblical Criticism on the Continent." In *Hebrew Bible, Old Testament: The History of Its Interpretation*. Vol. 2, *From the*

Renaissance to the Enlightenment, edited by Magne Sæbø, 875-901. Göttingen: Vandenhoeck & Ruprecht, 2008.

Burnet, Thomas. *Archeologia Philosophica sive Doctrina Antiqua de Rerum Originibus.* London: Kettilby, 1692.

———. "Review of the Theory of the Earth and of Its Proofs." In *The Sacred Theory of the Earth*, 380-412. 2nd ed. London: Kettilby, 1691.

———. *The Sacred Theory of the Earth*, 3rd ed. London: Kettilby, 1697.

Burstyn v. Wilson, 343 U. S. 495 (1950).

C., J. G. "Darwinism." *The Irish Ecclesiastical Record* N.S. 9 (1873) 337-61.

Cajetan, Tommaso de Vio. *In Pentateuchum Mosis iuxta Sensum quem Dicunt Literalem Commentarii.* Rome: Asulanus, 1531.

Calmet, Augustin, OSB. *Commentaire Littéral sur tous les Livres de l'Ancien et du Nouveau Testament.* Paris: Emery, 1726.

Calvin, Jean. *In Primum Mosis Librum, qui Genesis Vulgo Dicitur.* Geneva: Stephanus, 1554. Translation: *Commentaries on the First Book of Moses Called Genesis*, by John King. Grand Rapids: Eerdmans, 1948.

Chadwick, Owen. *The Victorian Church.* 2 vols. New York: Oxford University Press, 1966-70.

Chambers, Robert. *Vestiges of the Natural History of Creation.* London: Churchill, 1844.

Chattanooga Daily Times. "Plan Assault on State Law on Evolution." 4 May 1925. Page 5.

Chil y Naranjo, Gregorio. *Estudios Históricos, Climatológicos y Patológicos de las Islas Canarias.* Las Palmas, Spain: Miranda, 1876-91.

Christian Advocate. "Literary." 24/31 (22 May 1878) 1.

Christian Century. "Interpreting the Arkansas Anti-Evolution Law." 46/37 (1929) 1109.

Christian Reformed Church in North America. "Report 44: The Nature and Extent of Biblical Authority." In *Acts of Synod 1972.* Grand Rapids: Board of Publications of the Christian Reformed Church, 1972.

Clement of Alexandria. *Stromata, or Miscellanies of Notes of Revealed Knowledge in accordance with the True Philosophy.* Translation by William Wilson. *The Ante-Nicene Fathers*, edited by Alexander Roberts et al., 2:299-556. 10 vols. Buffalo: Christian Literature, 1885.

Cobb County (Georgia) School District. "Agreement Ends Textbook Sticker Case." Press Release, 19 December 2006.

Cosmas Indicopleustes. *Christianikē Topographia.* In *Patrologia Graeca*, edited by J.-P. Migne, 88:51-476. 161 vols. Paris: Migne, 1864.

Coyne, Jerry A. *Why Evolution Is True.* New York: Penguin, 2010.

Crowley v. Smithsonian Institution, 636 F.2d 738 (D.C. Cir. 1980).

Curtis, Christopher K. "Mississippi's Anti-Evolution Law of 1926." *Journal of Mississippi History* 48/1 (1986) 15-29.

Dabney, Robert Lewis. *A Caution against Anti-Christian Science.* Richmond, VA: Goode, 1871.

———. "The *Caution against Anti-Christian Science* Criticised by Dr. Woodrow." *Southern Presbyterian Review* 24/4 (1873) 539-86.

———. *Discussions: Evangelical and Theological.* Richmond, VA: Presbyterian Committee of Publication, 1890-1892.

———. "Geology and the Bible." *Southern Presbyterian Review* 14/2 (1861) 246-75.

Dana, James Dwight. *A Text-book of Geology.* New York: Ivison, 1863.

———. *Text-book of Geology*. 2nd ed. New York: Ivison, 1874.

Daniel v. Waters, 515 F.2d 485 (6th Cir. 1975).

Darrow, Clarence. *The Story of My Life*. New York: Scribner, 1932.

Darwin, Charles. *The Autobiography of Charles Darwin 1809–1882*. With original omissions restored. Edited by Nora Barlow. London: Collins, 1958.

———. Letter to John Fordyce, 7 May 1879. Darwin Correspondence Project, № DCP-LETT-12041. https://www.darwinproject.ac.uk/.

———. Letter to Joseph Hooker, July 1860. In *The Life and Letters of Charles Darwin*, edited by Francis Darwin, 2:324–325. 3 vols. London: Murray, 1887.

———. Letter to Thomas H. Huxley, 22 May 1861. In *The Correspondence of Charles Darwin*, edited by Frederick Burkhardt et al., 9:134 and 426. Cambridge: Cambridge University Press, 1994.

———. *On the Origin of Species by Means of Natural Selection, or The Preservation of Favoured Races in the Struggle for Life*. 1st ed. London: Murray, 1859. (Unless otherwise noted, all citations are to this edition.)

———. *On the Origin of Species by Means of Natural Selection, or The Preservation of Favoured Races in the Struggle for Life*. 3rd ed. London: Murray, 1861.

Darwin, Charles, and Alfred Russel Wallace. "Three Papers on the Tendency of Species to Form Varieties; and On the Perpetuation of Varieties and Species by Natural Means of Selection." *Zoologist* 16 (1858) 6293–308.

Darwin, Francis, ed. *Charles Darwin: His Life Told in an Autobiographical Chapter, and in a Selected Series of His Published Letters*. London: Murray, 1892.

———, ed. *The Life and Letters of Charles Darwin*. 3 vols. London: Murray, 1887.

Daubeny, Charles. "On the Final Causes of the Sexuality of Plants, with particular Reference to Mr. Darwin's Work 'On the Origin of Species by Natural Selection.'" In "Notices and Abstracts of Miscellaneous Communications to the Sections," published as the final part of *Report of the British Association for the Advancement of Science: 30th Meeting (1861)*, 109–10. London: Murray, 1861.

Davis, Percival William, and Eldra Pearl Solomon. *The World of Biology*. 3rd ed. Philadelphia: Saunders 1985.

Davis, Percival William, et al. *Pandas and People: The Central Question of Biological Origins*. Dallas: Haughton, 1989.

Dawkins, Richard. *The Blind Watchmaker: Why the Evidence of Evolution Reveals a Universe without Design*. New York: Norton, 1996.

———. *The God Delusion*. Boston: Houghton Mifflin, 2006.

Dawson, John William. *Archaia, or Studies of the Cosmogony and Natural History of the Hebrew Scriptures*. Montreal: Dawson, 1860.

De Camp, L. Sprague. *The Great Monkey Trial*. Garden City, NY: Doubleday, 1968.

De Ford, Miriam Allen. "After Dayton: A Fundamentalist Survey." *The Nation* 122 (1926) 604.

Dean, Dennis R. "The Age of the Earth Controversy: Beginnings to Hutton." *Annals of Science* 38 (1981) 425–56.

"Declaration of Students of the Natural and Physical Sciences." London: Simpkins, Marshall, 1865.

Dembski, William A. *The Design Inference: Eliminating Chance through Small Probabilities*. Cambridge: Cambridge University Press, 1998.

———. *Intelligent Design: The Bridge between Science & Theology*. Downers Grove: InterVarsity, 1999.

Dembski, William A., and Jonathan Will, *Intelligent Design Uncensored: An Easy-to-Understand Guide to the Controversy*. Downers Grove: IVP Books, 2010

De Morgan, Augustus. "Sir John Herschel and the New Test." *Saturday Review of Politics, Religion, Science and Art* 18 (1864) 386–87.

Dennett, Daniel C. *Darwin's Dangerous Idea: Evolution and the Meanings of Life*. New York: Simon & Schuster, 1995.

Denton, Michael. *Evolution: A Theory in Crisis: New Developments in Science Are Challenging Orthodox Darwinism*. Bethesda, MD: Adler & Adler, 1986.

Descartes, René. *Discours de la Méthode Pour Bien Conduire sa Raison, et Chercher la Vérité dans les Sciences*. Translation as *Discourse on the Method of Rightly Conducting the Reason*. In *The Philosophical Works of Descartes*, edited by Elizabeth S. Haldane and G. R. T. Ross, 79–130. 2 vols. Cambridge: Cambridge University Press, 1974.

———. *Principia philosophiae*. Translation: *Principles of Philosophy*, with explanatory notes, by Valentine Rodger Miller and Reese P. Miller. Synthese Historical Library 24. Dordrecht: Reidel, 1983.

Diderot, Denis. "Révolutions de la Terre." In *Encyclopédie, ou Dictionnaire Raisonné des Sciences, des Arts et des Métiers, etc.*, edited by Denis Diderot and Jean le Rond d'Alembert, 14:237–38. 28 vols. Neuchâtel: Faulche, 1765.

Dixon, A. C., et al., eds. *The Fundamentals: A Testimony to the Truth*. 12 vols. Chicago: Testimony, 1910–15.

Dobzhansky, Theodosius. "Nothing in Biology Makes Sense Except in the Light of Evolution." *American Biology Teacher* 35 (1973) 125–29.

Dopp, Katharine Elizabeth. *The Tree Dwellers*. Industrial and Social History Series. Chicago: Rand McNally, 1904.

Dow, Peter B. *Man: A Course of Study*. Vol. 1, *Talks to Teachers*. 9 vols. Washington, DC: Curriculum Development Associates, 1970.

Dowell, Spright. *A History of Mercer University, 1833–1953*. Macon, GA: Mercer University Press, 1958.

———. "Vital Information in the Fox Case." *Christian Index*, 16 October 1924, 26–28.

Draper, John William. *History of the Conflict between Religion and Science*. New York: Appleton, 1875.

———. *History of the Intellectual Development of Europe*. London: Bell, 1864.

———. "On the Intellectual Development of Europe, Considered with Reference to the Views of Mr. Darwin and Others, that the Progression of Organisms Is Determined by Law." Abstracted in "Notices and Abstracts of Miscellaneous Communications to the Sections," published as the final part of *Report of the British Association for the Advancement of Science: 30th Meeting (1861)*, 115–16. London: Murray, 1861.

Duhem, Pierre. "Léonard de Vinci, Cardan, et Bernard Palissy." In *Études sur Léonard de Vinci*, 1:223–53. 3 vols. Paris: Hermann, 1906–13.

———. "Léonard de Vinci et les Origines de la Géologie." In *Études sur Léonard de Vinci*, 1:281–357. 3 vols. Paris: Hermann, 1906–13.

———. "The Physics of a Believer." Translation: *The Aim and Structure of Physical Theory*, by Philip P. Wiener, 273–311. Princeton: Princeton University Press, 1991.

Edwards v. Aguillard, 482 U. S. 578 (1987).

Ellis, William E. *"A Man of Books and a Man of the People": E. Y. Mullins and the Crisis of Moderate Southern Baptist Leadership*. Macon, GA: Mercer University Press, 1985.

Engel v. Vitale, 370 U.S. 421 (1962).

Epperson v. Arkansas, 393 U. S. 97 (1968).

Eusebius of Caesarea. *Chronicon*. Translation: *Die Chronik des Eusebius aus dem Armenischen übersetzt mit textkritischen Kommentar*, by Josef Karst. Werke 5. Leipzig: Hinrich, 1911.

Everson v. Board of Education, 330 U.S. 1 (1947).

Fabre d'Envieu, Jules. *Les Origines de la Terre et de l'Homme*. Paris: Thorin, 1873.

Farag, Nadia. "The Lewis Affair and the Fortunes of al-Muqtataf." *Middle Eastern Studies* 8/1 (1972) 73–83.

Farr, A. D. "Early Opposition to Obstetric Anaesthesia." *Anaesthesia* 35/9 (1980) 896–907.

———. "Religious Opposition to Obstetric Anaesthesia: A Myth?" *Annals of Science* 40/2 (1983) 159–77.

Faventius, Valerius. *De Montium Origine*. Venice: Academia Veneta, 1561. Partial translation in Frank Dawson Adams, *The Birth and Development of the Geological Sciences*, 348–57. Baltimore: Williams & Wilkins, 1938.

Fawcett, Henry. "A Popular Exposition of Mr. Darwin on the Origin of Species." *Macmillan's Magazine* 3/14 (1860) 81–92.

Fellows, Otis E., and Stephen F. Milliken. *Buffon*. Twayne's World Authors Series 245. France. New York: Twayne, 1972.

Finegan, Jack. *Handbook of Biblical Chronology: Principles of Time Reckoning in the Ancient World and Problems of Chronology in the Bible*. Princeton: Princeton University Press, 1964.

Finnis, John. *Natural Law and Natural Rights*. Clarendon Law Series. Oxford: Oxford University Press, 1980.

Fiske v. Kansas, 274 U.S. 380 (1927).

Florida House of Representatives. House Concurrent Resolution № 7. In *General Acts and Resolutions Adopted by the Legislature of Florida at its Nineteenth Regular Session, April 3rd to June 1st, 1923*, 1:506–7.

Flower, William Henry. *Introductory Lecture to the Course of Comparative Anatomy Delivered at the Royal College of Surgeons of England, February 14, 1870*. London: Churchill, 1870.

Forrest, Barbara. "My Role in *Kitzmiller et al. v. Dover Area School District*." *Reports of the National Center for Science Education* 26/1–2 (2006) 47–48.

Fortune, Alonzo W. "The Kentucky Campaign against the Teaching of Evolution." *Journal of Religion* 2/3 (1922) 225–35.

Fosdick, Harry Emerson. "The Church Must Go beyond Modernism." *Church Monthly* 10/3 (1936) 43–48 and 55. Republished in *The Riverside Preachers: Fosdick, McCracken, Campbell, Coffin*, edited by Paul H. Sherry, 39–48. New York: Pilgrim, 1978.

———. "Shall the Fundamentalists Win?" *Christian Work* 102 (1922) 716–22. Republished in *The Riverside Preachers: Fosdick, McCracken, Campbell, Coffin*, edited by Paul H. Sherry, 27–38. New York: Pilgrim, 1978.

Frankenberry, Nancy, ed. *The Faith of Scientists in Their Own Words*. Princeton: Princeton University Press, 2008.

Fraser, A. M. "Evolution." In *Dr. James Woodrow as Seen by His Friends*, edited by Marion Woodrow, 41–46. Columbia, SC: Bryan, 1909.

Freiler v. Tangipahoa Parish Board of Education, 185 F.3d 337 (5th Cir. 1999). Petition for rehearing *en banc* denied, 201 F.3d 602 (5th Cir. 2000).

Freiler v. Tangipahoa Parish Board of Education, 975 F.Supp. 819 (E.D. La. 1997).
Garner, James W., et al. "Report on the University of Tennessee." *Bulletin of the American Association of University Professors* 10/4 (1924) 213–60.
Gaskin, J. M. "Baptist Messenger." In *Encyclopedia of Southern Baptists*, 1:117–18. 4 vols. Nashville: Broadman, 1958.
Gatewood, Willard B., Jr. *Controversy in the Twenties: Fundamentalism, Modernism, and Evolution*. Nashville: Vanderbilt University Press, 1969.
———. "The Evolution Controversy in North Carolina, 1920–1927." *Mississippi Quarterly* 17 (1964) 192–207.
Generelli, Giuseppe Cirillo. "De' Crostacei e dell'Altre Produzioni Marine, che sono ne' Monti." *Raccolta Milanese dell'Anno 1757*. Milan: Agnelli, 1757.
"Gesetz zur Verhütung erbkranken Nachwuchses." *Reichsgesetzblatt* 86 (1933) 529–31.
Gesner, Konrad. *Historiae Animalium*. 5 vols. in 4 bks. Zürich: Froschauer, 1551.
Gilkey, Langdon. *Creationism on Trial: Evolution and God at Little Rock*. Minneapolis: Winston, 1985.
Giraudet, Alexandre-Aimé. *Nouveau Traité de Géologie, ou Exposé de l'État Actuel de cette Science*. Tours: Mame, 1843.
Gish, Duane T. *Evolution: The Fossils Say No!* San Diego: Creation-Life Publishers, 1978.
———. Letter to the Editor. *Discover* 2/7 (1981) 6.
Gitlow v. New York, 268 U.S. 652 (1925).
Glick, Thomas F. "Spain." In *The Comparative Reception of Darwinism*, edited by Thomas F. Glick, 307–45. Chicago: University of Chicago Press, 1988.
Goldschmidt, Richard. *The Material Basis of Evolution*. Yale University Mrs. Hepsa Ely Silliman Memorial Lectures. New Haven: Yale University Press, 1940.
Goodstein, Laurie. "School Board: Evolution Slate Outpolls Rivals." *New York Times*, 9 Nov 2005, A24.
"Gorilla" (probably Sir Phillip de Malpas Grey-Egerton). "Monkeyana." *Punch* 40 (1861) 206.
Gottlieb, Sheldon F. Letter to the Editor included in the editors' "Denying Darwin: David Berlinski and Critics," 13–14. *Commentary* 102/3 (1996) 4–39.
Gould, Stephen Jay. "Fall in the House of Ussher." In *Eight Little Piggies: Reflections in Natural History*, 181–93. New York: Norton, 1993.
———. "Non-overlapping Magisteria." In *Leonardo's Mountain of Clams and the Diet of Worms: Essays on Natural History*, 269–83. New York: Harmony, 1998.
———. "The Return of Hopeful Monsters." In *The Panda's Thumb: More Reflections on Natural History*, 186–93. New York: Norton, 1980.
———. *Rocks of Ages: Science and Religion in the Fullness of Life*. The Library of Contemporary Thought. New York: Ballantine, 1999.
———. *Time's Arrow, Time's Cycle: Myth and Metaphor in the Discovery of Geological Time*. The Jerusalem-Harvard Lectures. Cambridge: Harvard University Press, 1988.
———. "The Titular Bishop of Titiopolis." In *Hen's Teeth and Horse's Toes*, 69–78. New York: Norton, 1994.
———. "The Upwardly Mobile Fossils of Leonardo's Living Earth." In *Leonardo's Mountain of Clams and the Diet of Worms: Essays on Natural History*, 17–44. New York: Harmony, 1998.
Grabiner, Judith V., and Peter D. Miller. "Effects of the Scopes Trial." *Science* N.S. 185/4154 (1974) 832–37.

Gray, Asa. *Elements of Botany for Beginners and for Schools*. New York: American Book Company, 1887.

Grayson, Donald K. *The Establishment of Human Antiquity*. New York: Academic Press, 1983.

Greetham, D. C. "The Concept of Nature in Bartholomaeus Anglicus." *Journal of the History of Ideas* 41/4 (1980) 663–77.

Gross, C. G. "Huxley versus Owen: The *Hippocampus minor* and Evolution." *Trends in Neurosciences* 16/12 (1993) 493–98.

Gross, Liza. "Scientific Illiteracy and the Partisan Takeover of Biology." *PLoS Biology* 4/5.e167 (2006) 680–83.

Gustafson, Robert K. *James Woodrow (1828–1907): Scientist, Theologian, Intellectual Leader*. Studies in American Religion 61. Lewiston, NY: Mellen, 1995.

Guyot, Arnold. *Creation; or, The Biblical Cosmology in the Light of Modern Science*. New York: Scribner, 1884.

Haeckel, Ernst. "Über die Naturanschauung von Darwin, Göthe, und Lamarck." *Tageblatt der 55. Versammlung Deutscher Naturforscher und Ärzte* (1882) 81–91.

Haldeman-Julius, Marcet. *Clarence Darrow's Two Great Trials: Reports of the Scopes Anti-Evolution Case and the Dr. Sweet Negro Trial*. Big Blue Book B-29. Girard, KS: Haldeman-Julius, 1927.

Hale, Matthew. *The Primitive Origination of Mankind Considered and Examined according to the Light of Nature*. London: Shrowsbery, 1677.

Haller, Albrecht von. *Vorrede über des Herrn von Buffon Lehre der Erzeugung* (1752). In *Sammlung Kleiner Hallerischer Schriften*, 91–131. Bern: Haller, 1756.

Halliburton, Rudia, Jr. "The Adoption of the Arkansas Anti-Evolution Law." *Arkansas Historical Quarterly* 23/3 (1964) 271–83.

———. "Attempts to Pass a Second Anti-Evolution Law in Oklahoma." *Proceedings of the Oklahoma Academy of Sciences for 1960* 40 (1960) 138–48.

———. "Kentucky's Anti-Evolution Controversy." *Register of the Kentucky Historical Society* 66 (1968) 97–107.

———. "The Nation's First Anti-Darwin Law: Passage and Repeal." *Southwestern Social Science Quarterly* 41/2 (1960) 123–34.

Hamilton v. Regents of the University of California, 293 U.S. 245 (1934).

Hansen, Thorvald. "Carl Peter Hoiberg." Danish Immigrant Archive. Des Moines: Grand View University Library.

Harman, Gilbert. "The Inference to the Best Explanation." *Philosophical Review* 74 (1965) 88–95.

Harrison, Peter. "The Development of the Concept of Laws of Nature." In *Creation: Law and Probability*, edited by Fraser Watts, 13–36. Theology and the Sciences. Minneapolis: Fortress, 2008.

Hart, Ariel. "Judge in Georgia Orders Anti-Evolution Stickers Removed from Textbooks." *New York Times*, 14 Jan 2005, A16.

Hays, Arthur Garfield. *City Lawyer: The Autobiography of a Law Practice*. New York: Simon & Schuster, 1942.

———. *Let Freedom Ring*. New York: Boni & Liveright, 1928.

———. "The Strategy of the Scopes Defense." *The Nation* 121/3135 (1925) 157–58.

Hebard, Roger D. "Stealey Controversy, Oklahoma." In *The Encyclopedia of Southern Baptists*, edited by Norman Wade Cox, 2:1297–98. 4 vols. Nashville: Broadman, 1958.

Herbert, Sandra. "Between Genesis and Geology: Darwin and Some Contemporaries in the 1820s and 1830s." In *Religion and Irreligion in Victorian Society: Essays in Honor of R. K. Webb*, edited by Richard W. Davis, 68–84. London: Routledge, 1992.

Herschel, John. *Preliminary Discourse on the Study of Natural Philosophy*. Cabinet Cyclopaedia. Natural Philosophy. London: Longman, 1831.

Herschel, William. "Catalogue of 500 New Nebulae, Nebulous Stars, Planetary Nebulae, and Clusters of Stars. With Remarks on the Construction of the Heavens." *Philosophical Transactions of the Royal Society of London* 92 (1802) 477–528.

Hooke, Robert. "Discourse on Earthquakes." In *The Posthumous Works of Robert Hooke*, 277–450. London: Smith & Walford, 1705.

Hooker, Joseph. Letter to Charles Darwin, 2 July 1860. In *Life and Letters of Sir Joseph Dalton Hooker*, edited by Leonard Huxley, 526. London: Murray, 1918.

Hunter, George William. *Civic Biology*. New York: American Book Company, 1914.

———. *A Civic Biology: Presented in Problems*. New York: American Book Company, 1914.

Hutton, James. *The Theory of the Earth*. 2 vols. Edinburgh: Creech, 1795.

Huxley, Thomas H. *Evidence as to Man's Place in Nature*. New York: Appleton, 1863.

———. Letter to Francis Darwin, 27 June 1861. In *Charles Darwin: His Life Told in an Autobiographical Chapter, and in a Selected Series of His Published Letters*, 240. London: Murray, 1892.

———. Letter to Frederick Daniel Dyster, 30 January 1859. In Huxley Papers, Imperial College, London, Control № 15.106.

———. "On the Reception of the 'Origin of Species.'" In Francis Darwin, ed. *The Life and Letters of Charles Darwin, including an Autobiographical Chapter*, 2:179–204. 3 vols. London: Murray, 1887.

———. Review of *The Origin of Species*. *Westminster Review* 17 (1860) 541–70.

———. Review of *The Vestiges of the Natural History of Creation*. *British and Foreign Medico-Chirurgical Review* 13/26 (1854) 425–39. Reprinted in *The Scientific Memoirs of Thomas Henry Huxley*, edited by Michael Foster and E. R. Lankester, 5:1–19. London: Macmillan, 1903.

Isidore of Seville. *Etymologiae*. In *Patrologia Latina*, edited by J.-P. Migne, 82:9–728. Paris: Migne, 1850. Translation: Stephen A. Barney, *The Etymologies of Isidore of Seville*. Cambridge: Cambridge University Press, 2006.

James, Frank A. J. L. "An 'Open Clash between Science and the Church'? Wilberforce, Huxley and Hooker on Darwin at the British Association, Oxford, 1860." In *Science and Beliefs: From Natural Philosophy to Natural Selection, 1700–1900*, edited by David M. Knight and Matthew Eddy, 171–93. Burlington, VT: Ashgate, 2005.

Jefferson, Thomas. Letter to Messrs. Nehemiah Dodge and Others, a Committee of the Danbury Baptist Association in the State of Connecticut, 1 January 1802 Reprinted in *Writings*, edited by Merrill D. Peterson, 510. Library of America 17. New York: Library of America, 1984.

Jeha, Shafik. *Darwin and the Crisis of 1882 in the Medical Department*. Translated by Sally Kaya. Beirut: American University of Beirut Press, 2004.

Jenkin, Fleeming. Review of *The Origin of Species*. *The North British Review* 46 (1867) 227–318. Reprinted in *Darwin and His Critics*, compiled by David L. Hull, 302–44. Cambridge: Harvard University Press, 1973.

John Paul II, Pope. "Ad Pontificiae Academicae Scientiarum Solidares." *Acta Apostolicae Sedis* 89 (1997) 186–90. Translation: "Revised Translation of Pope's Message on

Evolution to the Pontifical Academy of Sciences" in *Origins: CNS [Catholic News Service] Documentary Service* 26/25 (1996) 414–16.

Johnson, Phillip E. *Darwin on Trial*. Washington, DC: Regnery Gateway, 1991.

———. "Evolution as Dogma: The Establishment of Naturalism." *First Things* 6 (October 1990) 15–22.

Jones, James H. *Bad Blood: The Tuskegee Syphilis Experiment*. New York: Free Press, 1981.

Julius Africanus, Sextus. *Chronographiae*. Translation by Frederick Crombie. "The Extant Fragments of the Five Books of the Chronography of Julius Africanus." In *The Ante-Nicene Fathers*, edited by Alexander Roberts et al., 6:130–38. 10 vols. Buffalo: Christian Literature, 1886.

Kant, Immanuel. *Allgemeine Naturgeschichte und Theorie des Himmels*. Königsberg: Petersen, 1755. Translation: Stanley L. Jaki, *Universal Natural History and Theory of the Heavens*. Edinburgh: Scottish Academic Press, 1981.

Kellogg, Vernon L. *Darwinism To-day*. New York: Holt, 1908.

———. *Headquarters Nights: A Record of Conversations and Experiences at the Headquarters of the German Army in France and Belgium*. Boston: Atlantic Monthly Press, 1917.

———. "War and Human Evolution: Germanized." *North American Review* 207/748 (1918) 364–69.

Kemp, Kenneth W. "Scientific Method and Appeal to Supernatural Agency: A Christian Case for Modest Methodological Naturalism." *Logos* 3/2 (2000) 165–205.

Kenyon, Dean H., and Gary Steinman. *Biochemical Predestination*. New York: McGraw Hill, 1969.

Kevles, Daniel J. *In the Name of Eugenics: Genetics and the Uses of Human Heredity*. New York: Knopf, 1985.

Kidd, Benjamin. *The Science of Power*. London: Methuen, 1918.

Kidd, John. *Geological Essay on the Imperfect Evidence in Support of a Theory of the Earth*. Oxford: Oxford University Press, 1815.

———. *On the Adaptation of External Nature to the Physical Condition of Man*. 2nd ed. London: Pickering, 1833.

Kirwan, Richard. *Geological Essays*. London: Bremner, 1799.

Kitzmiller v. Dover Area School District, 400 F. Supp. 2nd 707 (M.D. Pa. 2005).

Korn, James H. *Illusions of Reality: A History of Deception in Social Psychology*. New York: State University of New York Press, 1997.

Kottler, Malcolm Jay. "Alfred Russel Wallace, the Origin of Man, and Spiritualism." *Isis* 65/2 (1974) 144–92.

Kramer, Stanley, dir. *Inherit the Wind*. Written by Nedrick Young et al. Los Angeles: United Artists, 1960.

Krutch, Joseph Wood. "The Monkey Trial." *Commentary* 43/5 (May 1967) 83–84.

La Peyrère, Isaac. *Pre-Adamitae*. Leiden: Elsevier, 1655.

Laba, Estelle R., and Eugene W. Gross. "Evolution Slighted in High-School Biology." *Clearing House* 24/7 (1950) 396–99.

Lacey, Alan. "Naturalism." In *The Oxford Companion to Philosophy*, edited by Ted Honderich, 604–6. Oxford: Oxford University Press, 1995.

Ladouceur, Ronald P. "Ella Thea Smith and the Lost History of American High School Biology Textbooks." *Journal of the History of Biology* 41/3 (2008) 435–71.

Lamarck, Jean Baptiste Pierre Antoine de Monet de. *Philosophie Zoologique, ou, Exposition, des Considérations Relatives à l'Histoire Naturelle des Animaux*. Paris: Dentu, 1809.

Lamb's Chapel v. Center Moriches School District, 508 U.S. 384.

Langford, Jerome J. *Galileo, Science, and the Church*. Ann Arbor: University of Michigan Press, 1971.

Lapide, Cornelius Cornelii a. *Commentaria in Pentateuchum Mosis*. Antwerp: Nutius and Meurisus, 1616.

Laplace, Pierre Simon de. *Exposition du Système du Monde*. 2 vols. Paris: Cercle-Social, 1796.

Larson, Edward J. *Summer for the Gods: The Scopes Trial and America's Continuing Debate over Science and Religion*. New York: Basic Books, 1997.

―――. *Trial and Error: The American Controversy over Evolution and Creation*. New York: Oxford University Press, 1989.

Lateran IV. *Constitutio de Fide Catholica*. 1215. Republished and translated in *Enchiridion Symbolorum Definitionum et Declarationum de Rebus Fidei et Morum*, 43rd ed., originally edited by Heinrich Denzinger, Dz 800–802. San Francisco: Ignatius, 2012.

Laughlin, Harry H. "Model Eugenical Sterilization Law." In *Eugenical Sterilization in the United States*, 446–51. Chicago: Psychopathic Laboratory of the Municipal Court of Chicago, 1922.

Lawrence, Jerome, and Robert E. Lee. *Inherit the Wind*. New York: Shumlin, 1955.

Lawrence, Philip. "Heaven and Earth—The Relation of the Nebular Hypothesis to Geology." In *Cosmology, History, and Theology*, edited by Wolfgang Yourgrau and Allen D. Breck, 253–82. New York: Plenum, 1977.

Le Conte, Joseph. *A Compend of Geology*. Appleton's Science Text-books. New York: Appleton, 1884.

―――. *Evolution and Its Relation to Religious Thought*. London: Chapman & Hall, 1888. Revised as *Evolution: Its Nature, Its Evidences, and Its Relation to Religious Thought*. Selected Library of Modern Science, Westminster edition. New York: Appleton, 1891.

―――. *Religion and Science: A Series of Sunday Lectures on the Relation of Natural and Revealed Religion, or The Truths Revealed in Nature and Scripture*. Christian Life Series 4. London: Ward, Lock, & Tyler, 1865.

Leavitt, Donald M. "Darwinism in the Arab World: The Lewis Affair at the Syrian Protestant College." *Muslim World* 71/2 (1981) 85–98.

Ledbetter, Cal, Jr., "The Antievolution Law: Church and State in Arkansas." *Arkansas Historical Quarterly* 38 (1979) 299–328.

Leeper v. State, 103 Tenn. 500 (1899).

Lemaître, Georges. *L'Hypothèse de l'Atome Primitif: Essai de Cosmogonie*. Neuchatel: Griffon, 1946. Translation: *The Primeval Atom: An Essay on Cosmogony*, by Betty H. and Serge A. Korff. New York: Van Nostrand, 1950.

Lemon v. Kurtzman, 403 U.S. 602 (1971).

Leo XIII, Pope. *Providentissimus Deus*. Acta Sanctae Sedis 26 (1893–1894) 269–92. Translation: *On the Study of Sacred Scripture*, by the National Catholic Welfare Conference. Boston: St. Paul Books and Media, 1992.

Leslie, John. "How to Draw Conclusions from a Fine-Tuned Cosmos." In *Physics, Philosophy and Theology: A Common Quest for Understanding*, edited by Robert Russell et al., 297–312. Vatican City: Vatican Observatory, 1988.
Leuba, James H. *Belief in God and Immortality: A Psychological, Anthropological and Statistical Study*. 1st ed. Boston: Sherman, French, 1916.
———. *Belief in God and Immortality: A Psychological, Anthropological and Statistical Study*. 2nd ed. Chicago: Open Court, 1921.
LeVake v. Independent School District #656, No. CX-99-763 (Minn. Dist. Ct. 20 June 2000).
LeVake v. Independent School District #656, 625 N.W.2d 502 (Minn. Ct. App. 2001).
Lewin, Roger. "Where Is the Science in Creation Science?" *Science* N.S. 215/4529 (1982) 142–46.
Lewis, C. S. "Religion and Science." In *God in the Dock: Essays on Theology and Ethics*, 72–75. Grand Rapids: Eerdmans, 1970.
Lewontin, Richard C. "Introduction." In *Scientists Confront Creationism*, edited by Laurie R. Godfrey, xxiii–xxvi. New York: Norton, 1983.
Lindberg, David C., and Ronald L. Numbers, eds. *God and Nature: Historical Essays on the Encounter between Science and Religion*. Berkeley: University of California Press, 1986.
Linder, Suzanne C. "William Louis Poteat and the Evolution Controversy." *North Carolina Historical Review* 40/2 (1963) 135–57.
———. *William Louis Poteat, Prophet of Progress*. Chapel Hill: North Carolina, 1966.
Linville, Henry R. *Biology of Man and Other Organisms*. New York: Harcourt Brace, 1923.
Lippmann, Walter. *American Inquisitors: A Commentary on Dayton and Chicago*. New York: Macmillan, 1928.
Lipton, Peter. *Inference to the Best Explanation*. 2nd ed. International Library of Philosophy. London: Routledge, 2004.
Lisenby, William Foy. "Brough, Baptists, and Bombast: The Election of 1928." *Arkansas Historical Quarterly* 32/2 (1973) 120–31.
Literary Digest. "No Evolution for Texas." 90 (1926) 30–31.
Livingstone, David N. *Darwin's Forgotten Defenders: The Encounter between Evangelical Theology and Evolutionary Thought*. Grand Rapids: Eerdmans, 1987.
Louisiana. Act № 685: Balanced Treatment for Creation-Science and Evolution-Science Act. In *Acts of the Legislature: Regular Session of 1981*, 2:1313–15.
Louisville Courier-Journal. "Tennessee Teacher Fired under Anti-Evolution Law." 15 April 1967. Page 9
Lucas, J. R. "Wilberforce and Huxley: A Legendary Encounter." *Historical Journal* 22/2 (1979) 313–30.
Luther, Martin. *Genesisvorlesung*. In *D. Martin Luthers Werke: Kritische Gesammtausgabe*, 42:1–673. Weimar: Böhlau, 1911. Translation in *Luther's Works:* Vol. 1, *Lectures on Genesis Chapters 1–5*, by George V. Schick. Edited by Jaroslav Pelikan. St. Louis: Concordia, 1958.
Lyell, Charles. *Geological Evidences of the Antiquity of Man*. London: Murray, 1863.
———. *Principles of Geology*. 3 vols. London: Murray, 1830–33.
Lynch v. Donnelly, 465 U.S. 668 (1984).
Lyon, James. "The New Theological Professorship, Natural Science in Connection with Revealed Religion." *Southern Presbyterian Review* 12 (1859) 181–95.

Lyon, John, and Phillip R. Sloan, trans. and eds. *From Natural History to the History of Nature: Readings from Buffon and His Critics*. Notre Dame, IN: University of Notre Dame Press, 1981.
Machen, John Gresham. *The Christian View of Man*. New York: Macmillan, 1937.
———. Papers. Westminster Theological Library, Philadelphia, Pennsylvania.
Mack, Joseph Bingham. "The Other Side." *Central Presbyterian* 19/51 (1884) 1.
Macnab, Robert M. "The Bacterial Flagellum: Reversible Rotary Propellor and Type III Export Apparatus." *Journal of Bacteriology* 181/23 (1999) 7149–53.
Malnak v. Yogi, 440 F. Supp. 1284 (D.N.J. 1977). *Aff'd per curiam*, 592 F.2d 197 (3d Cir. 1979).
Malone, Dudley Field. "Science, Evolution, and Religion." In *"Unaccustomed as I Am": Miscellaneous Speeches*, 139–70. New York: Little and Ives, 1929.
Mandell, Jonathan. "Inherit the Controversy." *Newsday* (17 March 1996) Page 10.
Mangenot, Eugène. "Hexaméron." In *Dictionnaire de théologie catholique*, edited by Alfred Vacant et al., 6:2325–54. 16 vols. in 25 bks. Paris: Letouzey, 1920.
Manson, Neil A., ed. *God and Design: The Teleological Argument and Modern Science*. London: Routledge, 2003.
Marsden, George. "Understanding Fundamentalist Views of Science." In *Science and Creationism*, edited by Ashley Montagu, 95–116. Oxford: Oxford University Press, 1984.
Martin, T. T. *Hell and the High Schools: Christ or Evolution, Which?* Kansas City, MO: Western Baptist, 1923.
Martini, Martino. *Sinicae Historiae Decas Prima*. Munich: Straubius, 1658.
Mather, Kirtley F. *Science in Search of God*. New York: Holt, 1928.
McCurdy, Jack. "Evolution or Creation? The Fight's Revived." *Los Angeles Times* (10 November 1972) Pages 3 and 23.
McLean v. Arkansas Board of Education, 529 F. Supp. 1255 (E.D. Ark. 1982).
McLean v. Arkansas Documentation Project. (www.antievolution.org/projects/mclean/new_site/).
McMullin, Ernan, ed. *The Church and Galileo*. Studies in Science and the Humanities from the Reilly Center for Science, Technology, and Values. Notre Dame, IN: University of Notre Dame Press, 2005.
———, ed. *Evolution and Creation*. University of Notre Dame Studies in the Philosophy of Religion 4. Notre Dame, IN: University of Notre Dame Press, 1985.
———. *The Inference That Makes Science*. Milwaukee: Marquette University Press, 1992.
———. "Introduction: Evolution & Creation." In *Evolution and Creation*, edited by Ernan McMulin, 1–56. University of Notre Dame Studies in the Philosophy of Religion 4. Notre Dame, IN: University of Notre Dame Press, 1985.
McVey, Frank L. "Statement to the People of Kentucky." *Louisville Evening Post* (13 February 1922).
Mémoires pour l'Histoire des Sciences et des Beaux-Artes [also called *Journal de Trévoux*]. Two reviews of *Histoire Naturelle, Générale et Particuliere, avec les Descriptions du Cabinet du Roi*, Volume 1, Articles CV and CXXV. 49 (1749) 1853–72 and 2226–45. Partially translated in *From Natural History to the History of Nature: Readings from Buffon and His Crtics*, edited by John Lyon and Phillip R. Sloan, 215–30. Notre Dame, IN: University of Notre Dame Press, 1981.

Mencken, H. L. Thirteen newspaper columns from and about Dayton. *Baltimore Sun* (29 June to 14 September 1925). Reprinted in *The Impossible H. L. Mencken: A Selection of His Best Newspaper Stories*, edited by Marion Elizabeth Rodgers, 560–611. New York: Doubleday, 1991.

Milgram, Stanley. "Behavioral Study of Obedience." *Journal of Abnormal and Social Psychology* 67/4 (1963) 371–78.

———. *Obedience to Authority: An Experimental View*. New York: HarperCollins, 1974.

Mill, John Stuart. *On Liberty*. London: Parker, 1869.

Miller, Arthur M. "Kentucky and the Theory of Evolution." *Science* N.S. 55/1416 (1922) 178–80.

Miller, Kenneth R. *Finding Darwin's God: A Scientist's Search for Common Ground between God and Evolution*. New York: Harper Perennial, 2007.

Millhauser, Milton. "The Scriptural Geologists: An Episode in the History of Opinion." *Osiris* 11 (1954) 65–86.

Milton, George Fort. "A Dayton Postscript." *Outlook:* 140 (1925) 550–52.

Mims, Edwin. *History of Vanderbilt University*. Nashville: Vanderbilt University Press, 1946.

Mississippi. Chapter 311. *Laws of the State of Mississippi: Appropriations, General Legislation and Resolutions Passed at a Regular Session of the Mississippi Legislature* (1926) 435.

Mitchell, Charles. "Evolution." In *Encyclopaedia Britannica*, 11th ed., 10:22–37. 29 vols. Cambridge: Cambridge University Press, 1910–1911.

Mivart, St. George Jackson. *On the Genesis of Species*. London: Macmillan, 1871.

Mochary v. Caputo, 100 N.J. 119 (1985).

Montgomery, James Riley. "John R. Neal and the University of Tennessee: A Five-Part Tragedy." *Tennessee Historical Quarterly* 38/2 (1979) 214–34.

———. *Threshold of a New Day: The University of Tennessee, 1919–1946*. University of Tennessee Record 74/6. Knoxville: University of Tennessee Press, 1971.

Moon, Truman J. *Biology for Beginners*. New York: Holt, 1921.

Moon, Truman J., et al. *Modern Biology*. New York: Holt, 1951.

———. *Modern Biology*. New York: Holt, 1956.

Moore, James R. "Of Love and Death: Why Darwin 'Gave Up Christianity.'" In *History, Humanity, and Evolution: Essays for John C. Greene*, edited by James R. Moore, 195–230. Cambridge: Cambridge University Press, 1989.

———. *The Post-Darwinian Controversies: A Study of the Protestant Struggle to Come to Terms with Darwin in Great Britain and America, 1870–1900*. Cambridge: Cambridge University Press, 1979.

Moore, John A. "Creationism in California." *Daedalus* 103/3 (1974) 173–89.

Moore, Ruth E. *Charles Darwin: A Great Life in Brief*. The Stratford Library. London: Hutchinson, 1957.

Moro, Anton-Lazzaro. *De' Crostacei e degli Altri Marini Corpi che si Truovano su' Monti*. Venice: Monti, 1740.

Moroni, Gaetano. *Indice Generale Alfabetico delle Materie del Dizionario di Erudizione Storico-Ecclesiastica*. Venice: Emiliana, 1878.

Morris, Henry M. *Applied Hydraulics in Engineering*. New York: Ronald, 1963.

———. *A History of Modern Creationism*. San Diego: Master, 1984.

———. "Intelligent Design and/or Scientific Creationism." Institute for Creation Research website (www.icr.org/).

Morrison, John L. "American Catholics and the Crusade against Evolution." *American Catholic Historical Society of Philadelphia Records* 64 (1953) 59–71.

Mozert v. Hawkins County Board of Education, 827 F.2d 1058 (6th Cir. 1987).

Mueller, Marvin. "The Shroud of Turin: A Critical Appraisal." *Skeptical Inquirer* 6/3 (1982) 15–34.

Mullins, Edgar Young. *Christianity at the Crossroads*. New York: Doran, 1924.

———. "President Mullins Address." *Baptist Messenger* 13/21 (1925) 5–7.

Nashville Christian Advocate. "The Vanderbilt Commencement." 38/22 (1878) 8.

National Association of Biology Teachers. "NABT Unveils New Statement on Teaching Evolution." *American Biology Teacher* 58/1 (1996) 61–62.

National Center for Science Education. "A New Fox News Poll on Evolution." 7 September 2011. National Center for Science Education website (https://ncse.ngo/new-fox-news-poll-evolution/).

Needham, John Turberville. Lettre de M. de Needham à M. de Buffon. In *Nouvelles Recherches Physiques et Métaphysiques sur la Nature et la Religion*, 1–26. London: Lacombe, 1769.

Nelkin, Dorothy. *The Creation Controversy: Science or Scripture in the Schools*. Boston: Beacon, 1982.

———. "The Science-Textbook Controversies." *Scientific American* 234/4 (1976) 33–39.

New York Times. "Act on Evolution Bills." 10 February 1927. Page 38.

———. "Author of the Law Surprised at Fuss." 18 July 1925. Page 1.

———. "Ban Evolution in Atlanta Schools." 10 February 1926. Page 10.

———. "Bryan in Dayton, Calls Scopes Trial Duel to the Death." 8 July 1925. Page 8.

———. "Bryan Loses Fight to Ban Darwinism in Church Schools." 23 May 1923. Pages 1 and 4.

———. "College Reinstates Evolution Exponent." 11 April 1923. Page 26.

———. "Cuts Evolution from Texas Books." 17 October 1925. Page 17.

———. "Death of Charles Darwin." 21 April 1882. Page 5.

———. "Ends Evolution Dispute." 13 May 1926. Page 8.

———. "The Evolution Arena at Dayton." 5 July 1925. Magazine Section, 1 and 10.

———. "Evolution Exponent Refuses to Retract." 10 April 1923. Page 22.

———. "Full Pay is Asked in Evolution Case." 16 April 1967. Page 61.

———. "Lays Scopes Trial to Publicity Thirst." 5 August 1925. Page 10.

———. "'Monkey Law' Ousts Tennessee Teacher." 15 April 1967. Page 1.

———. "Rush for Evolution Books Clears Tennessee Libraries." 18 July 1925. Page 1.

———. "School on S.I. [Staten Island] Dismisses 3 Nuns in Dispute on Teaching Evolution." 7 January 1969. Page 29.

———. "Tennessee Ending Its 'Monkey Law.'" 17 May 1967. Page 49.

———. "Tennessee Keeps Its 'Monkey Law.'" 21 April 1967. Page 41.

———. "Tennessee Takes Step to Repeal its 42-Year-Old 'Monkey Law.'" 12 April 1967.

———. "Tennessee Teacher Wins Support in Evolution Case." 30 April 1967. Page 68.

———. "Texas Schoolbooks Omit Evolution." 13 July 1926. Page 44.

New York World. "Darrow and Colby to Head Defense in Evolution Trial." 10 June 1925. Pages 1 and 4.

———. "The Strength of Mr. Bryan's Case." 12 June 1925. Page 8.

Newport, Frank. "In U.S., 46% Hold Creationist View of Human Origins." Gallup News. 1 June 2012.

Newton, Alfred. "Early Days of Darwinism." *Macmillan's Magazine* 57 (1888) 241–49.

Newton, Isaac. *Correspondence*. Edited by H. W. Turnbull et al. 7 vols. Cambridge: Cambridge University Press, 1959–1977.

———. "Four Letters from Sir Isaac Newton to Doctor Bentley Containing Some Arguments in Proof of a Deity." In *Isaac Newton's Papers and Letters on Natural Philosophy*, edited by I. Bernard Cohen, 279–312. Cambridge: Harvard University Press, 1958.

———. *Principia Mathematica Philosophiae Naturalis*. 2nd ed. 2 vols. Cambridge: 1713. Translation: Andrew Motte and Florian Cajori, *Sir Isaac Newtons Mathematical Principles of Natural Philosophy and His System of the World*. 2 vols. Berkeley: University of California Press, 1934.

Noll, Mark A. *A History of Christianity in the United States and Canada*. Grand Rapids: Eerdmans, 1992.

Nouvelles Ecclésiastiques. Review of Buffon's *L'Histoire Naturelle*. 6 and 13 February 1750. Pages 21–27. Translation in *From Natural History to the History of Nature: Readings from Buffon and His Crtics*, edited by John Lyon and Phillip R. Sloan, 235–52. Notre Dame, IN: University of Notre Dame Press, 1981.

Numbers, Ronald. L. "Cosmogonies from 1700 to 1900." In *The History of Science and Religion in the Western Tradition: An Encyclopedia*, edited by Gary B. Ferngren et al., 350–55. Garland Reference Library of the Humanities 1833. New York: Garland, 2000.

———. *Creation by Natural Law: Laplace's Nebular Hypothesis in American Thought*. Seattle: University of Washington Press, 1977.

———. *The Creationists: The Evolution of Scientific Creationism*. Berkeley: University of California Press, 1992.

———. *Darwinism Comes to America*. Cambridge: Harvard University Press, 1998.

———, ed. *Galileo Goes to Jail, and Other Myths about Science and Religion*. Cambridge: Harvard University Press, 2009.

Núñez, Diego. *El Darwinismo en España*. Biblioteca de Pensamiento 5. Madrid: Castalia, 1969.

Oklahoma. "Chapter 175: State Text Books." In *Session Laws of 1923 of the State of Oklahoma Passed by the Regular Session of the Ninth Legislature of the State of Oklahoma*, 292–98.

Origen, *Contra Celsum*. Translated by Frederick Crombie. In *The Ante-Nicene Fathers*, edited by Alexander Roberts et al., 4:395–669. 10 vols. Buffalo: Christian Literature, 1885.

Orr, H. Allen. "Darwin v. Intelligent Design (Again)." *Boston Review* 21/6 (1996–97) 28–31.

Orr, James. "Science and the Christian Faith." In *The Fundamentals: A Testimony to the Truth*, edited by A. C. Dixon et al., 4:91–104. 12 vols. Chicago: Testimony, 1910–15.

Ospovat, Alexander. "Werner, Abraham Gottlob." In *Complete Dictionary of Scientific Biography*, edited by Charles Coulston Gillespie et al., 14:256–64. 27 vols. Detroit: Scribner, 2008.

O'Toole, George Barry. *The Case against Evolution*. New York: Macmillan, 1925.

Otto, James H., and Albert Towle. *Modern Biology*. 6th ed. New York: Holt, Rinehart & Winston, 1965.
Owen, C. M., et al. "*Hippocampus Minor, Calcar Avis*, and the Huxley-Owen Debate." *Neurosurgery* 65/6 (2009) 1098–104.
Owren, Paul A. "Parahaemophilia. Haemorrhagic Diathesis due to Absence of a Previously Unknown Clotting Factor." *Lancet* 1/6449 (1947) 446–51.
Pagel, Mark. "Evolution." In *Encyclopedia of Evolution*, edited by Mark Pagel, 1:330–31. 2 vols. Oxford: Oxford University Press, 2002.
Paine, Thomas. *The Age of Reason; Being an Investigation* Owen *True and Fabulous Theology*. Paris: Barrois, 1794. In *Selected Writings of Thomas Paine*, edited by Ian Shapiro and Jane E. Calvert, 372–502. Rethinking the Western Tradition. New Haven: Yale University Press, 2014.
Paley, William. *Natural Theology: or Evidences of the Existence and Attributes of the Deity, Collected from the Appearances of Nature*. London: Fauldner, 1802.
Pallen, Mark, and Nicholas Matzke. "From *The Origin of Species* to the Origin of Bacterial Flagella." *Nature Reviews Microbiology* 4/10 (2006) 784–90.
Palmer, R. R. *Catholics and Unbelievers in Eighteenth Century France*. Princeton: Princeton University Press, 1939.
Patrick, Symon. *Commentary on the First Book of Moses, called Genesis*. London: Chiswell, 1695.
Peabody, James E., and Arthur E. Hunt. *Biology for Human Welfare*. New York: Macmillan, 1924.
Peay, Ausin. Message from the Governor (23 March 1925). *House Journal of the 64th General Assembly of the State of Tennessee*, 741–45.
Peirce, C. S. "The General Theory of Probable Inference" (1883). In *Philosophical Writings of Peirce*, edited by Justus Buchler, 190–217. New York: Dover, 1955.
Peloza v. Capistrano Unified School District, 37 F.3d 517 (9th Cir. 1994).
Peloza v. Capistrano Unified School District, 782 F.Supp. 1412 (C.D. Cal. 1992).
Penn, Granville. *Comparative Estimate of the Mineral and Mosaical Geologies*, 2nd ed. 2 vols. London: Duncan, 1825.
Peretó, Juli, et al. "Charles Darwin and the Origin of Life." *Origins of Life and Evolution of Biospheres* 39 (2009) 395–406.
Pereyra, Benito. *Commentariorum et Disputationum in Genesim Tomi Quattuor*. Rome: Populus Romanus, 1589–98.
Pew Research Center. "The Evolution of Pew Research Center's Survey Questions about the Origins and Development of Life on Earth," 6 February 2019 (www.pewforum.org/).
———. Pollwatch. "Reading the Polls on Evolution and Creationism." Press Release, 28 September 2005 (www.people-press.org/).
Pew Research Center and Pew Forum on Religion & Public Life. "July 2006 Religion and Public Life Survey" (see Legacy Questionnaire 287; www.people-press.org/).
Pfleiderer, Otto. "Evolution and Theology." In *Evolution and Theology, and Other Essays*, edited by Orello Cone, 1–26. London: Black, 1900.
Pickering v. Board of Education, 391 U.S. 563 (1968).
Pingré, Alexandre Guy. *Cométographie ou Traité Historique et Théorique des Comètes*. Paris: Imprimerie Royale, 1783–84.

Pius IX, Pope. *Quanta Cura. Acta Sanctae Sedis* 3 (1867) 160-76. Translation: *Encyclical Letter Quanta Cura & The Syllabus of Errors: Of the Supreme Pontiff Pius IX: Condemning Current Errors: December 8, 1846.* Kansas City: Angelus, 1998.

Pius XII, Pope. *Humani Generis. Acta Apostolicae Sedis* 42.11 (1950) 561-78. Translation: National Catholic Welfare Conference, *Some False Opinions Which Threaten to Undermine Catholic Doctrine.* Boston: Pauline, 1990.

Piveteau, Jean. "La Pensée Religieuse de Buffon." In *Buffon*, edited by Léon Bertin et al., 125-32. Paris: Muséum National d'Histoire Naturelle, 1952.

Plantinga, Alvin. *Where the Conflict Really Lies: Science, Religion, and Naturalism.* Oxford: Oxford University Press, 2011.

Plato. *Timaeus.* In *The Collected Dialogues of Plato*, edited by Edith Hamilton and Huntington Cairns, 1151-1211. Bollingen Series 71. Princeton: Princeton University Press, 1961.

Pliny. *Natural History.* Translated by H. Rackham. Loeb Classical Library. Cambridge: Harvard University Press, 1938-1963.

Popular Science Monthly. "Religion and Science at Vanderbilt." 13 (1878) 492-95.

———. "Vanderbilt University Again." 14 (1878) 237-38.

Presbyterian Church in the United States General Assembly. *Minutes of the General Assembly of the Presbyterian Church in the United States* [for 1886]. Richmond, VA: Presbyterian Committee on Publication, 1886.

Presbyterian Church in the United States of America General Assembly. *Minutes of the General Assembly of the Presbyterian Church in the United States of America* [for 1924]. New York: Presbyterian Committee on Publication, 1924.

Presbyterian Church in the United States Synod of South Carolina. *Minutes of the Synod of South Carolina at Its Annual Sessions at Greenville, S.C. October 22-28, 1884.* Spartanburg: Trimmier, 1884.

Price, George McCready. *The New Geology: A Textbook for Colleges, Normal Schools, and Training Schools; and for the General Reader.* Mountain View, CA: Pacific, 1923.

Provine, William B. "Response to Phillip Johnson." *First Things* 6 (October 1990) 23-24.

Puckette, Charles McD. "The Evolution Arena at Dayton." *New York Times*, 5 July 1925, Magazine Section, pages 1 & 10.

Pye Smith, John. *On the Relation between the Holy Scriptures and Some Parts of Geological Science.* London: Jackson and Walford, 1839.

Rappaport, Rhoda. "Geology and Orthodoxy: The Case of Noah's Flood in Eighteenth Century Thought." *British Journal for the History of Science.* 11/1 (1978) 1-18.

Rappleyea, George. Letter to the Editor. *Chattanooga Daily Times* (19 May 1925) Page 5.

Ratzsch, Del. *Nature, Design, and Science: The Status of Design in Natural Science.* SUNY Series in Philosophy and Biology. Albany: SUNY Press, 2001.

Reader, John. *Missing Links: The Hunt for Earliest Man.* 2nd ed. London: Penguin, 1988.

Reid, James M. *An Adventure in Textbooks, 1924-1960.* New York: Bowker, 1969.

Religion News Service. "Evolution Statement Altered." *Christian Century* 114/32 (1997) 1029.

Reventlow, Henning Graf. "English Rationalism, Deism, and Early Biblical Criticism." In *Hebrew Bible, Old Testament: The History of Its Interpretation.* Vol. 2, *From the Renaissance to the Enlightenment*, edited by Magne Sæbø, 851-74. Göttingen: Vandenhoeck & Ruprecht, 2008.

Bibliography

Reynolds v. United States, 98 U.S. 145 (1878).
Rhea County Court. *The World's Most Famous Court Trial, Tennessee Evolution Case. A Complete Stenographic Report of the Famous Court Test of the Tennessee Anti-Evolution Act, at Dayton, July 10 to 21, 1925, Including Speeches and Arguments of Attorneys.* Cincinnati: National Book Company, 1925.
Rice, E. L. "Darwin and Bryan—A Study in Method." *Science* 61 № 1575 (1925) 243–50.
Rice, William North. *Revised Text-book of Geology.* New York: American Book Company, 1897.
Riley, William Bell. "The Defense of Fundamentalism in the Matter of Evolution." *Christian Fundamentalist* 1 (1927) 8.
Rimmer, Harry. *Modern Science and the Genesis Record.* Grand Rapids: Eerdmans, 1937.
Robbins, Frank Egleston. *The Hexaemeral Literature: A Study of the Greek and Latin Commentaries in Genesis.* Chicago: University of Chicago Press, 1912.
Roberts, Jon H. "Conservative Evangelicals and Science Education in American Colleges and Universities, 1890–1940." *Journal of the Historical Society* 5/3 (2005) 297–329.
Robinson, A. Jean, et al. "Hageman Factor (Factor XII) Deficiency in Marine Mammals." *Science* N.S. 166 № 3911 (1969) 1420–22.
Robson, John. "The Fiat and Finger of God: The Bridgewater Treatises." In *Victorian Faith in Crisis: Essays on Continuity and Change in Nineteenth-Century Religious Belief*, edited by Richard J. Helmstadter and Bernard Lightman, 71–125. Stanford: Stanford University Press, 1990.
Roe v. Wade, 10 U.S. 113 (1973).
Rosenberg, Gary D., ed. *The Revolution in Geology from the Renaissance to the Enlightenment.* Memoir 203. Boulder, CO: Geological Society of America, 2009.
Rosentiel, Tom, et al. "On Darwin's 200th Birthday, Americans Still Divided about Evolution." Pew Research Center, February 5, 2009. Pew Research Center website (www.pewresearch.org/).
Royer, Clémence. "Préface." In *De l'Origine des Espèces ou Des Lois du Progrès chez les Êtres Organisés*, by Charles Darwin. Paris: Guillaumin, 1862.
Rudwick, Martin. "The Shape and Meaning of Earth History." In *God and Nature: Historical Essays on the Encounter between Christianity and Science*, edited by David C. Lindberg and Ronald L. Numbers, 296–321. Berkeley: University of California Press, 1986.
Rupke, Nicolaas A. *The Great Chain of History: William Buckland and the English School of Geology (1814–1849).* Oxford: Clarendon, 1983.
Ruse, Michael. "A Philosopher's Day in Court." In *Science and Creationism*, edited by Ashley Montagu, 311–42. New York: Oxford University Press, 1984.
Ruskin, John. *Works of John Ruskin.* Edited by E. T. Cook and Alexander Wedderburn. 39 vols. London: Longmans, Green, 1903–12.
Russell, Colin. "The Conflict of Science and Religion." In *The History of Science and Religion in the Western Tradition: An Encyclopedia*, edited by Gary B. Ferngren et al., 12–16. Garland Reference Library of the Humanities 1833. New York: Garland, 2000.
Russell, Jeffrey Burton. *Inventing the Flat Earth: Columbus and Modern Historians.* New York: Praeger, 1991.

Sanford, William F., Jr. "Dana and Darwinism." *Journal of the History of Ideas* 26/4 (1965) 531–46.

Sarayna, Torello. *De Origine et Amplitudine Civitatis Veronae*. Verona, 1540.

Sarton, George. "Introductory Essay." In *Science, Religion, and Reality*, by Joseph Needham, 3–22. New York: Braziller, 1955.

Scaliger, Joseph. *Opus de Emendatione Temporum*. Geneva: Roverian, 1629.

Science. "Proposed Legislation against the Teaching of Evolution." 55 № 1421 (1922) 318–20.

Scofield, C. I., ed. *Scofield Reference Bible*. New York: Oxford University Press, 1917.

Scopes v. State, 154 Tenn. 105, 289 S.W. 363 (1927).

Scopes, John T. "Reflections—Forty Years After." In *D-Days at Dayton: Reflections on the Scopes Trial*, edited by Jerry R. Tompkins, 17–31. Baton Rouge: Louisiana State University Press, 1965.

Scopes, John T., with James Presley. *Center of the Storm: Memoirs of John T. Scopes*. New York: Holt, Rinehart & Winston, 1967.

Se Boyar, G. E. "Bartholomaeus Anglicus and His Encyclopedia." *Journal of English and Germanic Philology* 19 (1920) 168–89.

Sedgwick, Adam. *Discourse on the Studies of the University*. Cambridge: Cambridge University Press, 1834.

Segraves v. California, № 278978 (Super. Ct. Sacramento County 1981).

Selman v. Cobb County School District, 390 F.Supp. 2nd 1286 (N.D.Ga. 2005).

Selman v. Cobb County School District, 449 F.3rd 1320 (11th Cir. 2006).

Semba, Umeko, et al. "Whale Hageman Factor (Factor XII): Prevented Production due to Pseudogene Conversion." *Thrombosis Research* 90/1 (1998) 31–37.

Shaw, Denis J. B., and Jonathan D. Oldfield. "Scientific, Institutional and Personal Rivalries among Soviet Geographers in the Late Stalin Era." *Europe-Asia Studies* 60/8 (2008) 1397–418.

Shields, Thomas Edward. "Note on Education: Text-books for Primary Grades." *Catholic University Bulletin* 15/3 (1909) 412–23.

Shipley, Maynard. "Growth of the Anti-Evolution Movement." *Current History and Forum* 32 (1930) 330–32.

———. *The War on Modern Science: A Short History of the Fundamentalist Attacks on Evolution and Modernism*. New York: Knopf, 1927.

Simpson, George Gaylord. "Evolution and Education." *Science* 187 № 4175 (1975) 389.

Simpson, J. A., and E. S. C. Weiner, preparers. *Oxford English Dictionary*. 2nd ed. 20 vols. Oxford: Clarendon, 1989.

Skoog, Gerald Duane. "The Coverage of Evolution in High School Biology Textbooks Published in the 1980s." *Science Education* 68/2 (1984) 117–28.

———. "The Coverage of Human Evolution in High School Biology Textbooks in the 20th Century and in Current State Science Standards." *Science & Education* 14/3–5 (2005) 395–422.

———. "The Topic of Evolution in Secondary School Biology Textbooks, 1900–1968." EdD diss., University of Nebraska, 1969.

———. "Topic of Evolution in Secondary School Biology Textbooks: 1900–1977." *Science Education* 63/5 (1979) 621–40.

Slaughterhouse Cases, 83 U.S. 36 (1872).

Smith v. Mississippi, 242 So.2d 692 (Miss. 1970).

Smith, Ella Thea. *Exploring Biology*. New York: Harcourt, Brace, 1938.

Smith, Roger. "Alfred Russel Wallace: Philosophy of Nature and Man." *British Journal for the History of Science* 6/2 (1972) 177-99.
Solinus, Gaius Julius. *De Mirabilibus Mundi*. Translation: *The Worthie Work of Iulius Solinus*, by Arthur Golding. London: Hacket, 1587.
Southern v. McCanless, № 44734, Knox County Chancery Court (1967).
Sprat, Thomas. *History of the Royal Society*. London: n.p., 1670.
Stengers, Jean. "Buffon et la Sorbonne." In *Études sur le XVIIIe Siècle*, edited by Roland Mortier and Hervé Hasquin, 113-24. Brussels: Éditions de l'Université de Bruxelles, 1974.
Stensen, Niels. *Canis Carchariae Dissectum Caput*. In *Nicolai Stenonis Opera Philosophica*, edited by Vilhelm Maar, 2:113-44. 2 vols. Copenhagen: Tryde, 1910.
———. *De Solido intra Solidum Naturaliter Contento Dissertationis Prodromus* (1669). In *Nicolai Stenonis Opera Philosophica*, edited by Vilhelm Maar, 2:181-226. 2 vols. Copenhagen: Tryde, 1910.
———. *Defensio et Plenior Elucidatio Epistolae de Propria Conversione* (1680). In *Nicolai Stenonis Opera Theologica*, 2nd ed., edited by Knud Larsen and Gustav Scherz, 1:380-437. 2 vols. Copenhagen: Nyt Nordisk, 1944-47.
———. *Nicolai Stenonis Epistolae et Epistolae ad eum Datae*, edited by Gustav Scherz. Copenhagen: Nyt Nordisk, 1952.
Stephens, Lester D. *Joseph LeConte: Gentle Prophet of Evolution*. Southern Biography Series. Baton Rouge: Louisiana State University Press, 1982.
Stewart, Balfour. Letter to James David Forbes, 5 July 1860. In Incoming Letters 1860, J. D. Forbes Collection, Special Collections Division, University of St. Andrews.
Stormorken, Helge. "The Discovery of Factor V: A Tricky Clotting Factor." *Journal of Thrombosis and Haemostasis* 1/2 (2003) 206-13.
Strabo. *Geography*. Translated by Horace Leonard Jones. Loeb Classical Library Cambridge: Harvard University Press, 1917-1932.
Street, T. Watson. "The Evolution Controversy in the Southern Presbyterian Church with Attention to the Theological and Ecclesiastical Issues Raised." *Journal of the Presbyterian Historical Society* 37 (1959) 232-50.
Suárez, Francisco. *De Opere Sex Dierum*. In *Opera Omnia*, 3:1-465. 28 vols. in 30. Paris: Vives, 1856.
Tablet. "Memoranda: Educational: Catholic University College, Kensington." 47 № 186 (5 Feb 1876) 182-83.
Tait, L. Gordon. "Evolution: Wishart, Wooster, and William Jennings Bryan." *Journal of Presbyterian History* 62/4 (1984) 306-21.
Tangipahoa Parish Board of Education v. Freiler, 530 U.S. 1251 (2000).
Temple, Frederick. *The Present Relations of Science to Religion: A Sermon Preached on Act Sunday, July 1, 1860, before the University of Oxford, during the Meeting of the British Association*. Oxford: Parker, 1860.
———. *The Relations between Religion and Science: Eight Lectures Preached before the University of Oxford in the Year 1884*. London: Macmillan, 1885.
Temple, Frederick, et al. *Essays and Reviews*. London: Longman, 1861.
Tennessee. Chapter № 27 (Butler Act). In *Public Acts of the State of Tennessee Passed by the Sixty-Fourth General Assembly* (1925), 50-51.
———. Chapter № 377: Act to Amend Tennessee Code Annotated §49-2008, Relative to the Selection of Textbooks (Textbook Selection Act). In *Public Acts of the State of Tennessee Passed by the Eighty-Eighth General Assembly* (1973), 1364-65.

Tennessee House of Representatives. House Bill № 48. In *House Journal of the Eighty-Fifth General Assembly of the State of Tennessee* (1967) 553–55.

Thaxton, Charles B., et al. *The Mystery of Life's Origin: Reassessing Current Theories*. New York: Philosophical Library, 1984.

Theophilus of Antioch. *Apology to Autolycus*. Translated by Frederick Crombie. In *The Ante-Nicene Fathers*, edited by Alexander Roberts et al., 2:85–121. 10 vols. Buffalo: Christian Literature, 1885.

Thomas Aquinas. *Summa Theologica*. Translation: *Summa Theologica*, by the Fathers of the English Dominican Province. 3 vols. New York: Benzinger, 1947.

Thompson, Ernest Trice. *Presbyterians in the South*. 3 vols. Richmond, VA: John Knox, 1973.

Thompson, James J., Jr. *Tried as by Fire: Southern Baptists and the Religious Controversies of the 1920s*. Macon, GA: Mercer University Press, 1982.

Thornhill, Richard H., and David W. Ussery. "A Classification of Possible Routes of Darwinian Evolution." *Journal of Theoretical Biology* 203 (2000) 111–16.

Tigert, John James. *Bishop Holland Nimmons McTyeire: Ecclesiastical and Educational Architect*. Nashville: Vanderbilt University Press, 1955.

Tindal, Matthew. *Christianity as Old as the Creation*. London: n.p., 1730.

Toulmin, Stephen. *The Return to Cosmology: Postmodern Science and the Theology of Nature*. Berkeley: University of California Press, 1982.

Tristram, Henry Baker. "On the Ornithology of North Africa. Part III. The Sahara (continued)." *Ibis* 1/4 (1859) 415–35.

Turner, Frank Miller. *Between Science and Religion: The Reaction to Scientific Naturalism in Late Victorian England*. Yale Historical Publications, Miscellany, 100. New Haven: Yale University Press, 1974.

United Press Associations. "Loses Job Because of Evolution." In *Oelwein* (Iowa) *Daily Register* (16 June 1925) Page 6.

United Press International. "Tennessee Teacher Is Rehired but Vows 'Monkey Law' Fight." *New York Times* (13 May 1967) Page 34.

Urquinaona y Bidot, José María. *Carta Pastoral*. Las Palmas, Spain: Victor Doreste y Navarro, 1876.

Ussher, James. *Annales Veteris Testamenti, A Prima Mundi Origine Deducti*. London, 1650.

Vai, Gian Battisa. "A Liberal Diluvianism." In *Four Centuries of the Word Geology: Ulisse Aldrovandi 1603 in Bologna*, edited by Gian Battisa Vai and William Cavazza, 220–49. Bologna: Minerva, 2003.

———. "Steno's Twofold Conversion." In *The Revolution in Geology from the Renaissance to the Enlightenment*, edited by Gary D. Rosenberg, 187–208. Boulder, CO: Geological Society of America, 2009.

Vallisneri, Antonio. *De' Corpi Marini, che su' Monti si Trovano*. Venice: Lovisa, 1721.

Van Fraassen, Bas C. "Constructive Empiricism Now." *Philosophical Studies* 106/1–2 (2001) 151–70.

———. *The Scientific Image*. Oxford: Oxford University Press, 1980.

Vatican I. *Constitutio Dogmatica de Fide Catholica ("Dei Filius")*. Translated in *Enchiridion symbolorum definitionum et declarationum de rebus fidei et morum*, 43rd ed., originally edited by Heinrich Denzinger, Dz 3000–3045. San Francisco: Ignatius, 2012.

Vignoles, Alphonse des. *Chronologie de l'Histoire Sainte et des Histoires Etrangères qui la Concernent depuis la Sortie d'Égypte jusqu'à la Captivité de Babylone.* Berlin: Haude, 1738.

Vincent of Lérins. *Commonitoria.* Translated by C. A. Heurtley. In *The Nicene and Post-Nicene Fathers,* edited by Philip Schaff and Henry Wace, 11:131–56. 14 vols. 2nd ser. Buffalo: Christian Literature, 1894.

Voltaire, François Marie Arouet De. *La Bible enfin Expliqué par Plusieurs Aumoniers.* London: Rey, 1776.

W., T. C. (probably Thornton C. Whaling). "Dr. Woodrow and the General Assembly." *Southern Presbyterian* (14 June 1888) Page 2.

Walker, Samuel. *In Defense of American Liberties: A History of the ACLU.* New York: Oxford University Press, 1990.

Wallace, Alfred Russel. *Contributions to the Theory of Natural Selection.* London: Macmillan, 1871.

Walz v. Tax Commission of the City of New York. 397 U.S. 664 (1970).

Warfield, Benjamin Breckinridge. "Creation, Evolution, and Mediate Creation." 1901. Reprinted in *Evolution, Scripture, and Science: Selected Writings,* edited by Mark A. Noll and David N. Livingstone, 197–210. Grand Rapids: Baker, 2000.

———. "The Manner and Time of Man's Origin." 1903. Reprinted in *Evolution, Scripture, and Science: Selected Writings,* edited by Mark A. Noll; David N. Livingstone, 211–29. Grand Rapids: Baker, 2000.

Wasmann, Erich. "Evolution: Attitudes of Catholics towards the Theory." *The Catholic Encyclopedia,* 5:654–55. 15 vols. New York: Appleton, 1909.

———. *Der Kampf um das Entwicklungsproblem in Berlin.* Freiburg im Breisgau: Herder, 1907. Translation: *The Berlin Discussion of the Problem of Evolution.* London: Kegan Paul, 1909.

Watson, Elbert L. "Oklahoma and the Anti-Evolution Movement of the 1920's." *The Chronicles of Oklahoma* 42 (1964–65) 396–407.

Watson, J. B., and P. Rayner, "Conditioned Emotional Reactions." *Journal of Experimental Psychology* 3/1 (1920) 1–14.

Webb, George E. "The Repeal of the Butler Act." *Journal of the Tennessee Academy of Sciences* 59/1–2 (1984) 14–17.

Webster v. New Lenox School District № 122, 917 F.2d 1004 (7th Cir. 1990).

Webster v. New Lenox School District № 122, Mem. op., 1989 WL 58209 (N.D.Ill. 1989).

Whaling, Thornton. *Science and Religion Today.* Chapel Hill: University of North Carolina Press, 1929.

Wheeler, Alwynne. "Wotton, Edward." In *Complete Dictionary of Scientific Biography,* edited by Connor Coulston Gillispie et al., 14:507–8. 27 vols. Detroit: Scribner, 2008.

Whewell, William. *History of the Inductive Sciences.* 3rd ed. New York, Appleton: 1858.

———. *The Philosophy of the Inductive Sciences.* 2 vols. London: Parker, 1840.

Whitcombe, John C., and Henry M. Morris. *The Genesis Flood: The Biblical Record and Its Scientific Implications.* Phillipsburg, NJ: Presbyterian and Reformed, 1961.

White, Andrew Dickson. *Autobiography of Andrew Dickson White.* 2 vols. New York: Century, 1914.

———. "The Battle-fields of Science." *New York Daily Tribune* (18 December 1869) Page 4.

———. *A History of the Warfare of Science and Theology in Christendom*. 2 vols. New York: Appleton, 1896.

———. *The Warfare of Science*. New York: Appleton, 1888.

White, Ellen Gould Harmon. *Patriarchs and Prophets*. Oakland, CA: Pacific, 1890.

Wilberforce, Samuel. Review of *On the Origin of Species*. *Quarterly Review* 108 № 215 (1860) 225–64.

Wilhelm, Richard D. "A Chronology and Analysis of the Regulatory Actions Relating to the Teaching of Evolution in the Public Schools." PhD diss. University of Texas, 1978.

Willoughby v. Stever. Civil Action № 1574–72 (D.D.C. 1972), aff'd mem., 504 F.2d 271 (D.C.Cir. 1974), cert. denied, 420 U.S. 927 (1975).

Wilson, Woodrow. Letter to Ellen Louise Axson, 26 June 1884. In *The Papers of Woodrow Wilson*, edited by Arthur S. Link et al., 3:216–18. 69 vols. Princeton: Princeton University Press, 1966–.

Winchell, Alexander. *Adamites and Preadamites: A Popular Discourse concerning the Remote Representatives of the Human Species and their Relation to the Biblical Adam*. Syracuse: Roberts, 1878.

———. *The Doctrine of Evolution: Its Data, its Principles, and its Theistic Bearings*. New York: Harper, 1874.

———. *Preadamites: A Demonstration of the Existence of Men before Adam; Together with a Study of their Condition, Antiquity, Racial Affinities, and the Progressive Dispersion over the Earth*. Chicago: Griggs, 1880.

———. *Reconciliation of Science and Religion*. New York: Harper, 1877.

———. "Science Gagged at Nashville." *Nashville Daily American* O.S. 3 № 881 (16 June 1878) 2.

Wiseman, Nicholas. *Twelve Lectures on the Connexion between Science and Revealed Religion*. London: Booker, 1836.

Wollaston, A. F. R. *Life of Alfred Newton*. New York: Dutton, 1921.

Wolleb, Johannes. *Compendium Theologiae Christianae*. Basel: Genathus, 1626.

Woodrow, James. *Evolution: An Address Delivered May 7th, 1884, before the Alumni Association of the Columbia Theological Seminary*. Columbia, SC: Presbyterian Publishing House, 1884.

———. "An Examination of Certain Recent Assaults on Physical Science." *Southern Presbyterian Review* 24/3 (1873) 327–77.

———. "A Further Examination of Certain Recent Assaults on Physical Science." *Southern Presbyterian Review* 25/2 (1874) 246–92.

———. "Geology and Its Assailants." *Southern Presbyterian Review* 15/4 (1863) 549–69.

———. "Inaugural Address." *Southern Presbyterian Review* 14/4 (1862) 505–31.

———. "Professor Woodrow's Speech before the Synod of South Carolina." *Southern Presbyterian Review* 36/1 (1885) 1–65.

Woodrow, Marion, ed. *Dr. James Woodrow as Seen by his Friends*. Columbia, SC: Bryan, 1909.

Woodward, John. *An Essay towards a Natural History of the Earth, and Terrestrial Bodyes, especialy Minerals; as also of the Sea, Rivers, and Springs. With an Account of the Universal Deluge, and of the Effects that it had upon the Earth*. London: Bettesworth and Taylor, 1723.

Wotton, Edward. *De Differentiis Animalium Libri Decem*. Paris: Vascosanus, 1552.

Wright v. Houston Independent School District. 366 F.Supp. 1208 (S.D. Texas 1972).
Wright v. Houston Independent School District. 486 F.2d 137 (5th Cir. 1973).
Wright, George Friedrich. "The Passing of Evolution." In *The Fundamentals: A Testimony to the Truth*, edited by A. C. Dixon et al., 7:5–20. 12 vols. Chicago: Testimony, 1910–15.
Wyllie, Irvin G. "Bryan, Birge, and the Wisconsin Evolution Controversy, 1921–1922." *Wisconsin Magazine of History* 35/4 (1952) 294–301.
Życiński, Józef. *Bóg i Ewolucja: Podstawowe Pytania Ewolucjonizmu Chrześcijańskiego.* Lublin: Towarzystwo Naukowe Katolickiego Uniwersytetu Lubelskiego, 2002. Translation: *God and Evolution: Fundamental Questions of Christian Evolutionism*, by Kenneth W. Kemp and Zuzanna Maślanka. Washington, DC: Catholic University of America Press, 2006.

Index

Abington v. Schempp, 146
Acland, Henry, 40
Acosta, José de, 51
Agassiz, Louis, 55, 89, 135
agnosticism, 15, 20, 72, 101, 107, 109, 117, 119, 190
Aguillard v. Edwards, 146, 164–67, 183
Aguillard v. Treen. See Aguillard v. Edwards
Albert of Saxony, 41
Albert the Great, 1, 31, 33–34, 41, 49, 64–65
Allen, Frederick Lewis, 36–37, 139
Ambrose of Milan, 34
American Association for the Advancement of Science, 128–29
American Civil Liberties Union, 98, 100, 102, 106–8, 110, 123, 154, 156, 163, 180
anesthesia, obstetric use of, 2–3, 34
Anglicanism, 39–40, 48, 54, 61, 76, 107
anthropogenesis. *See* man, origin of
anthropology, cultural, 76, 144
anthropology, philosophical and theological, 2, 130, 138–39, 185
anti-evolution campaign of the 1920s, 110–23
anti-evolution laws, 118–19. *See also under names of states*
Appellate Courts, U.S., 151–57
Aquinas, Thomas, 27, 34, 167
Arduino, Giovanni, 47–48
Aristotle, 40–41

Arkansas court cases. *See Epperson* and *McLean*
Arkansas Educational Association, 147
Arkansas Gazette, 108, 118, 123
Arkansas, anti-evolution laws in, 108, 117–18, 121–24, 128–29, 134, 147–50, 162–66
Armstrong, Orland Kay, 128–29
atheism, 2, 19–20, 25, 37, 40, 81, 112, 109, 112, 117–19, 128, 161, 182–83, 186–87, 190–91
Athenaeum, 75–76, 94
Augustine of Hippo, 34, 49, 65, 187–88
Ayala, Francisco, 163

Balanced Treatment Act (Arkansas), 162–65
Balanced Treatment Act (Louisiana), 165–66
Baltimore Sun, 102, 105
Baptists, 101, 113–14, 116, 118–20, 124–27, 139, 146
Barksdale, Rhesa Hawkins, 152
Barone, Cesare, 33
Barth, Karl, 15
Bartholomew the Englishman, 30–34
Bartlett, C. Julian, 183–84
Baylor University, 125
Beale, Howard K., 121–22, 137–39, 182
Bede the Venerable, 34, 46
Behe, Michael, 168–73, 177–80
Bellarmine, Robert, 1

221

Benedict XIV, 11, 30
Bentley, Richard, 12
Berg, Howard C., 178
Bird, Wendell, 159, 162, 165–66
Black, Hugo, 148–49
Blanchard, Howard H., Jr., 147
Bliss, Daniel, 84
Blount, Charles, 54
Bogard, Ben M., 118
Bonaventure, 64
Booth, William, 85
Borene, Bernard, 158
Brennan, William J., 166
Bridgewater treatises, 52, 57
Brigham, Albert P., 136
British Association for the Advancement of Science, 72
Brodie, Benjamin, 74, 79
Brooke, John Hedley, 23
Broughton, Len G., 149
Browne, Thomas, 46–48
Bryan laws, 108, 117–18, 121–25, 129, 147–50
Bryan, Mary, 111
Bryan, William Jennings, 2, 20, 96–98, 100–102, 104, 106–31, 159, 161, 183
Buckland, William, 55, 57, 62, 66
Buffon, Georges-Louis Leclerc, Comte de, 43–44, 47–48, 50, 56–58, 64, 66
Bultmann, Rudolf, 15
Burger, Warren, 146
Burnet, Thomas, 42, 50, 52, 54, 58, 60–64
Butler Act, 97–98, 103–4, 106, 108, 110, 118, 120–21, 128–29, 134, 136, 138, 148–50
Butler, John Washington, 97, 111–12, 124, 187

Cajetan (Tommaso de Vio), 49
Calmet, Augustin, 53, 64
Calvin, John, 50
Caputo, Nicholas, 174, 176
Carnes, Ed, 154
Catholicism, 10–11, 13–14, 16, 19, 26, 30, 50, 56–58, 61, 66, 68, 82–84, 94, 105, 113, 139–40, 163, 165–66, 170, 183–85
Chadwick, Owen, 40, 72
Chambers, Robert, 45, 66, 75
Chambliss, Alexander L., 134
Chattanooga Daily Times, 98–100
Chil y Naranjo, Gregorio, 82–83
Christian Century, 129
Christian Reformed Church, 184
chronology, Biblical, 45–48, 50
Clark, Steve, 165
Clark, Thomas, 146
Cobb County (Georgia), 153–54
Coffin, Harold, 163
Colenso, John, 40, 112
Columbia Theological Seminary, 82, 89–92
common ancestry, 20, 68–71, 74, 88, 110–11, 128, 134, 163, 168–73
conflict, kinds of, 3–6, 18–24, 30, 82–95, 190
Congregation for the Causes of Saints, 11–12
Constitution, Tennessee, 105–6
Constitution, U.S. *See* Establishment Clause, Free Exercise Clause, Free Speech Clause, *and* constitutionality of anti-evolution law
constitutionality of anti-evolution laws, 97–98, 100, 102–6, 108, 141, 145, 147–50, 152, 154, 156, 165–66, 181
Cooper, Clarence, 153
Cornell, Ezra, 28
Cosmas Indicopleustes, 34
Coyne, Jerry A., 22
Creation Science, 19, 141, 156–69, 180, 182, 184
creation, 10–11, 16–19, 23, 33, 63–64, 83, 134, 164
creation, six days of. *See* Hexaëmeron
creationism, old-earth, 123, 159–61
creationism, young-earth, 158–66. *See also* Creation Science
Cundiff, Bryce, 119, 124
Cuvier, Georges, 42, 52, 55, 62

Da Vinci, Leonardo, 51

Dabney, Roger L., 90
Dana, James Dwight, 135–36
Daniel v. Waters, 151
Darrow, Clarence, 97, 101–4, 109–10
Darwin, Charles, 1, 13, 15, 21, 39–40, 44, 68–73, 78–79, 85, 94, 112–13, 115, 168–71
Darwin, Francis, 79, 82
Daubeny, Charles, 73–74
Davidson, Randall, 77
Davis, Percival, 167, 180
Dawkins, Richard, 20–21, 169, 182
Dawson, John William, 159
De Luc, Jean-André, 50
De Morgan, Augustus, 77
De Vio, Tommaso, 49
Dean, Dennis R., 62–63
Declaration of Students of the Natural and Physical Sciences, 77
deism, 1, 7, 16, 39, 54. 63–66, 71, 114, 131, 133
Deluge. *See* Flood of Noah
Demaree, Ralph G., 126
Dembski, William A., 173–77, 179, 182
Dennett, Daniel, 20–21, 182
Denton, Michael, 169
Descartes, René, 1, 27, 41–43, 49–50, 63–65
design inference, 173–77, 179–80
design, 12–13, 19, 21, 49, 112–13. *See also* Intelligent-Design Theory
Diderot, Denis, 55
diluvialism, 51–55
District Courts, U.S., 152–58, 164, 166, 180–81
Dobzhansky, Theodosius, 23, 183
Dodge, David Stuart, 84
Dover (Pennsylvania) School District, 150, 180–81
Draper, John William, 20, 23, 25–26, 29–31, 34–36, 74–75, 82, 93
Duhem, Pierre, 13–14, 52
Duplantier, Adrian, 166
Dyck, William van, 85–86

earth, age of, 45–49
earth, sphericity of, 2, 34–35

earth, structure of, 41, 43–44, 47, 56–58, 63
Edwards v. Aguillard, 146, 164–67, 183
Edwards, George, 151
Élie de Beaumont, Léonce, 43
Ellington, Buford, 149
Ellis, George, 111, 119
Ellwanger, Paul, 162
endorsement test, 146, 152–53, 181
Episcopalianism, 163, 183
Epperson v. Arkansas, 148–51, 155, 161
Epperson, Susan, 117, 147–48
Essays and Reviews, 39, 79, 112
Establishment Clause, 145–46, 148, 151–55, 164–66, 180
eternalism, 48, 63, 53–54, 59, 160
ethics and evolution. *See* evolution and moral ideals
ethics, research, 3–5
Eusebius of Caesarea, 45–46
Everson v. Board of Education, 146, 159
evolution and moral ideals, 21, 114–16, 144
evolution and religious belief, 111–14
explanatory filter, 175–79

Fabre d'Envieu, Jules, 50–51
Farr, A. D., 34
Faventius, 41
Fawcett, Henry, 79
Ferguson, Miriam, 122
Ferguson, W. F., 99–100
Finnis, John, 22
First Amendment. *See* Establishment Clause, Free Exercise Clause, *and* Free Speech Clause
Flood of Noah, 36, 45, 48, 51–55, 61, 63–64
Florida, anti-evolution resolution in, 117–18, 120, 134
Flower, William Henry, 77, 133
Foley, Daniel, 157
Ford, Henry, 102
Fortas, Abe, 148
Fosdick, Harry Emerson, 125

fossils, 32, 44–45, 47, 51–55, 58, 136, 143, 159–60, 170. *See also* fossils, human
fossils, human, 71, 136, 142
Fox News, 184
Fox, Henry, 126–27
Fracastoro, Girolamo, 51–52
Free Exercise Clause, 145–46, 154–58, 164
Free Speech Clause, 145, 147, 154, 156–58
free speech, teachers' right of, 100, 107. *See also* Free Speech Clause
Freiler v. Tangipahoa Parish Board of Education, 146, 151–54
fundamentalism, 37, 99, 102, 108–10, 123, 125, 129, 137, 139, 159–60, 165, 183
Fundamentals, The, 123, 159

Galilei, Galileo, 1, 2, 42, 57, 58, 189
Gallup News, 183–85
Gatewood, Willard B., 126
Geisler, Norman, 164
Generelli, Giuseppe Cirillo, 58
geology, 27, 40–49, 50–63, 66, 135–36. *See also* fossils
Gesner, Konrad, 31–32
Gilkey, Langdon, 163
Giraudet, Alexandre-Aimé, 50
Gish, Duane, 158
Goldschmidt, Richard, 173
Gottlieb, Sheldon F., 8
Gould, Stephen Jay, 15–17, 23, 163
Grand View College, 126–27
Gray, Asa, 112–13, 135
Greetham, D. C., 32
Gross, Eugene W., 143
Guyot, Arnold, 159

Haeckel, Ernst, 21, 83
Hale, Matthew, 48
Haller, Albrecht von, 66
Hamilton, Albert, 146
Hays, Arthur Garfield, 102–3
Hein, George C., 122
Herbert, Sandra, 62–63
Herschel, John, 19

Herschel, William, 44, 46–47
Hexaëmeron, 35, 46, 49–50, 63, 83, 150
Hicks, Sue, 97, 101
Hippocampus Debate, 73–74, 77
Hoiberg, Carl F., 126–27
Holstead, James L., 162
Hooke, Robert, 51
Hooker, Joseph, 73, 74–75, 78–81
Hunter, George William, 3–4, 99, 121, 136–37
Hurani, Ibrahim, 85
Hutton, James, 48–49
Huxley-Wilberforce Exchange, 19, 35–36, 56, 72–82
Huxley, Leonard, 82
Huxley, Thomas H., 20–21, 25, 36, 45, 71–81, 94

inference to the best explanation, 8, 172–73, 179–80
Inherit the Wind, 37, 121
Intelligent-Design Theory, 12, 19, 141, 150, 159, 166–82
irenicism, 13–17
irreducible complexity, 170–73, 177–79
Isidore of Seville, 31, 34, 46

Jefferson, Thomas, 107, 146
Jenkin, Fleeming, 79
Jensen, V. S., 127
John Paul II, 15, 183, 185, 189
John V of Portugal, 30
Johnson, Philip E., 12, 168–70, 183
Jones, John E., III, 167, 180–81
Judaism, 1, 105, 166, 183
Julius Africanus, Sextus, 46

Keith, Senator Bill, 165
Kellogg, Vernon, 115–16
Kelly, Howard A., 111
Kentucky Wesleyan College, 126–27
Kentucky, proposed anti-evolution law in, 100, 111, 116–17, 119, 124–25
Kenyon, Dean H., 169
Kepler, Johannes, 27

Index

Kidd, Benjamin, 116
Kidd, John, 52, 55
Kirwan, Richard, 62
Kitzmiller v. Dover, 167, 180–81
Kitzmiller, Tammy 180
Knox, John, 75
Krutch, Joseph Wood, 37, 96–97

La Peyrère, Isaac, 87–88
Laba, Estelle, 143
Lacey, Alan, 6
Lactantius, 34
Lamarck, Jean-Baptiste de, 45, 119
Lambertini, Prospero. *See* Benedict XIV
Laplace, Pierre Simon de, 13, 44
Lateran Council, Fourth, 18–19
Lawrence, Jerome, 37
Le Conte, Joseph, 135
Lee, Robert E., 37
Lemaître, Georges, 17
Lemon test, 146, 151–53, 181
Lemon v. Kurtzmann, 146, 151–53, 181
Leo XIII, 19
Leopold, Nathan, 101
Leuba, James H., 111–12, 116
LeVake v. Independent School District #656, 107, 155, 157–58
LeVake, Rodney, 157–58
Lewis, C. S., 8–9
Lewis, Edwin, 82–85
Lewontin, Richard C., 8–9, 22
life, origin of, 69, 150–53, 169, 174, 176, 180
Linville, Henry R., 137
Lippmann, Walter, 104, 107
Livaudais, Marcel, 152
Loeb, Richard, 101
Louisiana court case. *See Aguillard v. Edwards*
Louisiana, anti-evolution law in, 165–66
Lucretius Carus, Titus, 40–41, 63
Luther, Martin, 50
Lutheranism, 126, 180
Lyell, Charles, 1, 43, 47, 58, 66, 72
Lyon, James A., 89

Machen, John Gresham, 124, 130, 138
Mack, Joseph Bingham, 90
Malone, Dudley Field, 101–2, 108
man, origin of, 17, 71–72, 116, 119, 130–38, 148, 165, 182
Manning, Henry Edward, 75
Marsden, George, 163
Martin of Tours, 30
Martin, T. T., 20, 120
Martini, Martino, 51
Martino, Alex, 156
materialism, 17, 63, 81, 83, 119, 125, 134, 138
Mather, Kirtley, 113, 116, 131, 138, 188
Matzke, Nicholas, 178
McDaniel, George W., 126
McKenzie, Ben, 103
McKinney, Colin P., 104
McLean v. Arkansas, 163–65, 183
McLean, William, 163
McMullin, Ernan, 17–18
McTyeire, Holland N., 85–88
McVey, Frank, 100, 119
Mencken, H. L., 102
Mercer University, 126
method, scientific, 6–13, 28–29, 32–35, 75, 93
Methodism, 85–86, 126, 146, 163, 165
Milgram, Stanley, 5
Mill, John Stuart, 187
Miller, F. A., 119
Miller, Kenneth, 180
miracles, 8–10, 11–12, 16–17, 22, 65, 114, 123, 130
Mississippi, anti-evolution law in, 108, 118, 121, 128, 134, 147, 150
Mitchell, Charles, 70
Mivart, St. George, 83–84, 133
Mochary, Mary, 174
modernism, 36–37, 102, 114, 125, 129, 139
Montgomery, J. L., 119
Moon, Truman J., 136–37, 143
Moore, James R., 35
Moro, Anton-Lazzaro, 58
Moroni, Gaetano, 68
Morris, Henry, 20, 159–61, 182–83

Moscow State University, Department of Geography, 5
Mueller, Marvin, 8
Mullins, Edgar Young, 119, 124–25, 127, 137

Nation, The, 37, 96
National Association of Biology Teachers, 181–82, 187
National Center for Science Education, 154
National Science Foundation, 143–44, 155
natural selection, 20–21, 69–73, 80–81, 114–16, 119, 161–63, 168–72, 181–82
naturalism, 6–13, 82–83
nature, theology of, 2, 10, 13–18
Neal, John Randolph, 100, 108
Needham, John, 50
Nelkin, Dorothy, 144, 163
New York Times, 39–40, 111, 115, 141, 187
New York World, 104, 107
Newman, John Henry, 75
Newton, Alfred, 80–81
Newton, Isaac, 1, 12, 50, 61, 64
Nicholas of Cusa, 32–33
Nietzsche, Friedrich, 116
Noll, Mark A., 141
non-overlapping magisteria, 15–17
North Carolina, proposed anti-evolution law in, 120
North Christian Advocate, 88
Numbers, Ronald, 169

O'Toole, George Barry, 72
Oklahoma Baptist Messenger, 125
Oklahoma Text-Book Law, 117, 119
Origen, 34
Orr, H. Allen, 178
Otto, James H., 147
Overton, William R., 163–66
Owen, Richard, 72–76, 79

Paine, Thomas, 65
Paley, William, 12, 168–69, 171
Pallen, Mark, 178

Palmer, R. R., 61–62
Pasteur, Louis, 69
Patrick, Symon, 48
Paul of Tarsus, 16, 65
Peay, Austin, 98, 105, 120–21
Peirce, C. S., 174
Peloza v. Capistrano Unified School District, 107, 155, 157
Peloza, John E., 156–57
Penn, Granville, 62–63
Perkins, John, 89
Perlus, Irving, 156
Pew Research Center, 183–86
Pfleiderer, Otto, 132
physicotheology, 12–13
Pierce, David H., 122
Pingré, Alexandre Guy, 44
Pius VII, 50
Pius IX, 26, 84
Pius XII, 11
Plantinga, Alvin, 181
Pliny the Elder, 31–32
Poole, D. Scott, 120
Porter, John W., 116, 124, 127
Poteat, William Louis, 113, 120, 127
Powell, E. L., 119
Pre-Adamitism, 85–89
Presbyterianism, 84, 89–94, 113, 123–27, 131, 133, 163
Price, George McCready, 160
providence, 2, 10, 54, 71–72, 86, 132, 182
Provine, William B., 21
Public Health Service, U.S., 5
public opinion, 184–86
Pye Smith, John, 47

Rappleyea, George, 98–100
Rash, James R., 119
Ratzsch, Del, 175
Raulston, John T., 102, 104, 106, 147, 163
Rayner, Rosalie, 4
Redi, Francesco, 58
Reed, Murray O., 147
Rehnquist, William, 166
Reichstag Fire Trial, 102
religion, nature of, 1, 16

Revolt of the Admirals, 5
Rice, William North, 136
Riley, William Bell, 101, 123–24, 127, 137, 159
Rimmer, Harry, 160
Ripple, Kenneth F., 156–57
Robinson, F. E., 99–100, 103
Rodholm, S. V., 127
Romanes, George, 112
Roosevelt, Theodore, 115
Rotenberry, A. L., 121–22
Roth, Ariel, 163
Royal Society of London, 66
Royer, Clémence, 21
Rupke, Nicolaas A., 62
Ruse, Michael, 163, 165
Ruskin, John, 40
Russell, Colin, 2–3

Sarton, George, 25, 78
Scalia, Antonin, 152–53, 164, 166
Scaliger, Joseph Justice, 46
science, nature of, 13–17
Scofield, C. I., 160
Scopes Trial, 19, 35–37, 56, 96–110, 114, 118, 121, 130–31, 187
Scopes v. State. 105, 134. *See also* Scopes Trial
Scopes, Lela, 122
Scopes, John T., 2, 37, 96–106, 110, 117, 121, 130, 187
Scott, Gary L., 117, 149
Scriptural Geology, 57
Seals, Woodrow B., 155–56
Segraves v. California, 156
Segraves, Kelly, 156
Selman v. Cobb County, 153–54
Shipley, Maynard, 37, 108, 122
Simpson, G. G., 144
Simpson, James Young, 34
Simpson, Wilfred Huddleston, 80
Singleterry, W. J., 117
Skoog, Gerald, 136, 142–43
Smith v. Mississippi, 150
Smith, Ella Thea, 142–44
Smith, Eugene A., 87
Smith, Hay Watson, 124, 127
Smith, Huston, 181

Smith, Mrs. Arthur G., 150
Snow, Parker, 72
solar system, origin of, 12–13, 42–44, 49, 58, 63
Solinus, Gaius Julius, 32
Sorbonne, College of, 56–58
soul, human, 6. 10–11, 14, 16–17, 72, 90–91, 111–12, 130–33, 138, 185
South Carolina, proposed antievolution law in, 119
Southern, Martin, 149
Soviet Academy of Sciences, Institute of Geography, 5
Sprowls, Jesse W., 100, 126–27
St. Louis Christian Advocate, 88
St. Mary of the Assumption School (Staten Island, New York), 222
State of Tennessee v. Scopes. See Scopes Trial
Steno, Nicolas. *See* Stensen, Niels
Stensen, Niels, 27, 43, 50–54, 56–61, 66
Stewart, Balfour, 76, 80
Stewart, Potter, 148
Stewart, Thomas, 104, 106, 109
Strabo, 44
Suárez, Francisco, 50
Sulpicius of Bourges, 30
Sulpicius Severus, 30
Summers, T. O., 86
Supreme Court, Arkansas, 118, 148
Supreme Court, Mississippi, 150
Supreme Court, Tennessee, 105, 134
Supreme Court, U.S., 118, 122, 145–50, 153, 166. *See also* names of individual cases
Syrian Protestant College, 82, 84–85

Tangipahoa Parish (Louisiana), 146, 151–54
Tangipahoa Parish Board of Education v. Freiler, 146, 151–54
teachers and teaching, 107–8, 117–18, 121, 134–38
Temple, Frederick, 79
Tennessee court case. *See* Scopes Trial and *Scopes v. State*

Tennessee, anti-evolution laws in, 96–111, 124, 128–29, 134, 149–51
Texas, anti-evolution measures in, 122, 142
textbooks, content of, 121, 135–37, 141–45, 150–54
textbooks, legal aspects of, 105, 119, 121–22
theology, definition and nature of, 1–2, 13–17
theology, method of, 28–35, 64–65
Theophilus of Antioch, 46
Thompson, James J., 127
Thornhill, Richard H., 179
Tindal, Matthew, 65
Toulmin, Stephen, 13
Towle, Albert, 147
transformation of species, 68–70, 81
Treen, David, 165–66
Tristram, Henry Baker, 80–81
Tyndall, John, 21, 77

unconstitutionality of anti-evolution laws. *See* constitutionality
Urban VIII, 2, 42
Urquinaona y Bidot, José María, 82–83
Ussery, David W., 179
Ussher, James, 46

Vai, Gian Battisa, 58, 61
Vallisneri, Antonio, 58
Van Fraassen, Bas, 14
Vanderbilt University, 82, 85–88
Vatican Council, First, 19, 26
Vignoles, Alphonse des, 46
Viviani, Vincenzo, 57–58
Vogt, Carl, 21
Voltaire, 32, 65

Wake Forest College, 113, 120, 127
Walker, Samuel, 36
Wallace, Alfred Russel, 70–71, 115, 135
Warfare Thesis (White's formulation), 28
Warfield, B. B., 131–33

Washington Star-News, 155
Wasmann, Erich, 68, 113, 133
Watson, John D., 4
Weber, Leona, 154–55
Webster v. New Lenox School District № 122, 107, 156–57
Webster, Ray, 107, 156–57
Weismann, August, 70, 115
Werner, Abraham, 47, 66
Whaling, Thornton, 92
Wheeler, Alwynne, 32
Whewell, William, 2, 158
Whiston, William, 54
Whitcomb, John C., 160
White, Andrew Dickson, 3, 21–23, 25, 27–36, 56–57, 77, 82–84, 86, 90, 92–93, 126, 182, 188
White, Ellen G., 160
White, Frank, 162
White, Walter, 99, 103
Whitfield, Henry L., 121
Wickramasinghe, Chandra, 163
Wilberforce-Huxley Exchange, 19, 35–36, 56, 72–82
Wilberforce, Samuel, 36, 75–81, 94
Wilhelm, Richard D., 122, 141
Williamson, Samuel F., 118
Willoughby v. Stever, 155
Willoughby, William, 155
Winchell, Alexander, 82, 85–89, 95
Wiseman, Nicholas, 42, 66
Wishart, Charles F., 124, 127
Wittgenstein, Ludwig, 15
Wolleb, Johannes, 134
Woodrow, James, 82, 89–93, 95, 133
Woodward, John, 54
Wooster College, 124, 127
World Christian Fundamentals Association, 101, 139
Wotton, Edward, 31–32
Wright v. Houston Independent School District, 154–56
Wright, George Friedrich, 159
Wright, Rita, 155–56

Zahm, John, 113
Życiński, Józef, 183

www.ingramcontent.com/pod-product-compliance
Lightning Source LLC
Chambersburg PA
CBHW022012220426
43663CB00007B/1054